W9-AVG-875

DYNAMIC ASIA: BUSINESS, TRADE AND ECONOMIC DEVELOPMENT IN PACIFIC ASIA

Dynamic Asia: Business, Trade and Economic Development in Pacific Asia

Edited by

IAN G. COOK
MARCUS A. DOEL
REX Y.F. LI
YONGJIANG WANG

Ashgate

Aldershot • Brookfield USA • Singapore • Sydney

Published by
Ashgate Publishing Company
Gower House
Croft Road
Aldershot
Hants GU11 3HR
England

HC
460.5
.D96
1998

Ashgate Publishing Company
Old Post Road
Brookfield
Vermont 05036
USA

British Library Cataloguing in Publication Data
Dynamic Asia : business, trade and economic development in
  Pacific Asia. - (Pacific Rim research series)
  1.East Asia - Economic conditions 2.East Asia - Commerce
  I.Cook, Ian G.
  338.9'5

Library of Congress Catalog Card Number: 97-77888

ISBN 1 85972 196 6

Printed in Great Britain by The Ipswich Book Company, Suffolk.

Contents

Figures and Tables

Contributors

Ian G. Cook is Reader in Urban and Regional Issues, Head of Geography, and Head of the Centre for Pacific Rim Studies at Liverpool John Moores University. From 1983 to 1990 he co-edited the journal *Contemporary Issues in Geography and Education*. His research interests cover community based economic development, as well as urban and regional issues in Pacific Asia, and he has written many papers on these topics. Dr Cook has given presentations at Peking University, the Chinese Academy of Social Sciences, and, more recently, was invited to present papers at international symposia held in Guangdong, Shanghai and Beijing. His most recent publications include a chapter in *China: Economic Growth, Population and the Environment* (Macmillan, 1998) and a co-edited volume *Fragmented Asia: Regional Integration and National Disintegration in Pacific Asia* (Avebury, 1996). He is currently working on several books, including one on the Human Geography of China.

Marcus A. Doel is Lecturer in Human Geography at Loughborough University. He was previously a Lecturer and Research Fellow at the School of Social Science, Liverpool John Moores University. He has published widely on new theoretical directions in cultural, economic, and political geography in such journals as *Environment and Planning A & D, Political Geography*, and *Transactions of the Institute of British Geographers*. His research interests centre on the relationship between space and social theory, modernity and postmodernity, virtual reality technologies, and the Holocaust. He is the author of *Poststructuralist Geography: The Harsh Law of Space* (Guildford, in press) and co-editor of *Fragmented Asia: Regional Integration and National Disintegration in Pacific Asia* (Avebury, 1996).

Simon Lee is Lecturer in Politics at the University of Hull. He taught previously at the Department of Political Theory and Institutions, Liverpool University, and has research interests in the politics and political economy of public expenditure, the political economy of local and regional development in England, and the politics of England and English identity. His most recent works include chapters in *Creating Industrial Capacity* (Oxford University

Press, 1996), *Industrial Policy in Britain* (Macmillan, 1996), and *The Politics of Social Policy in Europe* (Edward Elgar, 1997). He is the author of *The Political Economy of Manufacturing in the UK* (Macmillan, 1998), co-author of *The Political Economy of Modern Britain* (Edward Elgar, 1997) and is currently working on a book entitled *The Political Economy of Competitiveness*.

Rex Y.F. Li is Senior Lecturer in International Relations in the School of Social Science and Deputy Head of the Centre for Pacific Rim Studies, Liverpool John Moores University. Since 1996 he has served as an Associate Editor of *Security Dialogue* (International Peace Research Institute, Oslo/Sage). His research focuses on the domestic and international implications of China's reform, Chinese foreign relations, and economic and security issues in Pacific Asia, and his articles have appeared in such journals as *Asia Pacific Business Review*, *Contemporary Politics*, and *Security Dialogue*. He is co-editor of *Fragmented Asia: Regional Integration and National Disintegration in Pacific Asia* (Avebury, 1996) and the author of *The Pacific Rim in the Changing Global System* (Polity Press, forthcoming).

Geoffrey Murray is a Visiting Lecturer in the School of Social Science and a Research Associate of the Centre for Pacific Rim Studies, Liverpool John Moores University. A former international business journalist with thirty years experience in Asia, he has written seven books on business and economic development in the region, including works on China, Japan, Singapore and Vietnam. In 1996 and 1997 he was a Training Consultant for *Beijing Review*. Among his publications are *The Rampant Dragon: China's Long March to a New Economic Dynasty* (Minerva Press, 1993), *China: The Last Great Market* (China Library, 1994*)*, *Singapore: The Global City State* (Japan Library, 1996), and *Vietnam: Dawn for a New Market* (China Library, 1997).

Ngai-Ling Sum is Alex Horsley Research Fellow at the Political Economy Research Centre, the University of Sheffield. She has research interests in the political economy of Pacific Asia, newly industrializing countries, and the relationship between political economy and cultural politics. Dr Sum is on the Editorial Board of *The Pacific Review*, and has contributed to a number of edited volumes including *Fragmented Asia*, (Avebury, 1996),

Regionalism and World Order (Macmillan, 1996), *Beyond Markets and Planning* (Edward Elgar, 1997), and *Globalization and Its Critics: Views from IPE* (Macmillan, 1997). She is currently working on a book entitled *Capitalism in East Asian Newly Industrializing Countries: A Regional Perspective.*

Hock B. Tan is Lecturer in International Business in the Napier Business School, Napier University. He pursued his undergraduate study in Malaysia and received his MSc and PhD from the University of Stirling. Dr Tan has research interests in industrial and trade development with particular reference to ASEAN countries, technology transfer and networking of small and medium enterprises. His recent works include a study on the role of research and technology organizations in the UK, and the process of technology transfer to small and medium enterprises in Malaysia.

Yongjiang Wang is Senior Lecturer in Japanese Language and Business in the School of Modern Languages and Deputy Head of the Centre for Pacific Rim Studies, Liverpool John Moores University. He received his doctorate from the School of East Asian Studies, University of Sheffield, and was previously a Research Assistant at the University of Warwick, Research Fellow at the University of Stirling, and Visiting Lecturer at Kanazawa University, Japan. His research interests include foreign direct investment in China and Sino-Japanese joint ventures, and he has been consultant to a number of British companies on business practice in China and Japan.

Nicholas J. White is Lecturer in Economic and Social History in the School of Social Science and a Research Associate of the Centre for Pacific Rim Studies, Liverpool John Moores University. He received his doctorate from the History Department at Royal Holloway College, University of London, in 1993. His most recent publications include an article in the *Journal of Imperial and Commonwealth History* and two books: *Business, Government, and the End of Empire: Malaya, 1942-1957* (Oxford University Press, 1996) and *Decolonisation: The British Experience* (Longman, forthcoming). He is currently researching Anglo-Japanese economic relations in Southeast Asia after World War Two.

Henry Wai-Chung Yeung is Lecturer in Geography at the National University of Singapore. He received his doctorate from the School of

Geography, University of Manchester, and was previously a Visiting Associate at the Institute of Southeast Asian Studies, Singapore, and Visiting Scholar at the Centre of Asian Studies, University of Hong Kong. He has published extensively on transnational corporations from Asian developing countries and Hong Kong firms in Southeast Asia in such journals as *Economic Geography, International Business Review*, and *The Pacific Review*. His research interests include theories and the geography of transnational corporations, Asian firms and their overseas operations, and Chinese business networks in Pacific Asia. He is the author of *Transnational Corporations and Business Networks: Hong Kong Firms in the ASEAN Region* (Routledge, forthcoming).

Preface

This volume is the second of the Pacific Rim Research Series emanating from a series of international research seminars which were initiated and organized by members of the Centre for Pacific Rim Studies, Liverpool John Moores University, between 1993 and 1995. Funded by the Economic and Social Research Council (ESRC), the seminars brought together established and younger scholars from a host of disciplines and academic institutions in Britain and Pacific Rim countries, as well as government officials and representatives of the business community. A wide range of topics were covered by these meetings, including economic development, business challenges and opportunities, sustainable development, security issues, regional integration, transnational organizations, and, Europe and Pacific Asia.

The first volume of the Series, *Fragmented Asia: Regional Integration and National Disintegration in Pacific Asia*, was published in 1996 and focuses on the broader domestic and external challenges to the states in Pacific Asia in the light of the rapid pace of change within these countries and in the international system. The aim of this volume is, however, to examine specifically the challenges as well as opportunities for international business and trade in Pacific Asia, highlighting the dynamics and complexity of the changing economic and business environment of the region.

The chapters in the volume are drawn primarily from the seminars relating to business and trade in Pacific Asia. Once again we wish to thank all the paper presenters, discussants and participants, especially the local organizers at SOAS, University of London, the School of East Asian Studies, University of Sheffield, and the Centre for South-East Asian Studies, University of Hull. Special thanks are due to Professor Anne Booth, Professor Ian Gow, and Dr Mike Parnwell. We are also grateful to the contributors for their great effort in revising and updating the original papers for publication. In addition, we like to thank a number of colleagues at Liverpool John Moores University: Professor David McEvoy, Director of the School of Social Science, for his sustained support and encouragement; members of the University Research Committee for awarding a joint University Research Fellowship to Ian Cook and Rex Li which has enabled them to work on this book, among other projects; Phil Cubbin and Nicky

Davies for their technical advice; and Cathy Renton, Sue Meyer and Linda Pringle for their secretarial assistance.

Acknowledgements are also due to Japan Library for extracts from *Singapore: The Global City State*. Finally, the financial support of the ESRC for the Pacific Rim Seminar Series is gratefully acknowledged.

Ian Cook, Marcus Doel, Rex Li and Yongjiang Wang
Liverpool, October 1997

Abbreviations

ACI	Acer Computer International
AFTA	ASEAN Free Trade Area
AMC	American Motor Company
APEC	Asia-Pacific Economic Cooperation
ASEAN	Association of South-East Asian Nations
BANI	National Arbitration Board (Indonesia)
BAW	Beijing Automotive Works
BCIC	Bumiputera Commercial and Industrial Community (Malaysia)
BOT	Build, Operate, Transfer Arrangement
BQ	Business Headquarters
CASS	Chinese Academy of Social Sciences
CBO	Cooperative Business Operation (China)
CBU	Completely Built-Up Vehicle Unit
CCP	Chinese Communist Party
CEO	Chief Executive Officer
CFIUS	Committee on Foreign Investment in the United States
CJV	Contractual Joint Venture (China)
CKD	Complete-Knockdown Vehicle Assembly Kit
EANIC	East Asian Newly-Industrializing Country
EDB	Economic Development Board
EIU	Economist Intelligence Unit
EJV	Chinese-Foreign Equity Joint Venture
EOI	Export-Oriented Industrialization
EPZ	Export Processing Zone
EU	European Union
FDI	Foreign Direct Investment
FMM	Federation of Malaysian Manufacturers
G7	Group of Seven Industrialized Democracies (Canada, France, Germany, Italy, Japan, UK, US)
GATT	General Agreement on Tariffs and Trade
GDP	Gross Domestic Product
GNP	Gross National Product

GR-S	'General Purpose' Synthetic Rubber
ICI	Imperial Chemical Industries
IFDI	Inward Foreign Direct Investment
IMF	International Monetary Fund
ISI	Import Substitution Industrialization
JETRO	Japanese External Trade Organization
KLSE	Kuala Lumpur Stock Exchange
LDP	Liberal Democratic Party (Japan)
LPG	Liquefied Petroleum Gas
MIDA	Malaysian Industrial Development Authority
MITI	Ministry of International Trade and Industry (Japan)
MNE	Multinational Enterprise
MOSS	Market-Oriented Sector Selective
NAFTA	North American Free Trade Agreement
NIC	Newly-Industrializing Country
NIE	Newly Industrializing Economy
NGT	Northern Growth Triangle (Malaysia)
NTT	Nippon Telegraph and Telephone
OECD	Organization for Economic Cooperation and Development
OHQ	Operational Headquarters
OPP2	Second Outline Perspective Plan (Malaysia)
PLA	People's Liberation Army (China)
PRC	People's Republic of China
R&D	Research and Development
RHQ	Regional Headquarters
RO	Regional Office
RW	Ricardian Workfare
SES	Stock Exchange of Singapore
SEZ	Special Economic Zone (China)
SKD	Semi-Knockdown Vehicle Assembly Kit
SME	Small and Medium Enterprise
SW	Schumpeterian Workfare
TNC	Transnational Corporation
TVE	Township and Village Enterprise (China)
UK	United Kingdom
US/USA	United States of America
USTR	United States Trade Representative
VER	Voluntary Export Restraint
VIE	Voluntary Import Expansion

VMC   Vietnam Motors Corporation
WFOE   Wholly Foreign-Owned Enterprise (China)
WTO   World Trade Organization

Introduction

IAN G. COOK, MARCUS A. DOEL, REX Y.F. LI and YONGJIANG WANG

It is something of a commonplace to suggest that Pacific Asia is characterized by enormous dynamism and relentless transformation, metamorphoses which touch virtually every domain, from the routine practices that sustain the home to the macro-economic policy of governments. Whilst there is much scholarly debate on the explanations for the economic 'miracle' in the region (Appelbaum and Henderson, eds, 1992; Berger and Hsiao, eds, 1988; Haggard, 1990; Wade, 1990), the experience of Pacific Asian countries is generally looked upon as a model of development for other Third World countries to follow (World Bank, 1993). However, the achievement of rapid growth in Asia is not without its costs — social, economic, and environmental costs which have serious domestic, regional and global implications. Despite the huge economic progress made by many Asian countries over the past few decades, there are severe problems, such as environmental degradation, economic inequality, social instability, political uncertainty, which may threaten the continued growth of the region (Berger and Borer, eds, 1997). More fundamentally, scholars and analysts are beginning to question whether the economic growth in Pacific Asia can be sustained because of substantial institutional and structural constraints (Krugman, 1994; Lingle, 1996; Walton, 1997).

Apart from rising domestic challenges, East Asian elites have to come to terms with the impact of the potent forces of globalization on their culture, society and polity (Kofman and Youngs, eds, 1996; Robertson, 1992; Scholte, 1993; Rosenau and Czempiel, 1992). As Asian economies become more integrated into the world economy, they are increasingly influenced by the movement of global capital and the fluctuation of the stock markets (Agnew and Corbridge, 1995; Wolf, 1997). The recent financial crisis across Southeast Asia is but one example indicating the degree of vulnerability Pacific Asia faces in a globalized market (Cumming-Bruce, 1997). East Asian growth is also menaced by political change, regional tension and security uncertainty following the end of the Cold War and the

1

collapse of the bipolar international system. There is considerable concern over the strategic intentions of such regional powers as China and Japan. The post-Cold War arms build-up in the region, combined with many unresolved territorial disputes among Asian states, could also destabilize the region, thus having an undesirable effect on the investment environment in Pacific Asia (Li, 1998). For example, some observers are worried that democracy, civil liberties and the rule of law in Hong Kong cannot be maintained after its return to China (Szulc, 1997; Tsang, 1996), which will jeopardize the economic prosperity of the territory and of Pacific Asia more generally. As yet there has been no sign of political upheaval nor economic stagnation in Hong Kong since the Chinese takeover in July 1997. Nevertheless, the future of Hong Kong hinges ultimately upon the domestic situation in post-Deng China which is far from certain.

This is, however, not to suggest that Pacific Asia is about to decline and that the human and economic potential of the region has reached its limit. In fact, most East Asian governments are not unaware of the problems that they are facing and are prepared to find a solution to them if they can. At a regional level, there exist many institutions and channels such as the Asia-Pacific Economic Cooperation forum through which economic cooperation is pursued. Moreover, the enhancement of regional peace and security are being facilitated by numerous bilateral and multilateral security dialogues and mechanisms of which the ASEAN Regional Forum is the most prominent one. Essentially, what we are arguing here is that the prospects for further growth and business opportunities in Pacific Asia must be considered within the broader context of the rapid change taking place within individual countries and the region, as well as in the global system. Indeed, in the first volume of the Pacific Rim Research Series, we have analyzed the parallel trends in Pacific Asia of economic integration and security cooperation on the one hand, and growing pressure for decentralization and even disintegration in certain states on the other (Cook, Doel and Li, eds, 1996).

Pacific Asia is no doubt a dynamic area full of vitality and opportunities, but it is also a highly complex and diverse region which is not easy to comprehend. One major problem with Western perception of Pacific Asia, and indeed of other parts of the globe, is the failure to contextualize the nature of transformation in non-Western societies. Such an ethnocentric view of Pacific Asia has given rise to simplistic interpretations of events there, resulting in either excessive optimism of business and trade opportunities for foreign investors (Naisbitt, 1996) or extreme pessimism which sees the rise of East Asia as a formidable challenge and threat to Western economy, security, and even civilization (Huntington, 1996). Those who have been fascinated by the spectacular economic performance of Pacific Asia often fall into the trap of logocentrism. They tend to ascribe the East Asian 'miracle' to the subliminal, powerful influence of some Asian philosophies or cultural traditions (e.g. Confucianism). It is assumed that if one were to master the theory and practice of 'Asian values', one should be able to demystify oriental thinking and vastly excel other business competitors in the Asian market. However, the economic success of East Asia is a result of a unique combination of cultural, historical, political, social and economic factors. In any case, Asia's continued growth is not pre-determined and it is certainly not dependent upon something as vague and ill-defined as 'Asian values' (Robison, 1996; Rodan, 1996). East Asia has its distinct traditions and cultures but they are penetrated and challenged by external forces as the process of globalization evolves. Without integration with the global economy through which Western technology, investment and market become accessible, Pacific Asia would not have been so successful in its economic development. Thus, the changing business environment in Pacific Asia is so complex that it requires a careful reconsideration of many traditional assumptions and an in-depth analysis of the business institutions and actors within proper historical, social, economic and political contexts. As with the previous one, this volume is the product of multidisciplinary and multicultural collaboration which, we believe, is the most fruitful way of enhancing our understanding of the complexity of Pacific Asia in an increasingly globalized world. Thus, the authors in the book are drawn from Britain as well as Pacific Asian countries, and from various academic disciplines including business studies, history, human geography, political economy, political science and international relations.

Our first chapter is contributed by Nicholas White who focuses on the experience of some of the most significant and well-established British commercial firms operating in Southeast Asia — the so-called Agency Houses — as they struggle to disengage themselves from their locational and functional specificity as key agents of colonial capitalism and thereby transform themselves into fully-fledged transnational corporations operating efficiently within the Pacific Rim as a whole. White's detailed historical narrative is not only important because it attempts to take seriously issues of complexity and heterogeneity, but also because it is embedded within two interrelated contexts, whose lingering pertinence is frequently overlooked in many other accounts. The first of these two contexts is decolonization in

Southeast Asia. White is at pains to demonstrate how difficult it was for the 'linchpins of colonial capitalism' to reinvent themselves in a world that was undergoing major political, economic, social and cultural transformation. Moreover, the reworking of their forms, structures and strategies is usefully contrasted with the better known example of multinational enterprises, and White notes how integration and networking has always been a problem for the agency houses. As such, the experience of the agency houses cannot be reduced to a series of inevitable reactions to shifting horizons of risk and opportunity. To the contrary, White clearly demonstrates how the agency houses maintained a degree of relative independence of action — even in the most constrained circumstances - with a range of diverse outcome that such a situation entails.

The second context broached by White is that of structural change in the world economy in the third quarter of the twentieth century, and specifically the challenges posed to the agency houses by: the falling demand for primary commodities in the wake of the widespread adoption of synthetic materials; a widespread redirection of British investment and trade from the orbit of the colonial space-economies to the 'safer territories' of Europe, North America, and the White Commonwealth; and the declining competitiveness of British manufacturing in Southeast Asia. By giving both of these contexts due significance, White is able to construct a rich geographical and historical account of the reorientation in the 1950s and 1960s of the British agency houses centred on Southeast Asia. Needless to say, this account serves as a timely backdrop for many of the other chapters in the volume, and it also neatly demonstrates the sense in which numerous conducting and transforming bodies are affected by each other, often in unexpected and truly novel ways.

At first sight Ngai-Ling Sum's self-styled 'theoretical paper' stands in marked contrast to White's fondness for empiricism: abstract universality as distinct from concrete particularity. Yet the complimentarity between them is striking. Both refuse the temptation of ill-conceived simplification and reduction, and both endeavour to move away from the traditional Western perspectives. The West is inclined to occupy the place of the subject: the subject of action, history, knowledge, wisdom, passion, innovation, and so on and so forth. And the Western subject is inclined to view the world as *its* object; and all of those other peoples as *its* others. Indeed, the West tends to reproduce its own image in the 'other' and presents the other in its image. Much has been written from a host of perspectives which exposes this Western conceit and tries to reinforce the heterogeneity of points of view and the diversity and plurality of the world. The chapters by White and Sum partake in such a current of recent scholarship. So, whilst White's narrative locates itself within the orbit of the agency houses themselves, rather than the heart of empire which they served, Sum's theorization explicitly installs itself within the so-called 'periphery'. To her credit, Sum is not content simply to occupy the marginal position — the region of lack and incompleteness *vis-à-vis* the fullness of the centre as origin, exemplar, and destination. She not only attempts to construct a theory from the perspective of the periphery, giving this region of space-time its *full* due, so to speak; but in so doing, she causes the 'dominant perspectives' — in this case critical realism and regulation theory — to migrate from their privileged positions. In this way, Alain Lipietz's striking conception of 'peripheral Fordism' is forcefully challenged for its characterization of the 'periphery' in terms of a controlling centre located in the West, rather than in terms of its own specificity and singularity.

Specifically, Sum challenges the efficacy and relevance of the distinctions between the market and the state, and the private sector and the public sector, when it comes to describing and accounting for economic development in the East Asian newly-industrializing countries (EANICs). For Sum, these distinctions — which are often posed as oppositions — only have a consistency and a legitimate currency within very specific contexts: a number of Western societies viewed from the vantage of a certain Enlightenment heritage. Out of context, in East Asia for example, these distinctions not only fail to take on consistency, but they systematically block appropriate conceptions from coming into view. It is these latter that Sum propounds 'an alternative theoretical framework derived from a combined use of critical realism (methodologically) and the regulation approach (substantively)' (p. 41). Sum has much to say about the ethnocentricity of certain accounts of economic development in the EANICs, even the seemingly more 'progressive' and 'enlightened' ones, such as those based on French regulation theory or international political economy. In addition, her preference for an integral economy mode of society-wide research offers scope for an interesting refashioning of export-oriented economic development in the context of Fordist governmentality, regimes of accumulation, and social regulation. She concluded that dichotomizing and polarizing approaches are not helpful for our understanding of the relevance of the multiplicity and plurality of actors to the economic development of EANICs and the complex and specific contexts within which they operate and interact with each other. The chapter's high degree of abstraction does not foreclose, but positively demands, concrete case studies, not least of agency.

Amplifying themes picked up by both White and Sum, Henry Yeung provides a rich consideration of actor-networks in 'an increasingly important centre of gravity in the global economy'. His principal concern is to clarify how Hong Kong and Singapore are implicated in the changing spatial articulation of globalizing transnational corporations (TNCs). This concern is important because of the growing significance of TNCs in the manifold space-economies of Pacific Asia. Of all the chapters in this volume, Yeung's is the closest to mainstream economic geography, and it makes a useful contribution to ongoing debates, especially with regard to the interplay of corporate spatial organization and the attraction-repulsion of world cities as the 'controlling points' of the global economy. He clearly lays out the significance of location for TNCs and sets about marshalling a large array of mostly 1990s data to assess the changing organization of regional headquarters and regional offices of foreign firms in Hong Kong and Singapore, with particular emphasis on their number, activities, geographical responsibilities and country of origin. Furthermore, through a consideration of the relocation of RHQs from Hong Kong to Singapore, Yeung argues that the 'twin capitals' complement, rather than compete, with each other in the Pacific Asian region: Hong Kong remains the favoured location for securing access to East Asian markets, whereas Singapore appears to have become a centre for managing Southeast Asian operations. By embedding his study within the global economy Yeung is able to argue that locational decision making with respect to the RHQs of TNCs is less responsive to fiscal and tax incentives than it is to wider structural considerations and forces.

Geoffrey Murray sets aside the well known advantages for foreigners of doing business in Pacific Asia in order to concentrate on the negative side. Through a series of interlocking examples and anecdotes, which span a host of activities and a number of countries, Murray draws on thirty years of analyzing economic and business trends throughout Asia to highlight numerous sources of misunderstanding, frustration and disillusionment. Sometimes the difficulties hinge upon conflicting motives or inadequate infrastructure — physical, legal, informatory, etc.; sometimes they turn on unforeseen changes of context — political priorities, labour relations, policy goals, and so on and so forth. Perhaps surprisingly, the problems often rest on unquestioningly projecting one's taken for granted assumptions, experiences and expectations onto unfamiliar situations. One tends to act according to reflex, convention and habit without realizing that one is operating in an entirely different business environment. So, time and time again, Murray's experiential accounts demonstrate that whilst such difficulties can be overlooked and repressed in the initial stages of a business venture, one cannot prevent a return of the repressed in the longer term. Accordingly, many of those who have rushed to take advantage of what they imagined to be golden opportunities in the Pacific Asian region have been left disappointed as their object of desire dissolves into a markedly different, and frequently disillusioning, reality: the 'Beijing Jeep' joint (misad)venture between the now defunct American Motor Company and the Beijing Automotive Works being exemplary in this regard. However, when all is said and done, Murray's cautionary tales turn out to be much more than a warning about the complacency of Western ethnocentrism. As the account of the Vietnamese automotive industry makes clear, there is just as much scope for confusion within Pacific Asia as there is between Pacific Asia and the rest.

If Murray provides the reader with a negative take on business practices in Pacific Asia, Hock Tan strives for a much more balanced assessment of one area in particular: the structural characteristics of the Malaysian manufacturing industry. As with all the authors in this volume, Tan relates his principal theme to its wider social, economic, political and cultural contexts. Consequently, the chapter opens with a brief account of the structural changes to the Malaysian economy since the 1970s. Building on this account, Tan outlines what he characterizes as the threefold uniqueness of Malaysia's development path in contrast to that of Japan and Korea: its greater openness to foreign direct investment (FDI); its disinclination to second-guess trends in the global economy through a state-led industrial strategy; and the rapidity of the development of its financial markets. He then sets about situating the crucial role of manufacturing industry within this development path. After considering the most significant weaknesses of Malaysian manufacturing, especially its sectoral imbalance, over reliance on FDI, and extremely limited number of export markets, Tan then outlines a number of ways through which its profile, significance and competitiveness could be enhanced, with particular emphasis being placed on strengthening small and medium sized enterprises, developing the aptitude and skill of the country's human resources, improving the country's infrastructure, and securing the provision of sufficient capital at competitive interest rates for future rounds of industrialization. The chapter ends with a vision of the Malaysian economy in general, and manufacturing industry in particular, needing to continually foster a more highly-skilled workforce capable of producing high-technology and high value-added goods. Meanwhile, the spectre of capital and labour shortages, excessive foreign control, and rising wage-rates, hangs over 'the dream of full industrialization by 2020'.

Like Yeung and Tan, the chapter by Ian Cook and Yongjiang Wang recognizes the enormous significance of FDI on the restructuring of the space-economies of Pacific Asia. But whereas Yeung embeds FDI within the corporate and spatial organization of TNCs, and Tan positions it within the structural development of manufacturing industry, Cook and Wang are much more concerned with the agency of FDI itself: its changing form, characteristics, and affects. Their chapter begins with a brief consideration of foreign investment in the global economy of the 1980s and 1990s, noting that its growing volume and significance is an index of the increasing integration and deregulation of the space-economies comprising the global economy. It would be easy at this point to sound the death knell for territorially bounded space-economies, the possibility of effective state or governmental regulation, and the general advancement of an homogenizing borderless world, but Cook and Wang resist such ill-considered hyperbole. For amidst the maelstrom of flows, their principal concern floats to the surface: the incredibly dynamic and multiform space-economies of China. On the one hand, their chapter is a lucid rendition of the patterns and processes that has enabled so much FDI to circulate within China since 1979: its origins and nature, no less than its destination and form. Accordingly they give a detailed account of three great waves of FDI in China: 1979-1985, 1986-1988, 1989-94. On the other hand, their chapter offers not only an account of how this circulation is transforming the very fabric of the body that conducts it, but also attempts to draw up a balance sheet of the benefits and costs of FDI in China as a prelude to speculating on the future prospects of FDI in China. One of the most serious issues arising from Cook and Wang's study is the political ramification of the current transformation of the Chinese space-economy, which they view as being more or less irreversible: 'foreign investment may pose via the forces unleashed, a fundamental challenge to the bureaucratic-authoritarian system itself,' they say, 'a challenge which does not seek to *confront* state power, instead it increasingly bypasses and thus *subverts* it' (p. 204).

Assuming that it is still pertinent to give the most significant agency within the global economy to states, and that it is still meaningful to refer to space-economies as they were self-evidently centred on national territories — both of which are brought into question by recent scholarship and many of the chapters in this book, then China, Japan, and the United States of America would no doubt be three of the great players. Now, if Cook and Wang's chapter gives the reader a sense of the enormous challenges posed by thinking through the specificity of the Chinese situation, then it is apt indeed that this volume should close with Simon Lee's consideration of arguably the world's most important bilateral trade relation: that between the US and Japan.

Lee's chief concern is the US-Japanese trade negotiations during the first Bill Clinton's Presidency, set against the background of some major changes to the international governance of world trade. The chapter begins with a brief description of these changes, the performance of the US and Japanese domestic economies in the 1990s and the 'triple failure' of the Ronald Reagan and George Bush administrations to cut the US budget deficit, restrain calls for protectionism in the US, and maintain good relations with the Japanese. On this basis Lee argues that behind the free trade rhetoric lay a desire on the part of the US administrations for aggressive unilateralism, managed trade, and the tighter regulation of inward FDI to the US. Lee also maintains that these desires, which were initially motivated by self-interest, were both flawed in their reasoning and counter productive in their results. However, the first Clinton Presidency continued, rather than broke with, managed trade and aggressive unilateralism, seeking to reduce Japan's trade surplus with the US, and to increase foreign access to Japanese markets. In Lee's version of events, Clinton's strategy has inflicted damage on both US commercial interests and on the world trading system as a whole. And throughout the Reagan, Bush and first Clinton administrations, Lee argues that US trade policy was based on misunderstandings and faulty reasoning. He concludes by advocating multilateral negotiations, noting the current Japanese willingness to engage in further deregulation of economic activity, and the likelihood that the symbolic as well as economic significance of US-Japan trade relations may soon be eclipsed by US-China trade relations.

Taken together, the chapters in this volume give sustained consideration to numerous aspects of business, trade and economic development in Pacific Asia. Whilst it would be foolish to believe that the volume comprehensively covers these aspects, or provides a final solution to the problem of understanding the complexity and diversity of Pacific Asia itself, it is nevertheless evident that the chapters open up and pursue a host of fascinating research possibilities. Furthermore, given the enormous range of methodological, theoretical, substantive and political orientations expressed by the authors, it is remarkable how much consistency, resonance and complimentarity circulate amongst the various chapters. Hopefully we have addressed some of the key issues which are of interest to scholars and students of Pacific Asia as well as government officials and business people who have a professional interest in the region. Pacific Asia is indeed a vibrant and dynamic area, but dynamism implies rapid change and transformation which could at time be rather destabilizing and unsettling. One must therefore be aware of and prepared for the immense challenges facing Pacific Asian societies and their implications for the rest of the world. The most serious challenge ahead is arguably the social and environmental impact of economic development in this rapidly changing region which will figure centrally in the next volume of the Pacific Rim Research Series.

References

Agnew, J. and Corbridge, S. (1995), *Mastering Space: Hegemony, Territory, and International Political-Economy*, Routledge, London.

Appelbaum, R.P. and Henderson, J. (eds) (1992), *States and Development in the Asian Pacific Rim*, Sage, London.

Berger, M.T. and Borer, D.A. (eds) (1997), *The Rise of East Asia: Critical Visions of the Pacific Century*, Routledge, London.

Berger, P. and Hsiao, M.H.H. (eds) (1988), *In Search of an East Asian Development Model*, Transaction Books, New Brunswick, NJ.

Cook, I.G., Doel, M.A. and Li, R. (eds) (1996), *Fragmented Asia: Regional Integration and National Disintegration in Pacific Asia*, Avebury, Aldershot.

Cumming-Bruce, N. (1997), 'Malaysia Lets Demons Enter Its Doors Again', *The Guardian*, 5 September, p. 21.

Haggard, S. (1990), *Pathways from the Periphery: The Politics of Growth in the Newly Industrializing Countries*, Cornell University Press, Ithaca, NY.

Huntington, S.P. (1996), *The Clash of Civilizations and the Remaking of World Order*, Simon and Schuster, New York.

Kofman, E. and Youngs, G. (eds) (1996), *Globalization: Theory and Practice*, Pinter, London.

Krugman, P. (1994), 'The Myth of Asia's Miracle', *Foreign Affairs*, Vol. 73, No. 6, November-December, pp. 62-78.

Li, R. (1998), 'China's Investment Environment: The Security Dimension', *Asia Pacific Business Review*, Vol. 4, No. 1, forthcoming.

Lingle, C. (1996), 'The End of the Beginning of the "Pacific Century"? Confucian Corporatism and Authoritarian Capitalism in East Asia', *The Pacific Review*, Vol. 9, No. 3, pp. 389-409.

Naisbitt, J. (1996), *Megatrends Asia: The Eight Asian Megatrends That are Changing the World*, Nicholas Brealey, London.

Robertson, R. (1992), *Globalization: Social Theory and Global Culture*, Sage, London.

Robison, R. (1996), 'The Politics of "Asian Values"', *The Pacific Review*, Vol. 9, No. 3, pp. 309-27.

Rodan, G. (1996), 'The Internationalization of Ideological Conflict: Asia's New Significance', *The Pacific Review*, Vol. 9, No. 3, pp. 328-51.

Rosenau, J.N. and Czempiel, E.O. (1992), *Governance without Government: Order and Change in World Politics*, Cambridge University Press, Cambridge.

Scholte, J.A. (1993), *International Relations of Social Change*, Open University Press, Buckingham.

Szulc, T. (1997), 'A Looming Greek Tragedy in Hong Kong', *Foreign Policy*, No. 106, Spring, pp. 77-89.

Tsang, S. (1996), 'Maximum Flexibility, Rigid Framework: China's Policy Towards Hong Kong and Its Implications', *Journal of International Affairs*, Vol. 49, No. 2, Winter, pp. 413-33.

Wade, R. (1990), *Governing the Market: Economic Theory and the Role of Government in East Asian Industrialization*, Princeton University Press, Princeton, NJ.

Walton, M. (1997), 'The Maturation of the East Asian Miracle', *Finance and Development*, Vol. 34, No. 3, September, pp. 7-10.

Wolf, M. (1997), 'The Heart of the New World Economy', *Financial Times*, 1 October, p. 16.

World Bank (1993), *The East Asian Miracle: Economic Growth and Public Policy*, Oxford University Press, Washington, DC.

1 The Diversification of Colonial Capitalism: British Agency Houses in Southeast Asia During the 1950s and the 1960s

NICHOLAS J. WHITE

Introduction

During the 1950s and the 1960s, British commercial firms in Southeast Asia — known as agency houses — began to pursue corporate strategies which diversified their markets and investments away from traditional spheres in the region. In becoming less Southeast Asia specific they were transforming themselves into broad-based transnational corporations within the Pacific Rim as a whole. The British firms were re-aligning themselves toward emerging prospects in the Pacific Basin. In part, this was a defensive strategy and a negative response to political changes in Southeast Asia itself. As decolonization unfolded across the region, safe colonial investments were transformed into capital at risk. In addition, however, diversification was a prospective strategy and a positive response to structural changes in the international economy; the breakdown of old colonial economic systems with the economic 'disengagement' of metropole from periphery, and the development of what might be termed a 'Pacific economy'. The British business houses were not completely divesting themselves of markets and investments in Southeast Asia, but in many ways were developing new commercial linkages between Southeast Asia and the rest of the Asia-Pacific region.

The global role of the agency houses as 'investment groups' and their promotion and management of 'free-standing' companies in the period of British imperial expansion to World War One has spawned a lively and scholarly historical literature (On the investment group see Chapman, 1985; Chapman, 1988; Chapman, 1992. On the free-standing company see Wilkins, 1988; Hennart, 1994a; Casson, 1994; Corley, 1994; Hennart, 1994b). Few writers, however, have considered the survival and development of these firms down to the decolonization era and beyond.[1] The agency houses in Southeast Asia did not necessarily stagnate with the end of the British empire and the contraction of British global power. Some of the firms did find it difficult to adapt to a non-colonial world and, ultimately, failed. Others, however, through new strategies and directions transmogrified into multi-faceted Pacific Rim transnationals. The first part of this chapter examines the evolution of the agency houses from the early nineteenth century and provides examples of their diversification after World War Two. The second section surveys the changed political circumstances which proved a major factor in pushing geographical diversification. The third part of the chapter considers the structural or economic conditions which also precipitated the spatial shift in agency-house activities. These mutually reinforcing factors were: firstly, the contracting demand for commodities such as rubber and tin; secondly, the redirection of the British economy in general towards North America and Western Europe; and, thirdly, the declining competitivenesss of British manufactures in Southeast Asia which led the agency houses to seek greater links with businesses operating throughout the Pacific Basin.

The nature of the agency house

Before the chapter explores the corporate strategies of the British agency houses, this section analyses the nature of their development in the Southeast Asia region. What were the agency houses? Firstly, they were British merchant firms originating in the early nineteenth century and concentrating on purely trading activities. These firms became known as agency houses because they secured the agencies (i.e. rights) to sell the goods of metropolitan-based, western manufacturers. The existence of successful merchant firms with expert knowledge of Southeast Asia (in which the industrialized world had confidence) helped avoid the need for manufacturers to set up local sales branches, distributive networks and production units of their own. In exchange for western manufactures and capital goods, the agency houses marketed the primary products of the Southeast Asia region.

But from the mid-nineteenth century the agency houses took on new roles as promoters of fixed investments. The classic example of this phenomenon took place in *fin de siecle* Malaya. Following the signing of British treaties of protection with the rulers of the Malay States from 1874, the Singapore-based merchant firms expanded into the peninsula through diversification into primary production (Drabble and Drake, 1981, pp. 300-11; Stahl, 1951, pp. 81-121; Allen and Donnithorne, 1957, pp. 49-66; Puthucheary, 1960; van Helten and Jones, 1989). In so doing, Straits merchants such as Guthrie & Company, Boustead & Company, and Harrisons & Crosfield evolved into 'investment groups': those 'new kinds of organizational response to the boundless opportunities of the great age of imperialism' which appeared throughout British overseas trading networks during the last quarter of the nineteenth century (Chapman, 1985, p. 231). The reputations of these family firms were 'used to float a variety of subsidiary trading, manufacturing, mining or financial enterprises' (Chapman, 1985, p. 231). The Malayan merchants developed close links with the City of London as their 'expert knowledge' of local investment opportunities was channeled back to 'the centre of a global information network' where new plantation and mining companies were floated (Harvey and Press, 1990).

The case of Harrisons & Crosfield is particularly instructive. From humble beginnings as an importer of Indian tea, the firm transformed itself into a Malayan rubber producer via extensive issues on the London Stock Exchange. Hence by the 1910s, and through utilizing only limited amounts of capital, Harrisons had become the leading promoter of rubber companies in the City (Pugh, 1990, pp. 28-46; Chapman, 1985, p. 236). Many of the agency houses also extended their trading and investment interests from Singapore and the Malayan peninsula into the Borneo territories— Sarawak, Brunei and North Borneo — which were brought under formal British protection from the 1880s. However, up to the 1940s, European concessions were restricted by the protectionist idiosyncracies of White rajah rule in Sarawak, Chartered Company administration in North Borneo, and a British-advised Sultan in Brunei (Kaur, 1995; Tregonning, 1958; Horton, 1986). In addition, the 'Singapore grip' extended into the diverse islands comprising the Netherlands East Indies assisted by Anglo-Dutch trade treaties (Allen and Donnithorne, 1957; Tarling, 1993).

In Burma, similar developments took place from the 1860s. Steel Brothers & Company built up a vast commercial portfolio encompassing Burmese rice, timber, oil, cotton and tin, with ancillary interests in imports, shipping agencies, manufacturing, rubber planting, and insurance (Braund,

1975). The firm of Wallace & Company of Bombay (with its associated partnership in London, Wallace Brothers) floated the Bombay Burmah Trading Corporation in 1864 to develop forest concessions in Upper Burma (Pointon, 1964).[2] The teak industry, in particular, was given a fillip by the political stability consequent upon the British annexation of Upper Burma between 1885 and 1886. In the case of oil extraction from 1886, the Glasgow-based Burmah Oil Company's local affairs were handled by the managing agents 'on the spot', Finlay, Fleming & Company of Rangoon.[3] In nominally-independent Thailand there was also a strong British agency house presence. British formal rule was not necessarily a pre-requisite for British agency house success. The Borneo Company had developed close links with the King of Thailand from the 1850s and in the 1880s rapidly became the leading promoter of teak production in the country. During the 1880s two more British concerns, the Siam Forest Company (later styled the Anglo-Thai Corporation) and the Bombay Burmah Trading Corporation (and hence Wallaces) also became interested in exploiting Thailand's northern forests. In the 1900s, Guthries floated southern Thai tin companies in the City of London (Falkus, 1989).

Replicated in East Asia, South Africa, South America and India, these 'investment groups' provided security and 'on the spot' management expertise for distant City investors. The Southeast Asian houses, and their associated firms and partnerships in the metropole, were thus able to 'control' clusters of sterling and local currency, 'free-standing' companies they often did not 'own'. At the same time, however, it should be appreciated that the agency houses continued to handle huge volumes of import-export, shipping, and insurance business as the principals of European-based enterprises. So it was that the agency houses maintained their Janus-faced roles, firstly, as the agents for manufacturers and commercial service providers and, secondly, as the managing agents of fixed investments largely in primary production.[4] The agency houses were the linchpin of colonial capitalism linking metropolitan finance and manufacture with investment and trading opportunities in the periphery, and commanded financial resources equivalent to some of the larger industrial firms in metropolitan Britain (Chapman, 1988).

Up to the 1950s, these firms remained almost exclusively concentrated in and dependent upon Southeast Asia. The Malayan agency houses, for example, continued to promote rubber and oil palm companies to the 1930s.[5] Steel Brothers sponsored Burmese cement-making and tin-dredging firms on the eve of the war with Japan (Braund, 1975, pp. 82-4). The British agency houses in Southeast Asia were area-specific firms, and their competitive advantage hinged upon their expert knowledge of local trading and investment conditions. The need to economize on transaction costs, the frequency of transactions and the accumulation of market-specification knowledge, had propelled British multinationals such as Unilever and Imperial Chemical Industries to make the transition from contracts with agency houses to branch selling in interwar Southeast Asia (Nicholas, 1983). But the agency houses still retained their dominant position: Southeast Asian markets were generally too small to justify costly selling or manufacturing subsidiaries and the multinationals still faced severe competitive weaknesses through their lack of local expertise. Despite the termination of business between 1941 and 1945, during the Japanese occupation of the region, the agency houses quickly re-established themselves in post-war Southeast Asia. But from the 1950s significant shifts in corporate strategy were made by the majority of these firms. Immediately noticeable was a geographical diversification of both trading activities and investments. Interestingly, the general pattern of this expansion was not spatially random. Diversification was directed toward developing opportunities in the Pacific Basin. In the early 1950s, Guthries, for example, opened an Australian office (Cunnyngham-Brown, 1971, p. 308). Bousteads also posted a manager to Australia in the later 1950s to seek 'openings in that great Continent which may provide opportunities for the Company to expand its interests' (Boustead & Company Ltd., 1958). This led to the formation of a number of Australasian subsidiaries whose assets were finally brought under the control of Boustead Australia Ltd. in 1977 (Drabble and Drake, 1981, p. 315).

Harrisons & Crosfield — another British Malayan firm — laid the basis of its present-day manufacturing empire in North America (particularly in fine chemicals and fertilizers) in the early 1950s (Drabble and Drake, 1981, pp. 312-3; Pugh, 1990). Significantly, in 1957, the rubber baron, Sir Eric Miller, was succeeded as chairman of Harrisons & Crosfield by Sir Leonard Paton who was closely associated with the agency house's strategy of diversification into North American secondary industry. In the 1970s, when the independent Malaysian government placed restrictions on foreign investments, Harrisons & Crosfield executives comfortably switched the concentration of their holdings and agreed to a 30 per cent share in their former Malaysian interests (with Malaysian government agencies and associates, on behalf of the *bumiputera*, taking the remainder) (Coates, 1987, p. 358). In the 1930s, teak and rice in Thailand, continued to be the core businesses of the Anglo-Thai Corporation. After the war with Japan, however, the firm's policy-makers realized that they could no longer depend on primary production as the mainstay of the company and decided to expand its interests and 'return to the general trading of its forbears' (*History of the Anglo-Thai Corporation*, 1973, p. 17, 19). Initially, this involved establishing trading subsidiaries in Malaya, Singapore, Thailand, and India, but, in 1953, the Anglo-Thai's board took advantage of opportunities 'in other directions' leading to expansion in the dollar area, and opportunities were also explored in New Zealand.[6] By the 1970s, on the eve of the Anglo-Thai Corporation's absorption by the Inchcape group, light metal fabrication and window manufacture in Canada, and the import and the distribution of wines and spirits in Japan and Hong Kong, had been added to this agency house's diversified, Pacific Rim portfolio (*History of the Anglo-Thai Corporation*, 1973, p. 19).

Particularly instructive is the case of the Borneo Company which from the 1850s had developed a trading and investment empire spanning Southeast Asia in Sarawak, Malaya and Singapore, Thailand, and Indonesia. In the immediate post-war era the firm had actually expanded its interests in Southeast Asia. For example, it developed a number of local manufacturing interests in Singapore. From 1951, however, the Borneo Company was involved in a bold re-deployment of resources towards Canada. This involved the formation of a brick-making company to supply the Alberta state government. The Canadian brick-making venture in the event was never particularly successful.[7] Nevertheless, Borneo Company chairman, C. R. Akers, remained committed to expansion outside Southeast Asia. In 1955 the Borneo Company switched its investment from the Canadian brick plant to the Edmonton Concrete Block Company.[8] In 1958 the company acquired a controlling interest in the Alberta Oil Tool Company which provided repairs and replacements for rigs operating in western Canada.[9] In 1962 the Borneo Company's North American interests were brought together under a wholly-owned subsidiary, the Borneo Company (Canada) Ltd. (Griffiths, 1977, p. 141). In the 1960s the group diversified further; various timber interests were acquired in Australia, and the Hong Kong trading house, Gibb, Livingston & Company was taken over.[10] From 1952, the Borneo Company had also invested heavily in Cathay Pacific Airways Ltd. promoted by the Hong Kong-based Swire group.[11] As Figure 1.1 shows, on the eve of the Japanese interregnum in 1941 the Borneo Company, in terms of the spatial pattern of its subsidiary companies, was still an essentially pan-Southeast Asian firm. In contrast, Figure 1.2

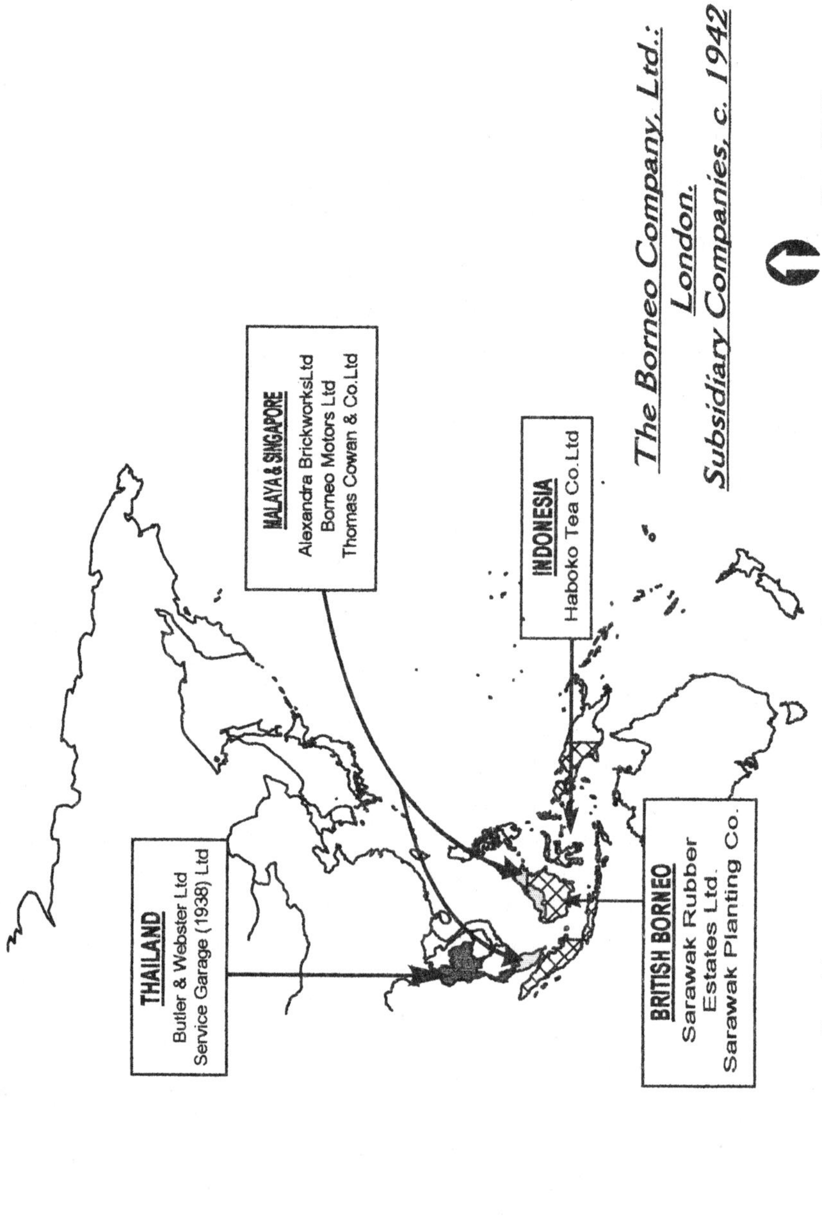

The Borneo Company, Ltd.: London.
Subsidiary Companies, c. 1942

Source: AR & A/Cs

MALAYA & SINGAPORE
Alexandra BrickworksLtd
Borneo Motors Ltd
Thomas Cowan & Co.Ltd

INDONESIA
Haboko Tea Co.Ltd

THAILAND
Butler & Webster Ltd
Service Garage (1938) Ltd

BRITISH BORNEO
Sarawak Rubber
Estates Ltd.
Sarawak Planting Co.

Figure 1.1

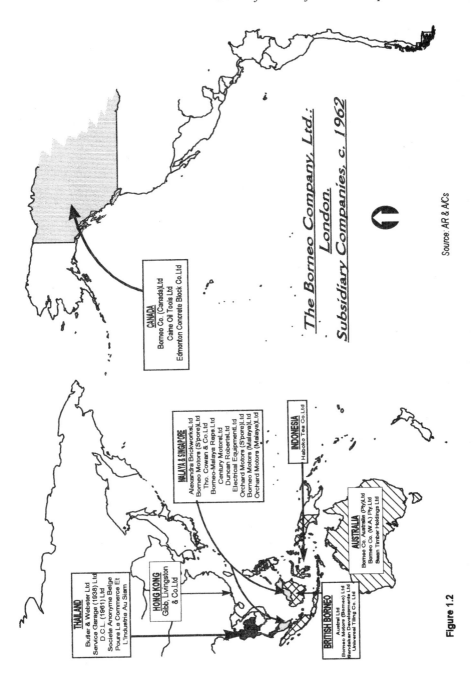

The Borneo Company, Ltd.:
London.
Subsidiary Companies, c. 1962

Source: AR & A/Cs

CANADA
Borneo Co. (Canada) Ltd
Caine Oil Tools Ltd
Edmonton Concrete Block Co. Ltd

MALAYA & SINGAPORE
Alexandra Brickworks Ltd
Borneo Motors (S'pore) Ltd
Tho. Cowan & Co. Ltd
Borneo-Malaya Reps. Ltd
Century Motors Ltd
Duncan Roberts Ltd
Electrical Equipment Ltd
Orchard Motors (S'pore) Ltd
Borneo Motors (Malaya) Ltd
Orchard Motors (Malaya) Ltd

INDONESIA
Haboko Tea Co Ltd

AUSTRALIA
Borneo Co. Australia (Pty) Ltd
Borneo Co. (W.A) Pty Ltd
Swan Timber Holdings Ltd

THAILAND
Butler & Webster Ltd
Service Garage (1938) Ltd
D.C.L. (1961) Ltd
Societe Anonyme Belge
Poure Le Commerce Et
L'Industrie Au Siam

HONG KONG
Gibb, Livingston
& Co. Ltd

BRITISH BORNEO
Austrel Ltd
Borneo Motors (Borneo) Ltd
Sandakan Developments Ltd
Universal Tiling Co. Ltd

Figure 1.2

illustrates that just twenty years later the Borneo Company was a far more widespread pan-Pacific entity. Merger with the successful Inchcape group was to follow in 1967 underlining this wider Pacific focus.

These corporate strategies of diversification into the Pacific Basin encountered considerable resistance, however, from conservative elements within the British agency houses. Such opposition was testimony to the radical departures away from Southeast Asia being engineered from the early 1950s onwards. After all, the strategy of diversification was what Ansoff would describe as a 'discontinuous change' representing a significant geographical, economic and cultural 'departure from the historical growth vector' (Ansoff, 1987, pp. 117-8). This is in contrast to an evolutionary process of strategic change, described as 'logical incrementalism' (Quinn, 1980). Before the Borneo Company's new policy of Canadian investment could be executed, for example, resistance had to be overcome from within the firm. In the Spring of 1952, A. R. Malcolm, formerly managing director,[12] expressed reservations to the Borneo Company board: he claimed that a world recession was imminent and that the firm's financial resources would be unreasonably strained by an investment which would 'tie up too much capital in a fixed asset, of which it would be difficult to dispose in hard times'. The scheme as a whole needed more investigation by 'someone resident on the spot'.[13] Moreover, Malcolm, who had been in the firm's employ since the 1920s, represented those elements which regretted the passing of the Borneo Company's Southeast Asian, colonial culture. The firm's prevailing 'values, expectations and objectives' — to use the terminology of strategic management analysts — appeared threatened (Johnson and Scholes, 1988).

Other stakeholders, such as the investors, also questioned the Canadian strategy because their confidence in the board rested on the expert knowledge which individuals like Malcolm possessed of Southeast Asian trading conditions. After all, the agency house would command at best only limited competitive advantages in the relatively uncharted territory of North America.[14] In June 1952, Malcolm took advantage of chairman Akers's absence in Canada to resist the implementation of the new strategy.[15] Yet, Akers remained convinced of his new vision for the Borneo Company and ignored the telegram from Fenchurch Street advising him to postpone the Canadian project.[16] By October a final draft of the agreement for the purchase of the Canadian plant had been received.[17] In the case of Guthries, the outspoken and cantankerous Sir John Hay, leading rubber baron and managing director of the premiere Malayan agency house from 1930, clashed with his chairman, Keith Anderson, concerning diversification away from Southeast Asia. Hay maintained that Guthries expertise in the 1950s still lay primarily in the natural rubber industry, the future of which was secure. Certainly there was a suggestion in the City that Hay 'held on too long to the belief in the supremacy of natural rubber in the face of the encroaching competition of the synthetic product'.[18] Given the strength of resistance, what were the telling motives and arguments that guided those who promoted geographical diversification in the Pacific region?

Changing political environments

Strategies of geographical diversification were partly designed to minimize political risk. By the early 1950s much of Southeast Asia was in political turmoil as colonialism crumbled (Stockwell, 1992; Tarling, 1993). In Indo-China the French were fighting a losing battle, despite large-scale American aid, against the Vietminh. By the early 1950s European planters were being murdered on French-owned rubber estates (Coates, 1987, p. 359). Indeed, anticipating the possible agonies of decolonization, French businesses had, from the early 1930s, reduced their assets in Indo-China (Marseille, 1985). In Malaya, the British firms faced communist insurgency which targeted rubber estates and tin mines, killing key personnel, slashing rubber trees and damaging valuable capital equipment (White, 1996, ch. 3) In Singapore, from the mid-1950s, strikes affected British industrial interests as the radical Peoples' Action Party and the more moderate Labour Front fought for the allegiance of the emerging trade union movement (White, 1996, pp. 228-30).

The examples of recently-independent Burma (1948) and Indonesia (1949) were far from reassuring as decolonization unfolded throughout the region. Both Burmese and Indonesian regimes had rapidly resorted to inward-looking development strategies with nationalization of foreign-owned enterprises as a central feature. As early as 1946 British business interests in Indonesia had decided that 'it would not be good business to put new money' into the islands, as the Dutch, determined to establish a loose federation under the Dutch crown, clashed with nationalists determined to establish a fully-independent republic.[19] In the early months of Indonesian *merdeka* (independence), British shipping agents in Singapore were relieved that the 'leading politicians... have ceased to be revolutionaries and are now dealing with practical politics'. Nonetheless, there remained a score of 'extremist elements... which might at any time cause a flare-up'.[20] Indeed, the Indonesian polity proved an unpredictable animal for the agency houses. The later 1950s, for example, were punctuated by boycotts of British and Dutch shipping and internal rebellions, causing anxiety and uncertainty for the British business community.[21] Most dramatically, in 1957-8 all Dutch firms were nationalized. It was only in the later-1960s, following President Sukarno's fall from power and his replacement by Suharto, that the Indonesian economy became reintegrated into western trading and investment networks (Brown, 1997, ch. 5).

The experience of Wallace & Company and its associated firm, the Bombay Burmah Trading Corporation, in Burma and Thailand, was an omen for the British business community throughout Southeast Asia. After independence in Burma on 4 January 1948, notice was given to all British lessees that the teak forests were to be nationalized within a period of three years commencing in June 1948. Given political instability 'up-country' in Burma, Wallaces made the decision to cut their losses as quickly as possible. In exchange for the unrestricted right to the proceeds from the marketing of some 45,000 tons of timber, all the firms assets in the forests — elephants, equipment, and up-country properties — were taken over by the government of the Union of Burma in February 1949. Thus ended Wallaces interest in Burmese teak which stretched back to 1862 when William Wallace obtained a forest lease from King Mindon in Mandalay. Developments in Thailand were no more encouraging for Wallaces. The Bombay Burmah Trading Corporation's leases were due to expire in Thailand in 1955, and it was decided not to renew them. The Thai government, faced by dwindling forest resources and pressures from economic nationalism, was no longer offering any new large-scale concessions to British firms (Pointon, 1974, pp. 80-3; Pointon, 1964, pp. 101-119).

Wallaces were thus forced into new directions by political changes and the emergence of economic nationalism. The timber business was compensated by a move into the jungles of North Borneo (still under British colonial administration) in the 1950s. Yet, significantly, Wallaces also branched outside Southeast Asia. An intelligence-gathering mission was dispatched to Canada in 1958 and a real estate business ensued (Pointon, 1974, pp. 80-3; Pointon, 1964, pp. 101-119). The experience of Steel Brothers under the socialist and military-socialist regimes in Burma was similar: government expropriation swept through the firm's activities between 1948 and 1963 where 'compensation was derisory' (Braund, 1975, pp. 31, 55, 79, 83). Steels diversified geographically into East Africa, South Asia, and the Middle East, but opportunities appeared more fruitful across the Pacific in Canada and Australia. In 1953, Steels established its Canadian head office on the Pacific coast at Vancouver, and by the 1970s, Steel Brothers Canadian Holdings Limited comprised interests in lime quarrying, aggregates, the manufacture of building materials, engineering, and imports. The majority of these holdings lay in the western, 'Pacific' provinces of Canada (Braund, 1975, pp. 101-7). Steels had been scouting for prospects in Australia from the 1950s, but the funds earmarked for this expansion were frozen by the Burmese government. As a result Steels were restrained from entering Australia until 1968, but insurance and manufacturing businesses swiftly developed (Braund, 1975, pp. 108-9).

Burma, of course, left the Commonwealth and retreated into isolationism. But the Southeast Asian firms found cold comfort in more managed decolonizations in other parts of Asia. Even in India, which had achieved independence within the Commonwealth in 1947, there proved to be no guarantees for long-established British business. The 1950s ushered in what the present Lord Inchcape has called the 'period of Indian restrictive economic policies patterned on the Soviet policy, which dominated the country for four decades' (Memoir in Jones, 1992, p. 370). Far from being a situation of neo-colonialism, the Indian government's assault on the British managing agencies illustrates the power of independent sovereign states over foreign private enterprise. Taxes soared: in 1948-9 Andrew Yule, its managed companies, employees, and shareholders paid one-sixtieth of the total revenue of the government of India in income tax. Commissions, new activities, and the number of companies an agent could manage were regulated and nationalization of coal and insurance ensued (Memoir of Lord Catto in Jones, 1992, p. 111).

The general climate, then, in the decolonization era was far from optimistic to the agency houses. British firms were faced with an increasingly uncertain and unpredictable Southeast Asian situation. Despite official assurances about the good treatment of foreign capital as the Federation of Malaya embarked on internal self-government from the summer of 1955, one British investor in the tin industry pointed out that:

> With the advent of Independence in Malaya, now promised, the office of High Commissioner will of course no longer exist, and the "present Govt. of Malaya" equally, may be expected to endure only to the first ensuing elections. We have seen often enough — in Indonesia, in the Argentine, in Brazil, in Egypt, in Persia — how much such promises are worth. In

particular surely we have now learnt, from the sad case of the Rubber Industry in the former Dutch colony of Indonesia, how solemn pledges given to foreign capital fly out of the window when Independence enters at the door...[22]

In such a world the 'keeping of all one's eggs in one basket' was inadvisable. In the case of the Borneo Company, re-deployment was clearly motivated by political developments in Southeast Asia. In February 1953, managing director, K. H. Simpson, wrote from Singapore proposing the formation of an engineering subsidiary in Malaya. The suggestion was not received favourably by the board in Fenchurch Street. Technical difficulties aside 'an important question of overall policy was involved'. As the board decided:

the Company's avowed aim had for some time been broadly speaking to reduce rather than increase its commitments in the East; and to invest any surplus proceeds of assets raised there in other safer territories.[23]

Those 'safer territories' usually referred to the White Commonwealth and the United States. Likewise, the Anglo-Thai Corporation's board in London had decided in 1953 to re-group its reserves 'to a level considered suitable in view of present conditions in the East'.[24]

These negative and defensive strategies in a sense represented a failing by British business in Southeast Asia to adapt to the political realities of the post-war decolonization epoque. Pre-war colonial cultures still pervaded the agency houses who refused to, or through neglect did not, co-operate with nationalists (whether moderate or radical). Cultural and ideological gaps between expatriate business leaders and nationalists are revealed in the reflections of one manager in Steels's oil department, who toured Burma in the immediate aftermath of 'liberation' in the summer of 1945:

Were they glad to see us back?... Well those Burmans who worked with Europeans [before the war] are glad, the rest I cannot answer for, as Tun Shwe says "The Jungle villager does not care as long as he is left alone and has food and clothes"... in the job of putting things to right, perhaps, the Burmese leaders will do some hard thinking on the real significance of such romantic slogans as Independence and Liberty. Our ideals cannot always be expressed in words, too often they are useless tools. If they do that hard thinking we will help in building a better Burma with such tools as affection and goodwill.[25]

The vain hope that Burmese nationalist leaders would somehow give up their struggle for independence, and concentrate, instead, on the task of economic reconstruction, in partnership with British businesses (who were far from sympathetic with their cause) was naive in the extreme! The young *Thakins* (civilian political leaders) led by Aungsan in the Anti-Fascist Peoples' Freedom League, with their innovative blend of socialism and buddhism, were hardly likely to see eye-to-eye with the conservative free-marketeers at the head of Burma's colonial firms. Nationalization, perhaps, was a self-fulfilling prophecy. The *Tuan Tuan Besar* (European commercial leaders) of Malaya and Singapore were no more accommodating to nationalism and, in the early 1950s, badgered British ministers and mandarins to slow down political advance to avoid the socialization schemes of independent India, Burma and Indonesia. British governments, however, took the opposite view and argued that precisely the way to defeat economic radicalism was to bring on moderate Malayan politicians (White, 1994; White, 1996, ch. 4). The Alliance of communal parties, led by Tunku Abdul Rahman, which came to power in the 1955 elections, soon proved its Anglophilia and its conservative, economic orthodoxy. Even so, Sir John Hay of Guthries feared the rush to independence since 'there was still a hard core of communist leadership which might seek other means of expression than through violence' and 'there did not exist the indigenous personnel qualified to administer the Government of a modern state'.[26] Despite the obvious political advantages of Asianization, the Malayan agency houses proved reluctant to employ local executives or introduce local capital into their businesses (White, 1996, ch. 6). The prejudices of the colonial past were still rife amongst top British executives. For example, A. R. Malcolm (managing director of the Borneo Company) chimed in March 1957 that 'integrity — particularly financial — is an ever present problem with Asians'.[27] In Malaysia, the British business community was indeed fortunate that the expropriation axe did not fall until the late 1970s and early 1980s when firms such as Guthries and Sime Darby were swiftly taken into local ownership and control (van Helten and Jones, 1989). As we will see in the next section, however, corporate strategic change was not solely provoked by negative responses to decolonization in Southeast Asia.

Changing economic environments

Alongside political developments in Southeast Asia, it should be appreciated how structural factors in the international economy, what might be termed 'embryonic globalization', stimulated change. The international conflict in Northeast Asia from mid-1950 had quadrupled export prices for strategic raw materials such as rubber and tin. By the end of 1951, however, the freak profits of the Korean war boom were coming to an end. Moreover, Southeast Asia's principal exports, rubber and tin, were declining in importance in the economies of western consuming nations. The Korean war witnessed a massive re-expansion of synthetic rubber output in the main market for Southeast Asia's plantation rubber, the United States. The quality of the synthetic rubbers had also vastly improved by the mid-1950s. In many uses, plantation rubber simply could not compete with the flame- and oil-resistant 'special rubbers', such as neoprene and nitriles, whilst butyl was generally held to be technologically-superior in the production of inner tubes. Claims for 'general purpose' synthetic (GR-S) were still made on the basis of dependability of source, stability of price, and uniformity of product. But by 1954 even the British Board of Trade believed there was a definite need for domestic synthetic manufacture (notwithstanding imperial and Commonwealth links with Malaya, Singapore, and the Borneo territories). The first British co-polymerization plant came on stream in 1958. By 1961 synthetic rubber had replaced its natural rival in both the United States and the United Kingdom in the manufacture of tyres and tyre products. This accounted for roughly three-fifths of the world's total consumption of rubber. In consequence of this drastic loss of competitiveness, Southeast Asian rubber producers became increasingly reliant on exports to the lesser-technology economies of the communist bloc. In the 1950s, no corporate policy-maker could have foreseen that the vast increase in the price of oil after 1973 would resuscitate demand for the products of plantation agriculture (White, 1996, ch. 5).

In the tin trade, the termination of buying by the United States of Straits tin for eight months from April 1951, and the widescale use of substitution and reclamation techniques by tin users during the boom years, further contributed to the economic insecurity of Southeast Asia. By the mid-1950s American manufacturers of tinplate could produce twice as much tinplate with the same amount of tin ore as in the late-1930s. Likewise, tin requirements in solders had been reduced by about half. Increased production of reclaimed secondary tin had been stimulated by low output in the immediate aftermath of the Japanese occupation as well as high prices during the boom years of 1950-1. Aluminium was also proving a cheaper and better substitute in the manufacture of containers for products ranging from motor oil to meats (Yip, 1969, pp. 338-9; Baldwin, 1983, pp. 49-54; Cleaveland, 1973, pp. 117-35). The economics, alongside the politics, of primary production were becoming increasingly uncertain.

Concurrently, the agency houses in Southeast Asia were forced to contend with the general economic 'disengagement' between the European metropoles and their decolonizing empires. Certainly, by the mid-1950s, Britain could no longer play the role of economic metropolis for the sterling area. With declining British industrial competitiveness even the Empire-Commonwealth trade bloc could not be relied upon to soak up British exports. Far from 'feather-bedding' British industry, by 1953 the sterling area was trading at a deficit with the rest of the world. In these circumstances, the stimulation of British exports to the dollar area — as opposed to the empire and Commonwealth — became the main focus of British trade policy as early as 1953. Freer trade naturally accompanied the free convertibility of sterling which began in stages from 1955 (Schenk, 1994, ch. 3, 5). Political, financial and industrial circles in Britain were turning away from sterling-area development and looking toward a new strategy for economic rejuvenation based upon the modernization of industry at home and the cultivation of markets and investments in the more sophisticated, and more remunerative economies, of Europe and North America (Holland, 1984). As Cain and Hopkins have written, the 'revival of the economies of continental Europe and Japan... was not just a matter of renewed growth but involved structural change, promoted by the United States, which gave rise to a new set of complementarities linking the advanced, highly specialized economies of the world' (Cain and Hopkins, 1993, p. 287).

British firms in Southeast Asia had made striking gains in terms of profitability in 1951-2. This is illustrated in the analyses of the pan-Southeast Asian Borneo Company's financial performance over the period, 1949-58, summarized in Tables 1.1A and 1.1B. All measures of profitability indicate a striking improvement in performance in 1951-2. The 'Parent' Figures in Table 1.1A (i.e. simply the Borneo Company's trading and investment activities through its overseas branches) should be contrasted with the 'Group' Figures in Table 1.1B (i.e. consolidated accounts incorporating all the subsidiary companies). The 'Parent' company Figures disguise the full extent of windfall gains.

Table 1.1A The Borneo Company Ltd. (Parent). Measures of Profitability, 1949-58

Year (to 31 Mar)	Net Profits	Return on Funds			Dividend Payment
		(1)	(2)	(3)	
	£	%	%	%	%
1949	93,998	4.04	7.96	9.40	4.13
1950	188,681	7.60	15.03	18.87	4.95
1951	333,318	10.62	24.57	33.33	4.42
1952	331,459	7.67	20.37	33.15	8.27
1953	187,852	3.79	10.05	18.79	6.53
1954	90,867	1.97	4.56	9.09	9.91
1955	125,825	2.73	5.80	12.58	10.28
1956	261,939	5.44	11.34	21.83	10.08
1957	216,687	4.09	9.00	15.48	8.63
1958	122,916	2.09	4.94	8.78	9.55

Table 1.1B The Borneo Company Ltd. (Group). Measures of Profitability, 1949-58

Year (to 31 Mar)	Net Profits	Return on Funds			Dividend Payment
		(1)	(2)	(3)	
	£	%	%	%	%
1949	236,430	7.39	15.74	23.64	4.13
1950	284,900	8.01	16.62	28.49	4.95
1951	519,548	11.63	26.52	51.95	4.40
1952	887,084	13.51	33.91	88.71	8.27
1953	599,528	7.49	17.78	59.95	6.53
1954	672,542	8.59	17.68	67.25	9.91
1955	658,225	8.67	16.02	65.82	10.28
1956	450,797	5.19	10.17	37.56	10.08
1957	392,824	4.29	8.18	28.06	8.63
1958	320,263	3.29	6.36	22.87	9.55

* The first post-war published accounts located are for 1948. Consolidated Accounts were also produced for the first time in that year, in adherence to the Companies Act, allowing us to compare 'parent' and 'group' Figures. However, this data still excludes the full financial position of those operating units, such as several tin and rubber companies, under the Borneo Company's 'control' but which were not, in law, subsidiaries.

Source: AR & A/Cs

Net Profit (NP) = (GP + OR) - (IA + D + TAX + CAE)

(1)

$$\frac{NP}{(A_1 + A_2)/2} \times \frac{100}{1}$$

(2)

$$\frac{NP}{(SE_1 + SE_2)/2} \times \frac{100}{1}$$

(3)

$$\frac{NP}{((OS + PS)_1 + (OS + PS)_2)/2} \times \frac{100}{1}$$

Dividend payments (OS + PS) = $\dfrac{(OSP + PSP)}{((OS + PS)_1 + (OS + PS)_2)/2} \times \dfrac{100}{1}$

Where:

GP	=	gross profit
OR	=	other revenue
IA	=	interest and amortization
D	=	depreciation
TAX	=	taxes not charged to operating expenses
CAE	=	central administrative expenses
A	=	total assets employed
OSP	=	ordinary share dividend payments
PSP	=	preference share dividend payments
Subscript 1	=	at the beginning of the year (1 April)
Subscript 2	=	at the year end (31 March)

Every indication would suggest that other British agency houses in Southeast Asia fared similarly. Despite heightened political uncertainties (e.g. the hiatus of Malayan Communist Party insurgency, nationalization scares, Indonesian independence, political instability in Thailand, and war in Vietnam and Korea) the high commodity prices resulting from the Korean war boom boosted income and profitability. However, this period represented the 'last gasp' of the old colonial economic system. Ironically, whilst Southeast Asia had generated vast incomes from 1950-2 for the British investment groups, these resources were to be re-invested outside Southeast Asia — in areas such as western Canada, the United States, Australasia, and Hong Kong — to reduce economic dependence on the region.

This is not to say that the British agency houses had given up on Southeast Asia. The Borneo Company, for example, never seriously contemplated divesting completely from the region. Chairman Akers informed his shareholders in November 1955 that the company intended to carry on and 'trade fully'; it was no use 'going backward' or trying to 'half trade'.[28] Strategies of geographical diversification within the Pacific Rim were also a response to the growing economic 'interconnectedness' of this wider region. In the 1950s, the UK remained the largest single source of manufactured imports for Malaya and Singapore. This reflected the traditional links of the agency houses, foreign exchange controls and imperial ties. In the 1960s Britain still supplied 22 per cent of Malaysia's imports (E. Kleiman, 'Trade and the Decline of Colonialism', *Economic Journal*, Vol. 86 (1976), p. 471 cited in Davenport-Hines and Jones, 1989, p. 7). Nevertheless, British products were becoming increasingly unpopular in many parts of Southeast Asia. For example, in the distribution of radios by the early 1960s, 'British makers persisted in trying to sell too expensive models which did not conform to highly specialized local tastes'. '[H]igh prices, protracted delivery periods and poor after-sale service' further contributed to declining British competitiveness (G. Borland, 'How to Regain a Market', *Singapore Trade* (May 1961), p. 33 cited in Huff, 1994, p. 284). As *merdeka* dawned in the Federation of Malaya, European agency house managers in the entrepot of Penang noticed the 'increased volume of trade between countries in the Far East namely India, Japan, Indonesia, Burma, China and Malaya' to the detriment of British sales. British industrials were unable to compete for reasons of 'distance and higher costs'.[29] As early as the summer of 1953, the UK Trade Commissioner in Malaya reported on declining market shares for British manufacturers which were being replaced by low-priced and high-quality German, Japanese and American goods (*Bulletin of the Association of British Malaya*, 25 August 1953). With British supplies declining in competitiveness — and becoming politically less desirable — it was necessary for the British agency houses to look elsewhere in the world. In the case of the Borneo Company, in the spring of 1955, the Malayan general manager advised London that the firm's *competitive strategy* should be to strengthen its extra-European agency list.[30] The company needed to be 'looking hard in the Americas for new lines and new ideas'.[31] Other British agency houses were developing North American connections: the Jardine Matheson subsidiary, Henry Waugh, had become the agents for Westinghouse Electric International Company's air-conditioning and refrigeration plants, forming a subsidiary in Singapore, Condair Engineering Ltd., with the American firm (*Straits Times* (Singapore), 5 April 1955). In the case of the Borneo Company, the search for North American sources proved shrewd and fortunate. At the time of the Suez crisis in October 1956, for example, the closure of the canal had little effect on the Borneo Company. Business was now heavily orientated towards the USA. The Borneo Company had secured lucrative agencies with Campbells, Richmond Chase, Sheaffer, and General Electric Refrigerators. The Malayan management, moreover, were increasingly interested in Australian sources of supply.[32] This was rational given Australia's growing trade with Southeast Asia in the post-war era.[33]

Equally important for the British agency houses was to tie up with the resurgent Japanese economy which, by the 1950s, was emerging reconstructed from the Allied occupation (Tsuru, ch. 1-2; Nakamura, ch. 2). Negative memories of the Pacific war discouraged Japan's immediate recovery in Southeast Asia's markets. In the aftermath of occupation, all Japanese properties were expropriated by the colonial authorities, and sold to local buyers as a contribution to reparations payments and war damage compensation. In addition, trade with Japan was strictly controlled to bolster the balance of payments of the sterling area. Japan only accounted for five per cent of Malayan and Singaporean exports and four per cent of their imports in 1954.[34] Nevertheless, the revival of Japanese business activities in Southeast Asia was remarkably rapid during the 1950s, and this allowed for the massive expansion of Japanese trade and investment — far beyond the levels of the 1930s — which occurred from the 1960s. As early as 1953 the Singapore Chamber of Commerce — mouthpiece of the British agency houses in the island colony — drew attention to Lancashire's dwindling share of the Malayan textile market. India and increasingly Japan were competing effectively for the cheap bulk trade, and out of 324 million square yards imported in 1952, about 254 millions came from these two countries. Japan was also entering the food market with potatoes, onions, oranges and even apples (*Bulletin of the Association of British Malaya*, 25 April 1953). In 1954 British firms in Malaya with British cement agencies (e.g. Guthries) were alarmed at the so-called 'dumping' of Japanese cement.[35] The future for British trade in the region looked increasingly dim. Reflecting on a tour of Southeast Asia at the end of 1957, Sir John Hobhouse senior partner in the Liverpool shipping empire, Alfred Holt & Company, feared and prophesized that 'European exports to Asia must be supplanted to an increasing extent by Japan and later China'.[36] The Japanese government-backed Japan External Trade Organization (JETRO) was established in Singapore to promote Japanese manufactures. During the 1950s a number of Japan's *zaibatsu*-linked general trading companies (the *sogo shosha*) set up in Singapore (Huff, 1994, p. 284). The first Japanese business to open an office in Singapore after the Pacific war was the huge Daiichi Trading Company, an offshoot of the former Mitusi and Company, in the summer of 1953. Daiichi was to export from Malaya rubber, tin, copra, latex, scrap iron and ilmenite, and to import machinery, textiles and foodstuffs (*Bulletin of the Association of British Malaya*, 25 June 1953). The Bank of England had to concede the establishment of a branch of the Bank of Japan in the island colony in 1955.[37]

British business houses in Southeast Asia were beginning to respond to the new realities: the Borneo Company acquired the shipping agency for the famous Nippon Yusen Kaisha (NYK) line when it resumed its passenger and cargo services to the *nanyo* in the summer of 1952 (*Bulletin of the Association of British Malaya*, 25 June 1952). Particularly noteworthy was the case of the Malayan agency house, Boustead & Company, which in 1958 floated the Oriental Mining Company, in partnership with the Japanese Kokan Mining Company, to supply the Japanese steel industry with the state of Kelantan's iron ore. The British government authorities had attempted to develop Malaya's iron mining industry as a sterling-area preserve. The Federation's High Commissioner, General Templer, viewed the Japanese interest in Malayan iron as representing 'the revival of their ideas on 'Co-Prosperity' in the East'.[38] But neither substantial British/Commonwealth markets or City sources of investment could be found. In June 1952 one Colonial Office mandarin had to accept that: 'I see no chance of developing iron ore in Malaya except on the basis of a Japanese market'.[39] Eventually, therefore, the British government conceded a fifty-one per cent shareholding in the new iron-mining venture to Bousteads (in partnership with the Tokyo-based British shippers, Andrew Weir & Company), with Kokan holding thirty-nine per cent of the share capital, and the remaining ten per cent of shares held by the Kelantan state government.[40] In 1959, the Oriental Mining Company produced over 400,000 tons of iron ore out of a Malayan total of over three and three-quarter million tons; the vast majority of which was destined for the revival and expansion of Japan's heavy industries (Ooi, 1963, Table 52, p. 310). And, Japanese trade and investment generally with the Southeast Asia region were to greatly expand. Recognizing this trend, by 1975, both Guthries and Harrisons & Crosfield had established interests and branches in Japan (Drabble and Drake, 1981, Table 4, p. 313).

Conclusion

This chapter has traced the reorientation of the British business houses in Southeast Asia during the 1950s and the 1960s. Corporate strategies of geographical diversification within the Pacific Rim were partly responses to the political realities of decolonization. They were also, however, a product of economic rationale and structural changes in the international economy. In a sense the expansion of the agency houses can be explained by the general upturn in the international economy from the early 1950s (Ashworth, 1987, ch. 10; Kenwood and Lougheed, 1992, chs. 16-21; Foreman-Peck, 1983, chs. 9-10). But the Southeast Asian firms primarily sought opportunities within an emerging Asia-Pacific regional economy. This is not to say that the British agency houses were aware of a geographical or economic construct called the 'Pacific Rim', or that they consciously directed their investments to economies which fronted the Pacific, but the firms sought the most lucrative and secure opportunities and these tended to be found in or around the Pacific Basin.

Strategies of geographical diversification were not always successful. The big Burmese firms ultimately failed outside Burma. Competitive advantages based upon 'expert knowledge' of Southeast Asian conditions and opportunities were clearly of little utility when investing in Canada and Australia. By the 1980s Wallaces and Steels could not survive as independent entities. Guthries and Sime Darby, which diversified least, could not retain their identity as British firms when Malaysian economic nationalism became more radical from the 1970s. But other agency houses successfully developed new sources of competitive advantage, based upon an extension of skills learned through the operation of investments in Southeast Asia: Harrisons & Crosfield diversified into areas, such as North American fertilizers and fine chemicals, where they had accumulated expertise as the manager and supplier of rubber and oil palm plantations; the Borneo Company and the Anglo-Thai Corporation joined forces with the Inchcape group and so benefited from vast, pan-Pacific intelligence and capital resources. The reasons for post-colonial success and failure will only be fully assessable when business records for the 1970s and 1980s are opened. The experiences of Harrisons & Crosfield and the Inchcape group, at least, illustrate that, despite relative British industrial decline after 1945, certain international business sectors of the British economy remained vigorous and efficacious.

Notes

An earlier version of this chapter was presented to the Economic and Social Research Council British Pacific Rim Research Group Seminar at Liverpool John Moores University, March 1995. I am grateful to the participants at this seminar for their comments on this paper.

1. An exception is Drabble and Drake (1981). This article, however, devotes little space to the important transitional period of the 1950s and 1960s.
2. At the end of the nineteenth century the firm promoted rubber companies on the Dutch-controlled island of Java. Pointon (1964), pp. 50-2.
3. Direct control from the London office of Burmah Oil was finally established in 1928. Corley, (1983); Corley, (1980).
4. On the agency house role in the provision of commercial services, I am particularly indebted to Lee Kam Hing of Universiti Malaya and his paper 'The beginnings of the insurance industry in Malaysia'.
5. An important point made in Hennart (1994b, p. 125) concerning the continued vibrancy, post-1914, of free-standing companies and, hence, the agency houses which managed them.
6. Annual Report & Accounts (hereafter AR & A/Cs) 1953; Inchcape Archives, Guildhall Library, London (hereafter IA), Ms. 27008/11, Board of Directors Minutes, 14 October 1953, 13 January, 7 April and 7 July 1954.
7. The company's loss balance amounted to CAN $167,000 at 31 March 1955. IA, Ms. 27178/25, Board of Directors Minutes, 21 July 1955.

8.   IA Ms. 27178/25, Board of Directors Minutes, 18 May, 7 September, 19 October 1955. The minutes of 17 July 1957 reported that the company's shareholding in the Alexandra Brick and Tile Company was sold. IA, Ms. 27178/25

9.   AR & A/Cs 1958.

10.   AR & A/Cs for 1960s; Jones (1986), p. 271.

11.   IA, Ms. 27178/24, Board of Directors Minutes, 16 April 1952. The initial Borneo Company investment was £40,000.

12.   Malcolm was Managing Director in London from 1946 to 1950, and again from October 1953.

13.   IA, Ms. 27178/24, Board of Directors Minutes, 7 May 1952.

14.   The AGMs for this period do not survive in the Inchcape Archives, but in 1955 Akers referred to being 'criticised severely by shareholders' for investing outside Southeast Asia. IA, Ms. 27182, AGM, 30 November 1955.

15.   IA, Ms. 27178/24, Board of Directors Minutes, 18 June 1952.

16.   Ibid.

17.   IA Ms. 27178/24, Board of Directors Minutes, 1 October 1952.

18.   Obituary in *The Times*, 27 May 1964.

19.   Rubber Growers' Association Council Minutes, Tropical Growers' Association, London (hereafter RGACM), 58, 19 December 1946.

20.   Merseyside Maritime Museum, Liverpool, Ocean Steam Ship Company, 4. B. 111/1, 'Political Report on Indonesia, 3 February 1950' enclosed in H. J. C. K. Toms, Straits Steamship Company Ltd., Singapore to R. S. MacTier, Glen Line Ltd., London.

21.   E.g. see Merseyside Maritime Museum, Liverpool, Blue Funnel Line, 4. C. 1112, Copy of Meyer & Co.'s Scheepvaart Maatschappij N. V., Amsterdam to Alfred Holt & Company, Liverpool, 15 November 1956; MacLaine, Waston & Company, N. V., Djakarta to Alfred Holt & Company, Liverpool, 19 February 1958, 4 June 1958, and 30 April 1960.

22.   Merseyside Maritime Museum, Liverpool, Ocean Steam Ship Company, 4.B.111/1, Copy of Letter from Lt.-Col. S. E. Scammell to the Shareholders of Tekka Taiping Ltd., 14 July 1956 enclosed in Mansfield & Company (Singapore) to Sir John Hobhouse, Alfred Holt & Company (Liverpool), 10 August 1956.

23.   IA, Ms. 27178/24, Board of Directors Minutes, 24 February 1953.

24.   AR & A/Cs, 1953.

25.   Steel Brothers Archive, Guildhall Library, London, Ms. 29255, Steel Brothers News Letter, No. 36, August, September, October 1945, 'Burma News. Oil Department (by W. Grant)', n. d.

26.   RGACM, 64, 15 April 1954, Report of Malaya Committee, p. 4.

27.   Enclosure of 8 March 1957, IA, Ms. 27259/4, BCL 43.

28. IA, Ms. 27182, AGM, 30 November 1955.
29. Arkib Negara Malaysia, Kuala Lumpur, AE 99/M, Penang Chamber of Commerce Confidential Minutes, 'Notes of a Meeting between members of the Chambers Committee and J. N. Davies, Trade Commissioner for Malaya in the UK, 22 November 1956'.
30. Competitive strategy is the level of strategy below corporate strategy concerned with 'how to compete in a particular market...whereas corporate strategy involves decisions about the organization as a whole, competitive strategy is more likely to be related to a unit within the whole'. Johnson and Scholes (1988), p. 9.
31. IA, Ms. 27259/1, BCL 305, Donald to MacEwen, 2 May 1955.
32. IA, Ms. 27297, BCL 581, Young to Malcolm, 2 October 1956.
33. For example, the most important post-war change in the pattern of Malayan and Singaporean imports was the higher percentage supplied by the overseas sterling area, which accounted for about a fourth of the total by the 1950s, compared with a 1934-38 average of 16 per cent. The largest gain was made by Australian exporters. Economic Cooperation Administration Special Mission to the United Kingdom, (1951), p. 375 and Table 163, p. 388.
34. Bank of England Archives, Threadneedle Street, London (hereafter BoE), OV 65/4, Note by Hughes for Loynes, 19 July 1955.
35. Arkib Negara Malaysia, Kuala Lumpur, AE/99/M, Penang Chamber of Commerce Confidential Minutes, 9 February 1954.
36. Merseyside Martime Museum, Liverpool, Blue Funnel Line, 4. C. 2107, Handwritten note of 20 November 1957.
37. BoE, OV 65/4, Note by Hughes for Loynes, 19 July 1955.
38. PRO, CO 1022/179, 'Note of a Meeting in the Colonial Office', 5 November 1953. In 1945 one senior official in the British Military Administration Malaya believed that: 'There can probably never again be any question of export of this valuable iron ore to Japan, and it ought to be our policy to endeavour to obtain an Empire market for this ore...' National Archives Singapore, MSA 004 BMA Civil Affairs 88/45, P. A. B. McKerron to H. C. Willan, 17 September 1945.
39. PRO, CO 1022/179, Minute by Hugh Harding, 9 June 1952.
40. PRO, CO 1030/183, Savingram from High Commissioner, Federation of Malaya to Secretary of State for the Colonies, 8 May 1956.

References

Allen, G. C. and Donnithorne, A. (1957), *Western Enterprise in Indonesia and Malaya*, Allen & Unwin, London.

Ansoff, H. I. (1987), *Corporate Strategy*, Penguin, Harmondsworth, Middlesex.

Ashworth, W. (1987), *A History of the International Economy since 1850*, 4th edn., Longman, London.

Baldwin, W. L. (1983), *The World Tin Market. Political Pricing and Economic Competition*, Duke University Press, Durham, North Carolina.

Boustead & Company Ltd (1958), *East India Merchants Established 1828*, Boustead & Company Ltd, Southampton.

Braund, H. E. W. (1975), *Calling to Mind: Being Some Account of the First Hundred Years (1870-1970) of Steel Brothers and Company*, Pergamon Press, Oxford.

Brown, Ian (1997), *Economic Change in Southeast Asia, c. 1830-1980*, Oxford University Press, Kuala Lumpur.

Bulletin of the Association of British Malaya, 1952-3.

Cain, P. J. and Hopkins, A. G. (1993), *British Imperialism: Crisis and Deconstruction, 1914-1990*, Longman, London.

Casson, M. (1994), 'Institutional Diversity in Overseas Enterprise: Explaining the Free-Standing Company', *Business History*, Vol. 36, No. 4, pp. 95-108.

Chapman, S. D. (1985), 'British-based Investment Groups before 1914', *Economic History Review*, Second Series, Vol. 38, pp. 230-51.

Chapman, S. D. (1988), 'The Agency Houses: British Mercantile Enterprise in the Far East, c. 1780-1920', *Textile History*, Vol. 19 , pp. 239-54.

Chapman, S. D. (1992), *Merchant Enterprise in Britain from the Industrial Revolution to World War One*, Cambridge University Press, Cambridge.

Cleaveland, N. (1973), *Bang! Bang! in Ampang. Dredging Tin During Malaya's 'Emergency'*, Symcon Publishing, San Pedro, California.

Coates, A. (1987), *The Commerce in Rubber. The First Two Hundred and Fifty Years* , Oxford University Press, Singapore.

Corley, T. A. B. (1980), 'Communications, Entrepreneurship and the Managing Agency System: the Burmah Oil Company, 1886-1928', Paper presented to the Business History Seminar, Polytechnic of Central London, May 1979 summarised in *Business History*, Vol. 22, No. 1, pp. 104-5.

Corley, T. A. B. (1983), *A History of the Burmah Oil Company, 1886-1924*, Heinemann, London.

Corley, T. A. B. (1994), 'Free-Standing Companies, their Financing, and Internalization Theory', *Business History*, Vol. 36, No. 4, pp. 109-17.

Cunnyngham-Brown, S. (1971), *The Traders. A Story of Britain's Southeast Asian Commercial Adventure*, Newman Neame, London.

Davenport-Hines, R. P. T. and Jones, G. (1989), 'British Business in Asia since 1860' in Davenport Hines, R. P. T. and Jones, G. (eds), *British Business in Asia since 1860*, Cambridge University Press, Cambridge.

Drabble, J. H. and Drake, P. J. (1981), 'The British Agency Houses in Malaysia: Survival in a Changing World', *Journal of Southeast Asian Studies*, Vol. 12 , pp. 297-328.

Economic Cooperation Administration Special Mission to the United Kingdom (1951), *The Sterling Area: An American Analysis*, London: Economic Cooperation Administration Special Mission to the United Kingdom.

Falkus, M. (1989), 'Early British Business in Thailand' in Davenport-Hines, R. P. T. and Jones, G. (eds.), *British Business in Asia since 1860*, Cambridge University Press, Cambridge.

Foreman-Peck, J. (1983), *A History of the World Economy. International Economic Relations since 1850*, Wheatsheaf, Brighton.

Griffiths, Sir P. (1977), *A History of the Inchcape Group*, Inchcape, London.

Harvey, C. E. and Press, J. (1990), 'The City and International Mining, 1870-1914', *Business History*, Vol. 32, pp. 98-119.

Hennart, J-F. (1994), 'International Financial Capital Transfers: A Transaction Cost Framework', *Business History*, Vol. 36, No. 1, pp. 51-69.

Hennart, J-F. (1994b), 'Free-Standing Firms and the Internalization of Markets for Financial Capital: A Response to Casson', *Business History*, Vol. 36, No. 4, pp. 118-32.

History of the Anglo-Thai Corporation Limited, 1834-1971, Typescript, 1973, Inchcape Archives, Guildhall Library, London, Ms. 27032.

Holland, R. F. (1984), 'The Imperial Factor in British Strategies from Attlee to Macmillan, 1945-63', *Journal of Imperial and Commonwealth History*, vol. 12, pp. 165-86.

Horton, A. V. M. (1986), 'British Administration in Brunei, 1906-1959', *Modern Asian Studies*, 20, 2 , pp. 353-74.

Huff, W. G. (1994), *The Economic Development of Singapore. Trade and Development in the Twentieth Century*, Cambridge: Cambridge University Press.

Johnson, G. and Scholes, K. (1988), *Exploring Corporate Strategy*, Prentice Hall International, London.

Jones, S. (1986), *Two Centuries of Overseas Trading. The Origins and Growth of the Inchcape Group*, Macmillan, London.

Jones, S. (1992), *Merchants of the Raj: British Managing Agency Houses in Calcutta Yesterday and Today*, Macmillan, London.

Kaur, A. (1995), 'The Babbling Brookes: Economic Change in Sarawak, 1841-1941', *Modern Asian Studies*, Vol. 29.

Kenwood, A. G., and Lougheed, A. L. (1992), *The Growth of the International Economy, 1820-1990*, 3rd edn., Routledge, London.

Lee Kam Hing (1994), 'The beginnings of the insurance industry in Malaysia, 1826-1941', 13th International Association of Historians of Asia Conference, Tokyo, 5-9 September.

Marseille, J. (1985), 'The Phases of French Colonial Imperialism: Towards a Periodization', *Journal of Imperial and Commonwealth History*, Vol. 13, No. 3, May, pp. 127-41.

Nakamura, T. (1981), *The Post-war Japanese Economy*, Tokyo University Press, Tokyo.

Nicholas, S. (1983), 'Agency Contracts, Institutional Modes, and the Transition to Foreign Direct Investment by British Manufacturing Multinationals Before 1939', *Journal of Economic History*, Vol. 43, No. 3, September, pp. 675-86.

Ooi Jin Bee (1963), *Land, People and Economy in Malaya*, London: Longman.

Pointon, A. C. (1964), *The Bombay Burmah Trading Corporation 1863-1963*, Millbrook Press, Southampton.

Pointon, A. C. (1974), *Wallace Brothers*, Oxford University Press, Oxford.

Pugh, P. et al. (1990), *Great Enterprise. A History of Harrisons & Crosfield*, Harrisons & Crosfield, London.

Puthucheary, J. J. (1960), *Ownership and Control in the Malayan Economy*, Donald Moore for Eastern Universities Press, Singapore.

Quinn, J. B. (1980), *Strategies for Change: Logical Incrementalism*, Irwin, Illinois.

Schenk, C. R. (1994), *Britain and the Sterling Area. From Devaluation to Convertibility in the 1950s*, Routledge/London School of Economics, London/ New York.

Stahl, K. M. (1951), *The Metropolitan Organization of British Colonial Trade: Four Regional Studies*, Faber, London.

Stockwell, A. J. (1992), 'Southeast Asia in War and Peace: The End of European Colonial Empires' in Tarling, N. (ed), *The Cambridge History of Southeast Asia. Vol. II. The Nineteenth and Twentieth Centuries*, Cambridge University Press, Cambridge.

Tarling, N. (1993), *The Fall of Imperial Britain in Southeast Asia*, Oxford University Press, Singapore.

Tregonning, K. G. (1958), *Under Chartered Company Rule, North Borneo, 1881-1946*, University of Malaya Press, Singapore.

Tsuru, S. (1993), *Japan's Capitalism: Creative Defeat and Beyond*, Cambridge University Press, Cambridge.

van Helten, J. J. and Jones, G. (1989), 'British Business in Malaysia and Singapore since the 1870s' in Davenport-Hines, R. P. T. and Jones, G. (eds), *British Business in Asia since 1860*, Cambridge University Press, Cambridge.

White, N. J. (1994), 'Government and Business Divided: Malaya, 1945-57', *Journal of Imperial and Commonwealth History*, Vol. 22, No. 2, May, pp. 251-74.

White, N. J. (1996), *Business, Government, and the End of Empire: Malaya, 1942-1957*, Oxford University Press, Kuala Lumpur.

Wilkins, M. (1988), 'The Free Standing Company, 1870-1914', *Economic History Review*, Second Series, Vol. 61, pp. 259-82.

Yip Yat Hoong (1969), *The Development of the Tin Mining Industry of Malaya*, University of Malaya Press, Kuala Lumpur and Singapore.

2 Theorizing Export-Oriented Economic Development in East Asian Newly-Industrializing Countries: A Regulationist Perspective

NGAI-LING SUM

Introduction

This is a theoretical paper which seeks to challenge the orthodox choice between market- and state-oriented explanations of economic development in East Asian newly-industrializing countries (EANICs). In order to develop this argument I will, first of all, criticize the market-state dichotomy used in the 1970s/1980s to interpret the political economy of EANICs as being rooted in Enlightenment categories of thought. I then propose an alternative theoretical framework derived from a combined use of critical realism (methodologically) and the regulation approach (substantively). I discuss briefly the concept of Fordism but pay special attention to its peripheral variant. Here, Lipietz's conception of 'peripheral Fordism' is discussed and criticized for interpreting the periphery in terms of the dynamics of a centre located in the 'West'. Given the totalizing nature of this conception of the peripheries, I seek to provide a more historically contingent account of one part of the periphery (i.e. EANICs) focusing on its export-oriented industrialization (EOI) stage. I hope to break with the Atlantic-fordist bias of regulationism by revealing the internal-external complexities of EANICs through the concept of 'exportism' in organizing capital accumulation in these economies. The chapter then concludes with some pointers for a possible new research agenda on the political economy of EANICs.

The Enlightenment categories in liberal and statist discourses

Although some refinements have been made since the late 1980s, the generic concepts deployed in market- or state-led accounts of economic development are still indebted to the Enlightenment. It is assumed that modern society is characterized by an institutional separation between a market economy (an unrestrained sphere of exchanges among formally free and equal economic subjects), a unified sovereign state (a constitutionalized political order with a monopoly of legitimate violence in a given territorial area), and a civil society (comprising individuals, families, and voluntary associations based on bourgeois individualism). Assuming this triple institutional separation, the emphasis could be on laissez-faire or interventionism, neo-classical models or governed markets, liberal or developmental states, private or public power, and market rational or plan rational economies. In this context, the state can play one of two roles: it can act from outside the economy to maintain the legal and political framework within which a market-generated economic order operates (with its own market-driven, self-regulating dynamic) or it can become a dominant economic player through its combined and privileged use of economic and extra-economic resources (e.g. taxes and laws). In the first case one has a laissez-faire economy, in the second a governed (mixed or command) economy and some form of interventionist state. From this viewpoint civil society is sometimes seen as an external environment in which market forces operate and which can act as a source of exogenous shocks; and sometimes as a source of animal spirits motivating entrepreneurs and/or providing demand to which they respond. In the EANIC context, this is reflected in ideas such as Confucian capitalism or diasporic capitalism.

From an agency-oriented viewpoint, the above market- or state-led approaches can be further criticized. The first approach, which has been used by Balassa (1986, 1991) and Page (1993) in relation to the EANICs, can be criticized for ignoring the social and political embeddedness of economic activities in the state and civil society, for reducing economic behaviour to the rational-maximizing Enlightenment subject, and for its exaggerated concern with self-directed markets as the principal mode of economic regulation. The second approach, which has been adopted by White (1988), Amsden (1989), Wade (1990), and Applebaum and Henderson (1992) in their studies of the EANICs, can be criticized for treating the state as an autcmonous actor able to stand outside and above other social actors and successfully pursue the best development option. In its most extreme form, it considers the state in a social vacuum and neglects processes both internal and external to the state. It conceptualizes the state apparatus as being unified and state power as being 'monistic' (i.e. whilst recognizing differences among state managers, it sees these as constrained by the unity of state power). It also tends to accept the same 'developmentalist' and 'statist' discourses as the so-called 'development state' itself deploys, thereby privileging the positions of bureaucrats/state managers/experts and so ignoring other power relations rooted in international forces, labour, gender, etc.

Can one really reduce the complexities of political economy to a simple external relation between state (or society) and economy? Or is there a more complex internal-external dialectic or even a set of internal relationships at work? Recent theoretical developments (the regulation approach in institutional economics, theories of governance in political science) as well as longer established traditions of evolutionary and/or institutional economics or the historical school in sociology would suggest that something more is required to deal with European and American political economy. I want to argue that this is even more true of East Asian economies, which lack the Enlightenment intellectual construction and institutional configuration of state-economy-society relations. If a reflexive social science attuned to the social reality is appropriate (and I believe it is), then one needs to search for the different patterns and practices beyond the separation of economy, state, and civil society. One way beyond this stifling trichotomy is through the analysis of networks.

A regulation approach and the study of export-oriented development in East Asian Newly-Industrializing Countries

Rather than adhere to reified concepts, I propose that a more appropriate form of analysis of the political economies of EANICs is to focus on economic and political networks which have greater or lesser centrality within an economic mode of growth, and a set of political and economic networks which have a greater or lesser centrality within a mode of governance (Campbell, Hollingsworth and Lindberg, 1991; Kooiman, 1993). Theoretically, I draw on two broader perspectives: regulation theory and governance theory. The first of these can be described as 'integral economics' (i.e. economics in its inclusive sense), which focuses on the socially embedded, socially regulated character of economic activities: the economy in its social context. The second can be described as 'integral politics' (i.e. politics in its inclusive sense) and focuses on the socially embedded, socially regulated character of political activities: the state in its social context. These perspectives provide a potentially society-wide analysis of economics and politics respectively without ignoring the distinctive institutional logics of specific economic or political orders. In the first case, economic development can be seen as providing the core of an accumulation strategy which then informs and subfuses political and social life. Economic principles become the basis of societalization, i.e. they come to structure political and social life and subordinated them to the pursuit of economic success. In the second case, economic development can be seen as a subordinate element within an integral political project: this does not mean that economic forces are totally controlled by the state but that the economy must be analyzed as politically embedded and politically regulated at the same time as the economy, with its relatively autonomous dynamic, generates economic resources for the political project.

Whilst integral economics and integral politics can be seen as competing perspectives, I also want to suggest that there has been a shift in their overall relevance to the EANICs. Specifically, whereas their early growth was organized under the dominance of security states as in Taiwan and South Korea, current growth perspectives are better seen as organized under the dominance of an integral economic project. Thus I will suggest that the organization of EANICs since the 1980s can be understood in terms of a movement from an economic strategy which was an essential element in a dominant political strategy to one which has itself become the dominant organizational principle for the social formation, with the result that politics is increasingly oriented to the need to secure the conditions of an increasingly dynamic economy. The key to this transition can be seen in the declining dominance of national security (whether phrased in economic or military terms) and the increased importance of different technological complexes that may enhance structural competitiveness, economic flexibility, and global competition. And this in turn is associated, I will argue, with a shift away from a Ricardian workfare regime towards a Schumpeterian workfare regime in the EANICs. This distinction between workfare regimes was initially developed from within a regulation-theoretical approach to 'integral economics'. As the latter term has been defined above, a regulationist approach shares the concern of integral economics more generally with the socially embedded, socially regularized character of economic activities; but it is especially interested in the social mode of economic regularization as opposed to the role of market forces in the self-reproduction of the economy or that of the juridico-political in economic regulation (in the conventional sense). The latter is best understood as a general research programme within radical political economy and, as such, embraces several schools with similar approaches to the socially embedded, socially regulated nature of capitalism (Hodgson, 1993; Grabher, 1993; Camagni, 1995). All these schools are interested in the historically contingent ensembles of complementary economic and extra-economic mechanisms and practices that enable capital accumulation to occur in a relatively stable manner over long periods despite the fundamental contradictions and conflicts generated by the capital relation itself. In particular, whilst far from neglectful of the essentially anarchic role of exchange relations in mediating capitalist reproduction, regulationists also stress the complementary role of other mechanisms (institutions, norms, conventions, networks, procedures, and modes of calculation) in structuring, facilitating, and guiding capital accumulation (Jessop, 1990). Thus one could suggest that regulationists study the structure of capitalist economies as a complex ensemble of social relations comprising an accumulation regime embedded in a social structure of accumulation; and that they analyze accumulation dynamics as a complex process involving the self-valorization of capital in and through regulation. Hence the regulation approach goes well beyond a narrow concern with production functions, economizing behaviour, and pure market forces to investigate the wide range of institutional factors and social forces imbricated in capital accumulation (Sum, 1994).

The Eurocentricity of the regulation approach: the time and space of Fordism/Peripheral Fordism

The national time/space of Fordism

At the centre of most work within the regulation approach is the model of Fordism, which describes a primarily national mode of growth which was consolidated in the post-war period. Fordism involves mass production of complex consumer durables based on moving assembly line techniques operated with the semi-skilled labour of the mass worker. Thus, at the heart of the Fordist dynamism is mass production, rising productivity based on economies of scale, rising incomes linked to productivity, and increased mass demand owing to rising wages. This represents a nationally-framed compromise between capital and labour. In the Fordist period, national wages were linked to productivity gains and inflation with the effect that workers benefited from cooperation with capital and capital in turn benefited from that cooperation and the full employment levels of demand which higher wages permitted within nationally-oriented spatial economies. At the same time, the welfare state indexed income support in line with the private wage and also expanded other forms of welfare provision and public employment. In conjunction with Keynesian techniques of demand management and infrastructural provision, these factors helped to create the basis for a relatively autocentric mode of growth. This entered into crisis in the advanced capitalist economies in the late-1960s and the crisis became more acute in the 1970s.

Boyer provides a useful summary of the Parisian explanation for the crisis of Fordism under four headings. First, the Fordist technical regime became relatively exhausted. This can be seen in a decline in the output/capital ratio and a slowdown in the growth of labour productivity related to the 'gigantism' of Fordism. Secondly, there was growing obsolescence of national-oriented economic management in an age of internationalization and this is related to the increasing social and economic contradictions within Fordist regulation. Thirdly, Fordism is subject to a growing conflict between rigid techniques and uncertain macroeconomic prospects as consumer demand became more differentiated and products were renewed at faster rates. Fourthly, there has been a breakdown of the international order related to the loss of international cooperation with regards to economic policies, exchange rate dynamics and monetary controls (Boyer, 1991).

Fordism as a heuristic device has been variously applied to different historically-specific conjunctures of post-war capitalist accumulation in Europe, Canada, Latin America and even Africa (Tickell and Peck, 1992). In line with Marxist radical political economy, regulationists are also interested in the restructuring of capital accumulation and models of growth. This can be seen in more recent work which has considered possible new models under the rubric of post-Fordism. Although various Fordist/post-Fordist scenarios have been proposed, I will focus on Lipietz's account of 'bloody Taylorism' and 'peripheral Fordism' in the developing countries (Lipietz, 1984, 1986, 1987). This is more relevant for my purpose in developing a regulationist account of export-oriented growth in EANICs.

Globalizing the time/space of Fordism

For Lipietz (1984), the crisis of central (metropolitan) Fordism emerged in the late-1960s. His explanation gives a more value-theoretical twist to the standard regulationist argument and puts particular emphasis on the profitability crisis of firms in advanced capitalist economies. Lipietz claims that this crisis triggered a worldwide search for higher rates of profit. Key agents in this regard were multinational firms and banks. They adopted strategies to locate and finance production processes in peripheral countries in southern Europe and East Asia.[1] Their global search for higher rates of profit led them to implant first 'bloody Taylorism' and then 'peripheral Fordism' in these countries and prompted the growth of 'global Fordism' (Lipietz, 1987). Bloody Taylorism was intended to transform selected peripheral countries into export platforms for manufactured goods, using a cheap female labour force with no prior experience of the capitalist labour process, and thereby integrating these countries into an international division of industrial labour. Noting the re-orientation in their exports from primary goods (raw materials, food, etc.) to manufactured exports, Lipietz termed this approach to growth an 'export-substitution strategy'. Its deregulated labour markets, labour force repression, and detailed division of semi-skilled labour led him to describe its associated labour process as 'bloody Taylorism'.

Two further features were special concessions in purposefully-established export-oriented economic zones and a marked reliance on female labour. According to Lipietz, this strategy enjoyed limited success for two main reasons. First, as the export advantage was based on the super-exploitation of labour, it was socially unstable and generated growing social costs. Second, since it was solely oriented towards exports, it did not lead to significant expansion of the internal market. To this we might add, third, that it was vulnerable to competition from even cheaper export platforms. Lipietz himself notes that bloody Taylorism also prompted a conjunctural protectionist reaction at the centre as the latter's domestic markets were penetrated by exports but there was no reciprocal access to expanding NIC markets. Avoiding a functional analysis, Lipietz suggested that the replacement of 'bloody Taylorism' by 'peripheral Fordism' in some countries in the 1970s could be variously explained as a 'legacy of the old-styled import-substitution policies, the outcome of an export-substitution programme based on bloody taylorization or any other specific reasons' (1984, p. 101).

The global-national diffusion: the discourse of 'Peripheral Fordism'

Lipietz's non-functionalist account of peripheral Fordism, which is alleged to be the trajectory of economic development in developing countries with some features of Fordism (e.g. mechanized mass production and/or assembly line techniques), needs careful scrutiny. I will first present a more detailed account of this concept as found in Lipietz's work and then present four key criticisms of its general meta-theoretical underpinnings, its overall analytical coherence, its missing institutional dynamic in countries where it seems most relevant, and its particular historical relevance to EANICs.

To begin with, Lipietz relates his account of peripheral Fordism to the dynamic of an alleged 'global Fordism'. Yet, without more specific historical analyses of those economies/societies which were able to achieve this form of integration into the emerging global Fordist economy, the notion of global diffusion regards the periphery essentially as a collection of sites for assembling cheap, mass-produced consumer goods for export. According to Lipietz (1987), this new mass production role for the periphery in the global division of labour contributed to the rise of the intensive regime of accumulation. This is associated with monopoly capitalism and the expansion of the market for consumer durables in these economies. This seemingly Fordist production-consumption relation was allegedly sustained by the presence of a sizeable urban middle class,[2] a significant element of a skilled working class/rural reserve army, and the existence of autonomous local capital. Whilst peripheral Fordism is similar to central Fordism in its reliance on some degree of mechanization and/or assembly line production and an expanding internal market for consumer goods, it is also said to differ in several respects. Table 2.1 provides an overview of these alleged differences as distilled from Lipietz's various arguments.

Three factors are particularly important for our purposes. First, regarded as a labour process, only the less skilled part of the Fordist production process is performed in the periphery, with research and development, design, management, skilled labour, etc., remaining either in the centre or the Southern European 'semi-periphery' (sic). Second, considered as an accumulation regime, it is not autocentric and departs from the logic of mass production and mass consumption within national boundaries. Instead, the dynamic of peripheral Fordism is articulated to the global circuits of capitalism.[3] Third, considered as a social mode of economic regulation, the expanding internal market is not constituted by the rising wages of the working class but rather by the rising incomes of the urban middle class.

Table 2.1 A Stylized Comparison between Central and Peripheral Fordism

	Central Fordism	Peripheral Fordism
Process logic	Virtuous cycle of mass production within the domestic economy	Mass production articulated to the global circuits
Labour process	Mass production by assembly lines	Mass production by assembly lines/Taylorist practices
Production	Skilled and research-oriented processes. Mainly for domestic consumption	Semi-skilled production processes with R&D located overseas. Mainly for export
Consumption	Mass consumption by working class	Consumption by urban middle class
Working class	Responsible trade unionism	Embryonic working class
Mode of regulation	Keynesian welfare state	Unstable international regulation

In part this is due to the organizational weakness of the working class and thus the absence of the trade union link in the mass-production-mass-consumption cycle. According to Lipietz, Keynesian-welfare policies also played a limited role (if at all) in securing the conditions for mass consumption in peripheral Fordism. Inspired in part by Lipietz's analysis, there has been a growing body of work concerned with peripheral Fordism. This covers economies ranging from Southern Italy (Dunford, 1988) and Ireland (Perrons, 1988) to East Asia (Cho, 1988; Douglass, 1991, 1993; Rodgers, 1994) and South Africa (Gelb, 1991). But its obvious appeal ought not to distract attention from some serious problems with the concept of peripheral Fordism.

A centre with a view: the Eurocentricity of 'Peripheral Fordism'

Despite its originality, Lipietz's construction of peripheral Fordism is problematic on four grounds. First, the concept is linked to theoretical currents based on dualistic accounts of the world (e.g. centre vs. periphery, global vs. national, developed vs. underdeveloped societies). These define the 'periphery' in terms of its functions in the global system and/or in terms of its assumed difference from (and inferiority to) the 'centre': they consider it from the viewpoint of the dynamic of the centre and its role in structuring the dynamic of the global system as a whole. Yet this sort of dualism is actually criticized within the French regulation school — including Lipietz himself in relation to the concepts of imperialism and dependency (Lipietz, 1986). It seems odd to criticize it in one context and adopt similar lines of argument in another. This might be justified if the focus on the periphery were to emphasize its own internal differentiation, e.g. between 'bloody Taylorism' and 'peripheral Fordism' (Lipietz, 1984) or between pre-industrial, rentier, intraverted industrialization, bloody Taylorist, and mixed regimes (Ominami, 1986). But, in making such a justified effort to break with simple dualism, Lipietz runs the risk of reifying 'peripheral Fordism'. This would reduce its dynamic to one of serving the functional needs of the Fordist centre or, more generally, of the world market shaped by the dynamic of that centre. Some afterthoughts and passing comments about conjunctural features of the periphery do not really enable Lipietz to escape this problem even though it allows him to distinguish various 'peripheral fordisms' (Lipietz, 1984).

Second, he defines and interprets the periphery in terms of the dynamics of the centre (Amsden, 1990; Larrain, 1991). This is achieved by emphasizing the presence of certain 'Fordist' features in the peripheral labour process at the expense of other, non-Fordist features. Even so, three characteristics of central Fordism — i.e. autocentricity, working-class consumption and the Keynesian welfare state — are missing in 'peripheral Fordism'. The combined effect of this approach is to portray the periphery as a form of incomplete Fordism in ways that would make sense to a Western/Western-oriented audience. This sort of logic of 'Fordism of the missing half' is Eurocentric and thereby ignores the diversity and the distinctive temporality/spatiality/identity of the various spaces that comprise the 'other half' of Atlantic Fordism.

Third, Lipietz's account posits urban middle class consumption — a notion which, in his hands at least, lacks any firm institutional grounding — as the key internal link in the virtuous circle of production-consumption. He thereby marginalizes other factors shaping the economic and social regulation of the periphery such as the key role of the articulation between the internal-external dynamics (see below). 'Peripheral Fordism' can therefore be regarded as a politically vacuous concept because Lipietz decontextualizes the dynamics of the periphery and simply analyses it in terms of the ideal type of metropolitan Fordism, judging the dynamic to be incomplete. In this sense his approach basically defines the periphery in relation to the time and space of Atlantic Fordism. This leads him to see other forms of development in terms of their incompleteness or, at best, their relative complementarity or coherence with the Fordist model. This logic of 'Fordism's missing half' is a typical example of research limited by its own categories.

Fourth, 'peripheral Fordism', as a concept, is not specific enough, given that Lipietz tries to restrict it 'to the countries where the expansion of the local market played a real part in the national system of accumulation' (1984, p. 102). It is unclear what a 'real' part could mean for countries as diverse in time and space as those in Latin America, Southern Europe, East Asia and Africa. The following comparison of the development paths of Latin America and East Asia (Gereffi and Wyman, 1990) aims to demonstrate that Lipietz's concept needs to be more specific in time and space. I would suggest that Lipietz's 'bloody taylorism' seems to dominate in the primary EOI stage as enclaves in the periphery become export-processing zones. Various forms of peripheral Fordism may come to dominate the secondary ISI stage as a large middle class expands the domestic market. This leaves unresolved in his work the question of whether a third form of integration into the world market would be possible, e.g. economies where export-oriented industrialization is the dominant force, especially in East Asia after the 1970s (cf. Hurtienne, 1988). In this way, Lipietz's peripheral fordism conception is spatially unbound and temporally overbound. This means that the spatial concept of 'periphery' is too loose for serious research to be possible and it is also too specific for depicting the key features of the secondary ISI stage in the NICs' growth path (see Figure 2.1).

Figure 2.1   The Temporal-Spatial 'Specificities' of Lipietz's Concept of Peripheral Fordism

Latin America

Mexico and Brazil 1880-1930	1930-1955	Mexico 1955-70 Brazil 1955-68	Mexico 1970-present Brazil 1960 - present

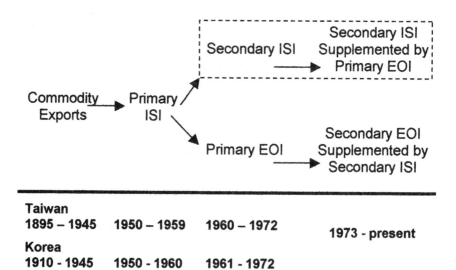

Taiwan 1895 – 1945	1950 – 1959	1960 – 1972	1973 - present
Korea 1910 - 1945	1950 - 1960	1961 - 1972	

East Asia

```
┌ ─ ─ ─ ─ ─ ┐
│           │   Peripheral Fordism
└ ─ ─ ─ ─ ─ ┘
```

Note: Original Idea from Gareffi, G. & Wyman, D. 1990: 18

Periphery with a response: a regulationist approach towards 'exportism' as a mode of growth[4]

Given these problems with the concept of 'peripheral Fordism' either in isolation or as part of a periodization of third world development, I am hesitant to provide another umbrella concept for the periphery. Instead I will offer a more historically contingent account of one part of the periphery (i.e. EANICs) with reference to the period when they adopted an EOI strategy. Coincidentally, Boyer also recognized such a need and proposed that one should emphasize the originality of the growth model of the newly industrializing countries (1994). In developing this account I will attempt two more limited tasks bearing on an adequate analysis of EANICs. First, on an ideal-typical level, I will introduce the concept of exportism. This is not intended to provide an historical description of EANICs but to provide a heuristic device for interpreting certain dominant features of their development. Second, I will offer some specific, historically informed claims about the development of EANICs in the 1960s — especially Hong Kong and Singapore. In separating ideal-typical and historical arguments in this way I hope to avoid one of the problems in the concept of post-Fordism which tends to conflate these issues. Let us start with an ideal-typical account of exportism.

An ideal-typical account of exportism from a regulationist perspective

In developing this account, I propose to use regulationist concepts to study the international division of labour as a hierarchically structured system of unequally developed national (or regional) social formations and to emphasize that accumulation regimes are best understood as being pluri-national in character (Sum, 1997). I will examine this hierarchy in terms of the reciprocal influence, the complementarities, and the contradictions between different national (or regional) formations and emergent transnational regimes and structures. And I will analyze the historical development of each national/regional formation in terms of its (changing) position within the overall international division of labour. But I also stress that the insertion of all social formations (or economic spaces) into the global order must be related to the specificity of their own historically developed social relations, classes, and structures of domination (cf. Aglietta, 1982; Hirsch, 1995). In the light of these remarks I propose that the mode of growth in EANICs can be better understood in terms of an 'exportist' accumulation regime as opposed to a 'peripheral Fordist' regime.

The second set of preliminary observations concerns the state. There are two senses in which the state can Figure in a political economy of East Asia:

as a sovereign actor in an international community of states (where statehood entails the mutual recognition of states) and/or as a particular, highly autonomous configuration of apparatuses within a domestic political order. I do not necessarily want to deny the statehood of East Asian states in the first sense (although Hong Kong would certainly be located with some difficulty in this schema); but I do want to consider whether the EANICs can be said to have a domestic political order which corresponds to a state in the second sense.[5] The problem with asserting the existence of a state in this strong, autonomous sense is the crucial role of economic and political networks in co-determining the policy-making process and securing the 'governmentalization' of society.

I want to suggest in this context that the archetypal East Asian state may be recognized as a state in the international community but has few features of a highly autonomous state which acts as the ultimate political power in society. Whether in the form of a monistic, but not monolithic, military dictatorship or an authoritarian, corporatist, labour-repressive regime or emerging, one-party dominant plebiscitary regime, East Asian governance lacks a clearly differentiated, autonomous state. When one sees the 'state' intervening, one is actually observing a particular institutional mediation of the exercise of social power which reflects a complex balance of forces whose composition goes well beyond the formal boundaries of the state (even presupposing these can be easily identified in societies where the public-private distinction is not strongly developed) and where the decision-making process is based on cooptation, consultative mechanisms, and organizational intelligence and learning capacities that are widely diffused through society. State managers and specific state apparatuses enter partnerships in a network of relations, they are not the ultimate and absolute power. In this sense it is important not to mistake formal, juridical structures for real power centres: instead one should be looking for 'parallel power networks' that cross-cut formal hierarchies and bridge apparently separate institutional spheres (cf. Poulantzas, 1978). Thus it is misleading to talk about the 'state' doing this or that. State power is always a complex institutional and organizational mediation of relations among those within and beyond the boundaries of the state. Thus one needs to examine the regimes, modes of governance, networks, etc., which are involved in exercising power.[6] And one should typically expect to find a complex of overlapping hierarchies and horizontal power networks which have no single, unitary, and unified peak. Rather than search for a mythical state, I believe in looking at the 'governmentalization' of economic power (i.e. the many and varied ways in which government agencies, state managers, and government resources are interwoven into technological trajectories and circuits of capital) and the interlocking networks and strategic capacities which enable the so-called 'state' to project its power beyond its boundaries into the furthest reaches of economic and social relations and to overcome or minimize resistance.

This theoretical critique is intended to highlight the need for a post-Enlightenment conceptual approach which is concrete enough to serve as an initial starting point for studying the EANICs. One possible way is through the combined use of critical realism and the regulation approach. Methodologically, critical realism involves the articulation of variables in a spiral movement from the 'abstract-simple' to the 'concrete-complex' (Bhaskar, 1979, 1986; Asheim and Haraldsen, 1991). In the search for more concrete-complex concepts located at a meso-level of analysis, the regulation approach identifies, on a substantive level, an ensemble of historically contingent practices that co-ordinate the economic and extra-economic regularities in a mode of growth. This means that it attributes primacy or success neither to the market nor to the policies of the state. Instead, both the market and the state are respecified institutionally and historically so that they are no longer seen as transhistorical phenomena with universal significance but as integral, inter-related, and more or less changing parts of the structure of global capitalism. In this sense, it is the distinctive structural coupling of the economic and extra-economic regularities in a specific conjuncture that make a mode of growth effective.

More specifically, a regulation-theoretic account of a mode of growth (such as national/Atlantic Fordism or exportism) requires one to look at the following areas: a) the organization of the labour process considered as a specific articulation of the technical and social division of labour; b) the accumulation regime, i.e. the macro-economic relationship obtaining between production and consumption; c) the social mode of economic regulation, with special reference to the reproduction and dynamic of the wage relation, the money form, the organization of capital and forms of competition, the role of the state, and international regimes; and d) the mode of societalization or broader implications of an accumulation regime and its mode of regulation for the wider society (Boyer, 1990; Dunford, 1990; Jessop, 1992). When dealing with 'exportist' accumulation regimes in which extraversion has a key role, it is particularly useful to focus on the 'mode of global connection' and its interiorization within a social formation. Although the above concepts may presently comprise little more than a list of desiderata for study, it should be obvious how looking at them will help one transcend the orthodox market/state dichotomy by focusing on the socially embedded, socially regulated character of economic activities. Given the merits of the regulation approach over the market/state dichotomy, the exportist mode of growth enables us to explore the articulation of the internal and external as well as the economic and the extra-economic regularities. In particular, I suggest that the concept of 'exportism' enables us to explore the international articulation of capital accumulation during the recent and crucial export-oriented industrialization (EOI) of global capitalist development. In this regard, the exportist mode of growth is extraverted and can be analyzed in terms of how different global moments are interiorized in the organization of the labour process, the regime of accumulation, the social mode of economic regulation, and the mode of societalization. These areas can only be an initial starting point for concrete research and so must be respecified for individual case studies on the EANICs. Limitations of time and paper mean that I will focus below on a stylized model of 'exportism' and its social mode of economic regulation in EANICs. Two new terms — the Ricardian and Schumpeterian workfare regimes — will be introduced to indicate how these ideas could be further developed (for more detailed arguments, see Jessop, 1993; Sum, 1994, 1995).

'Exportism' as a mode of growth

The concept of 'exportism' is intended to highlight the key role of the internationalization of production during the EOI stage of global capitalism. It is this role which provided a distinctive spatial form to the organization and dynamic of capital accumulation in the NICs. Without the coincidence of internationalization of production and a specific opening of the world market to exports of consumer durables, the exportist takeoff could not have occurred. Capital accumulation always tends to be a precarious phenomenon: it is especially so in the case of the East Asian exportist NICs because of the complexities and contradictions involved in balancing the need to import capital goods and transfer technology with the need to maintain the flow of exports and/or to deal with the crises resulting from an imbalance by reducing imports, cutting costs, or boosting demand. However, precisely because the virtuousness of this circle depends on a specific mix of complementary phenomena (which can vary from case to case), it cannot be grasped in terms of a determinate theoretical model.

Instead one needs to examine how the complementarity arises in specific cases from the interaction between the internal and external moments of a specific economic formation. In general, the uneven development of ISI-EOI orientations proceeds in different forms. On a more concrete level, one can usefully distinguish two spatially specific forms of exportism in the NICs, namely, simple and complex exportism. The former (to be called exportism from now on) is characterized by an historical conjuncture or ensemble of complementary phenomena which are related primarily, if not exclusively, to an EOI project (this is the case of Hong Kong in the 1950s and Singapore in the 1960s). Complex exportism, however, is characterized by a specific articulation of EOI-ISI projects (examples here would include South Korea and Taiwan after the 1960s).

Exportism as an ideal type cannot be compared directly with 'bloody Taylorism' and 'peripheral Fordism', which are historical concepts that capture the key features of dependent capitalist economies especially in relation to their ISI strategy. Nonetheless certain common features can be noted insofar as there are elements of extraversion in the economic dynamics of all three. Thus we need to be clear about the specific dynamic of extraversion in exportism.[7] In this regard, I want to emphasize that exportism, as an extraverted mode of growth, depends on the advanced capitalist countries for production of key investment goods and access to foreign markets to sell goods at a profit. Articulation with the international sphere of exchange for their exports means that demand (consumption) is beyond the control of local capital in the aggregate and/or the control of the local state. Exportist logic is more or less uncoupled from domestic consumption (which can be partly non-commodified in nature) and links production to investment and reinvestment. In other words, the exportist cycle proceeds from investment (for the production of export goods), actual production, effective realization of profits, to reinvestment; consumption itself is flexible and subject to international terms of trade. It is worth noting here that, in so far as demand in open economies lies beyond internal control, more emphasis in reproduction-regulation falls on the adjustment of supply.

Given its supply-side adjustment, the motivating force behind exportism is not primarily related to working/urban middle class consumption which are pertinent to the demand-led logic of Fordism and peripheral Fordism.[8] As an extraverted mode of growth, exportist logic is primarily external and production-related rather than internal and consumption-related. However, this argument is not to deny the possible significance of middle class

Table 2.2 A Stylized Comparison between Peripheral Fordism and Simple/Complex Exportism

	Peripheral Fordism	Simple/Complex Exportism
Relation to Fordism	Incomplete Fordism	Beyond Fordism
Nature	'Export-substitution' mode of growth. From raw material to manufactured products	Extraverted mode of growth. Articulated to international circuits
Process logic	Mass production for export & middle-class consumption	Depends on interna/-external linkages between investment, production and reinvestment
Motivating force	Supply of cheap consumer goods to the centre and middle-class consumption within the peripheries	Production constituted by competitive strategies and technological change
Industrial paradigm	Taylorism	Diffused & flexible Taylorism
Regime of accumulation	Intensive and monopolistic practices. Intensification of the labour process through Taylorist practices in economic production zones	Exploitation of product cycles in the succesion of long waves of growth

Consumption	Lack of working-class consumption. Middle-class consumption	Flexible consumption
Mode of regulation	Unstable international regulation	Ricardian and Schumpeterian workfare regime(s)
Class relations	Demobilized working class, strong urban middle class, and rural reserve army	Weak working class
Time and space	Fordism in terms of global diffusion	Product cycle preparing for the next long wave
Governing of time and space	Markets + hierarchies in economic and political spaces	Networks in social and cyber space
Nature of discourse	Rhetoric of the centre	Rhetoric of the NICs
Construction of NIC identity	Incomplete identity. 'Fordism of the missing half'	Simple/complex exportism

consumption especially in more historically-specific and concrete analyses. For example, complex exportism in Taiwan and South Korea in the 1980s may be motivated by a hybrid of production and consumption-related dynamics, though still with greater priority to the distinctive features of the reproduction-regulation of production in newly industrializing economies and how these are shaped by their insertion into the global division of labour as innovators of new processes and organizational practices.

The supply-side emphasis of exportism further highlights the importance of all forms of the flexibilization of production — most notably those relating to the organization of production within and across firms. Yet the concept of 'bloody Taylorism' displays an exaggerated concern with the flexibility of the labour force as grounded in repression, deregulation, and feminization. Likewise, although the concept of peripheral Fordism also refers to the impact of the domestic-foreign mix of demand on export-substitution growth dynamics, it focuses on flexibility rooted in a deregulated, partly feminized semi-skilled work force as part of an international division of Fordist labour. Conversely the concept of exportism as deployed here attempts to go beyond Fordist dynamics. As an extraverted mode of growth, it is articulated to the international circuits, being inserted into an external demand-driven virtuous cycle. In this regard, its process logic depends on the internal-external linkages between investment, production, and reinvestment. It also depends on its various sources of flexibilized production to produce an extensive regime of accumulation which is associated with competitive capitalism. It exploits product cycles in the context of an orientation to the succession of long waves of growth rather than simply to mature Fordist products (Vernon, 1966; Sum, 1994). Given its productionist orientation, its virtuous cycle is actively constituted by the competitive-driven strategies of networks of individual capitals, capital in the aggregate, and state/quasi-state actors to coordinate the time and space of production. In order to guide understanding, Table 2.2 summarizes the stylized differences between peripheral Fordism and exportism.

Some analytical foci of exportism

Given its extraverted dynamic, it is important to relate exportism in different EANICs to their respective 'modes of global connection'. If one understands a mode of growth to refer to the accumulation dynamic of a national economy considered in terms of its position in the international division of labour, then the 'mode of global connection' focuses on the internationalized moments of the mode of growth. Thus, we need to incorporate the global moment into the regulation approach, and its related four analytical foci of economic organization, namely, the labour process, the accumulation regime, its social mode of economic regulation, and its mode of societalization (or economic mode of presence in the social) (Jessop, 1992). Due to the limitation of time and space, this chapter can only emphasize the mode of global connection, the labour process, and the social mode of regulation. Let us start with the mode of global connection which involves internal-external linkages that are related to an exportist virtuous cycle.

Mode of global connection   On a concrete level, these internationalized moments display a variety of forms that can be captured with reference to the following: a) the interiorization of the internationalization of capital, politics (global power of capital) and ideology; b) the extraverted nature of the regime of accumulation and the exogeneity of its virtuous cycle basing on investment, production and re-investment; and c) the manner and extent to which a mode of regulation assists international competitiveness. In a tripartite economic-political-ideological space, the mode of global connection typically involves contingent internal-external linkages between a complex, nested internal formation (that, depending on the precise analytical focus, could be a local/regional/national space) and a more encompassing economic-political-ideological space organized under the dominance of a hegemonic power. Thus the mode of global connection can be defined as a spatially-specific form of internal-external structuration which expresses the distinctive, contingent articulation of a domestic social formation with the processes of the internationalization of capital, politics (the global power of capital), and ideology.

The economic dimension of the mode of global connection depends on the precise forms and degrees of the threefold internationalization of capital (production, trade, and allocation of money capital) under the auspices of transnational corporations and banks. There are various ways in which these three circuits of capital (production, realization, and reinvestment) can be articulated (for a comprehensive, sixfold typology of virtuous exportist cycles, see Sum, 1994; see also Bryan, 1987). In a pure Fordist regime none of these circuits is internationalized; at the opposite extreme one can envisage a 'footloose' global capital for which all economic activities are potentially mobile across economic space. Of particular relevance to the East Asian cases, however, are the implications of a mode of global connection which mainly involves domestic or TNC production of goods using transferred technology and/or investment goods in the hope of exporting the former at a profit. In such cases there are a complex set of constraints, opportunities, contradictions, and dilemmas which need to be confronted if accumulation is to proceed. These will also change over time as past success or failure changes the terms of international competition and the demand for imports and exports.

The political space is especially important in studying NICs because economic links with advanced capitalist countries are usually associated with political links of various kinds (Norcliffe, 1985). For present purposes one must be content to note the geo-political position occupied by EANICs because of their strategic positions in the Cold War era that involves the dominance of the US and the impact of communist China and Japan upon the security of Taiwan, South Korea, Hong Kong, and Singapore. Given time and space, I can only highlight the differential significance of US control over raw material and energy (especially oil) supplies, loans, aid, military protection, exchange-rate linkages, trade pacts, most favoured nation status, and so on. It is important to note that these factors do not function simply as external pressures but are often internalized as part of the rules of the game and self-understanding of economic and political forces within the EANICs as subordinate or peripheral countries. As such they constitute opportunities as well as constraints and have proved to be significant as sources of technology transfer and other learning opportunities.

Ideologically, the global process of capital accumulation is linked to a global process of ideological domination with its own distinctive dynamic. In addition to the more obvious structural phenomena (such as global news or telecommunications regimes), it is also worth noting the role of pervasive discursive formations. These formations can be recognized by a certain 'regularity in dispersion' in behaviour as social conduct is normalized in and through specific power/knowledge systems. Regardless of the historical constitution of discursive formations, we must also study how discursive formations operate in specific contexts. In the context of EANICs, it is useful to consider three aspects of how their identities are being constructed. The first aspect concerns the pervasive postwar discourse which has developed around modernization, growth, and security (Escobar, 1985, 1995; Ferguson, 1990; DuBois, 1991). The second aspect concerns the need to stablize these identities if they are to have lasting effects and influence. The third aspect concerns how these identities are embodied in communication and information technology, especially the mass media, television and commercial cinema. An analysis of these mechanisms in terms of power and knowledge would be of great importance in understanding the form of subjection in the NICs (see Sum, 1994).

The labour process Exportism, by its very nature, is extraverted and thus subject to dynamic changes induced by the external conditions. Externally, the coincidence of technological change and the internationalization of production triggers the transfer of production of mature goods from advanced industrial economies. As such, production takes the form of imitation (Ting, 1986) which is combined with a 'flexible Taylorist' (numerical and wage flexibility) labour process. This distinct type of production, which may be termed 'flexible imitative production', may change from a within to across border existence. In addition, the dynamism embedded in imitation is continually re-oriented in the light of technological advances abroad and domestic learning capacities and lessons (Ernst and O'Connor, 1989; Hobday, 1994, 1995). In this context I present a synoptic Table of a set of industrial/technological complexes in the EANICs (Table 2.3):

I use this framework to specify the nature of dominant commodity chains found in the industrial/technological production of these economies (Gereffi and Korzeniewicz, 1994). For example, the development of flexible imitative production of labour-intensive products is associated with labour processes that are dominanted by 'flexible Taylorism' (not to be confused with the sort of flexible specialization discussed by Piore and Sabel (1984)). This means that the Taylorized fragmentation of tasks does not take the form of a rigid assembly line within one plant but of a fragmented division of labour across many production sites, often small or miniscule in size. This process is often organized through subcontracting and putting-out and mediated through informal social networks with little official regulation; but it can also occur within larger plants controlled by powerful local and/or foreign capital able to exploit weak unions at home and abroad. It seeks to exploit labour flexibility at each stage of the minutely divided (or Taylorized) technical process. Other developments of flexible imitative production are associated with new forms of work organization: they include the deepening of flexible Taylorization (through the multiplication and stratification of subcontracting chains), and the growth of a neo-Taylorist Toyotism (in which production engineers come to play a key role in shopfloor management).

The mode of social regulation Let us turn from the micro- to the macro-economic aspects of the East Asian integral economy and examine change in the mode of regulation. The imitation and modification production complexes are associated with the dominance of a Ricardian workfare (RW) regime, whereas other industrial complexes based on technologically more sophisticated production systems are associated with the dominance of a Schumpeterian workfare (SW) regime. In ideal-typical terms, without implying an absolute difference in the real world, this chapter deploys the conceptual couplet of workfare and welfare to highlight the distinction

Table 2.3 Industrial/technological complexes in the EANICs

Imitator	Modifier	Improver	Innovator
Mature products	Modified prodcuts & processes	Improved products & processes	New products & processes
Low technology	Medium technology	High technology	Very high technology
Flexible Taylorism	Flexible Taylorism & Flexible Taylorism with externalization	Neo-Taylorism	Toyotism? Sonyism?
Subcontractors/ subsidiaries from TNCs	Joint ventures, licensing of new technology package	Strategic alliances, development	Original innovation
Cost-oriented, feature-oriented	Technical oriented	Product-quality oriented	Niche-market oriented
Technical & vocational/ industrial & production engineering	Adaptive design engineering, process engineering	Advanced production engineering, R&D capability	Frontier R&D
Market follower	Market follower	Market anticipator	Market leader

between the Ricardian workfare regimes in EANICs from the Keynesian welfare system in advanced capitalism in the Atlantic Fordist region. Table 2.4 shows the contrast between the RW regime and Keynesian welfare state:

Table 2.4 A Stylized Comparison of the Ricardian Workfare Regime and the Keynesian Welfare State

	Ricardian workfare regime	Keynesian welfare regime
Context	Open economy	Closed economy
Goals	Competitiveness and low-cost production	Economic growth and full employment
Mode of regulation	Supply-side	Demand-side
Nature of wage	Cost of production	Source of demand
Consumption	Privatized and individualized	Collectivized as citizen rights
Social policy	Subsidized wage in the form of workfare shelters	Social protection in the form of welfare shelters

In contrast to the Keynesian welfare state, the basis of regulation or governance of RW regimes is related to supply-side intervention that subordinates social policy to the building of competitiveness in the context of open economies. In this sense RW regimes seek competitive advantages by exploiting the cheapest and most abundant factor of production in the search for competitive economic advantage. In the resource-poor EANICs, this factor is labour power; and, as noted above, it is subject to numerical and wage flexibility within the more general context of 'flexible Taylorism'. On a different basis of regulation or governance of the supply-side conditions, the SW regime seeks structural competitiveness through permanent innovation and re-skilling. Both regimes treat wage-labour mainly as a cost of production rather than a source of demand and adopt a productivist rather than a consumerist or welfare rights approach to labour power. Given this distinction (which is based on, but goes beyond, the work of Jessop on Schumpeterian and Keynesian regimes, see Jessop, 1993),[9] I suggest that there is a tendency for EANICs to move from a Ricardian to a

Schumpeterian workfare regime. Specific cases are, however, always hybrid or mixed in character.

The dominance of a labour-intensive exportism will typically be associated with a Ricardian workfare regime whose primary functions are determined by the NICs' position in the internal-external linkages of the mode of global connection. This will typically involve the 'interiorization' of mature standardized production in low-cost production sites dominated by small firms/medium-sized enterprises—production which is financed by privately-owned/state-sponsored capital and which functions in a monetary framework with a distinctive national-international linkage. In regulation-theoretic terms, one would expect this regime of accumulation and its associated regulatory aspects to be closely linked to distinctive extra-economic regulatory or governance mechanisms in regard both to valorization of capital and the reproduction of labour-power. In exploring this role, however, one must be careful not to fall into Eurocentrism in general or, at least, mistakenly to transfer concepts from the Fordist/peripheral Fordist model to the exportist case. In addition, I would argue that using abstract and dichotomous categories such as market-state may not be very helpful in analyzing the complexities of NIC modes of growth. These are better grasped through an institutionalist account of governance or regulation which dissolves the dichotomy between market and state. In insisting upon the socially embedded, socially regulated character of markets and the socially embedded, socially governed character of political orders, the complexities of transition can be revealed. This can be seen especially clearly in the forms of social reproduction of labour-power in EANICs. For example, collective consumption is not seen as a citizen right in EANICs; and 'workfare shelters' are not so much provided to satisfy needs as to subsidize low wages in an exportist regime.[10] The imperative of staying at some sort of work or reskilling in order to re-enter the labour market rather than rely on a social wage and/or collective consumption entails that consumption in a Ricardian workfare regime occurs primarily through individualized and privatized channels. In the early stages of exportism, as previously noted, a low-cost accumulation strategy is structurally-coupled and strategically coordinated with the Ricardian workfare regime.

In abstract terms one can define the Ricardian workfare regime as involving reliance on a network of private and public actors sponsoring a flexible mix of formal and informal social reproduction mechanisms oriented to maintaining and expanding a low-cost workforce and low-cost production in a factor-driven form of time-based competitiveness. Thus, the reproduction-regulation of exportism is focused on economic and political networks which have a greater or lesser centrality within an economic growth dynamic (or mode of growth) and a set of political and economic networks which have a greater or lesser centrality within a mode of governance. Whether or not these can be unified, coordinated, and conformed to produce a coherent and well-functioning political economy is debatable. This latter doubt is, of course, reinforced by the openness of East Asian economies (rendering them especially vulnerable to shocks) and the increasing transnationalization of political relations (with the emergence of (sub)regional blocs).

As a mode of governance, the Ricardian workfare regime may involve private-public networks with capacities to: (a) adjust the labour market through practices related to flexi-wage, flexi-time and flexi-space (e.g. housewives producing at home at a low wage and/or cheap labour across borders); (b) give rise to spontaneous organizational networks of firms organized around international subcontracting/trading and subcontracting management; and (c) to facilitate mutual learning between the private and public sectors in strategizing the reproduction of low-cost labour-power through subsidized wages and close orientation to the needs of the labour market, and reproduction of general conditions of low-cost production through indirect subsidies to capital by state and corporate concerns. This mode of governance has implications for the economic and social policies pursued in the NICs. For economic policy, the strong supply-side-orientation of the RW regime leads to provision of private-public structural supports for low-cost exports. In particular this involves the deployment of industrial, tax, investment, infrastructural, immigration, exchange rate and trade development policies. For social policy, the RW regime is involved in subordinating this policy to the accumulation strategy of exportism and this means the commodification of policies such as housing, medical and health, education and social welfare (Deyo, 1992).

In abstract terms, as the NICs re-strategize and articulate with commodity chains that are more technologically sophisticated, a new form of competition is emerging. Spurred on by time-based competition and a global drive for competitiveness based on process/product/ organizational innovation, more than 'entrepreneurial spirits' are required for technological upgrading. Far more importance comes to be attached to the collective learning capacities of organizations and institutional ensembles. In this regard the Schumpeterian workfare regime acquires a role in promoting collective learning capacities and thereby advancing the structural competitiveness of the exportist economy. This entails public support for product, process, organizational and market innovation to promote structural competitiveness and state provision or sponsorship of social reproduction mechanisms oriented towards maintaining and expanding the flexibility of the workforce. Specifically, then, reproduction-regulation is focused on the following sites of intervention: a) reproduction of innovation through industrial, infrastructural, technological, and trade policies; and (b) reproduction of workforce flexibility through labour market and manpower policies. In general, the distinction between the RW and the SW regimes is summarized in Table 2.5:

Table 2.5 A Stylized Comparison between the Ricardian and Schumpeterian Workfare Regimes

	Ricardian workfare regime	Schumpeterian workfare regime
Techno-identity	Imitator/market follower	Leader/market anticipator
Level of technology	Low/standardized	High
Form of competition & competitiveness	Factor-driven by low-cost workforce. Turnover-time competition	Process and product innovation-driven. Compressed-time competition
Time and space	Flexi-wage, time, and space. Importance of social space. Economic processing zones	Fast-in-time-&-space, lead-time. Importance of social and cyber space. Learning/technological regions within and across borders
Social policy	Residual state spending on workfare shelters	State and corporate spending on reskilling and retraining

It must be noted that the transition from RW regime to SW regime typically involves the continual adjustment of policies to new structural and/or conjunctural problems and the changing balance of forces. This is reflected in different strategy mixes in moving towards the emerging SW regime just as there were different mixes in establishing the Ricardian workfare regime. This may take the form of varying degrees of restructuring of public-private networks with the capacities to: (a) innovate through new products and process with high-waged labour; (b) the spontaneous emergence of new organizational and market innovations based on the formation of a more complex network of firms organized around strategic alliances/licensing/etc.; (c) the emergence of financial innovations linked to the internationalization of the money circuit; and (d) co-operation between the private and public sectors. For the often private-dominated regimes, it involves privatization where feasible and, for other cases, adoption of commercial criteria or market proxies. In addition, regarding state economic policy as opposed to direct state economic activity, this path involves: (a) manpower policy based on the reskilling of the labour force in the direction of higher technological and managerial capacities; (b) policies oriented to diversification of products and markets; and (c) a political framework to provide for passive support for market solutions. This sort of private-dominated strategy is well exemplified in Hong Kong and is associated with a growing number of quangos and apparatuses oriented to innovation, reskilling, and competitiveness.

As for the public-dominated regime which involves greater public involvement in building networks with the private, this is best exemplified by Singapore. Here one finds a public-dominated approach in which the regime actively pursues cooperation with private capital (foreign or domestic) so as to steer the economy in a high-tech direction. This can involve the following policies and activities that enable expanded economic reproduction to occur: a) the state pursuing industrial policy by picking winners, such as certain capital-intensive industries, research organizations and new high-technology sectors, to be supported by fiscal incentives, subsidies, loans, import controls, etc. (Wade, 1990); (b) the state pursuing manpower policy by reskilling the labour force so as to bring about a flexi-skill rather than flexi-price labour market; (c) the management of trade in the global context by avoiding exchange rate overvaluation and by using export subsidies and other measures to offset the anti-export bias from import protection (Thomas and Nash, 1992); (d) cooperation of government and business in promoting growth and a consistent set of goals; (e) the co-ordination of various semi-public and private agencies ranging from educational institutions, research institutes, enterprises, and banks in order to promote new technologies, technology transfer, etc.; and (f) some degree of de-regulation and liberalization of government control. Regardless of the strategy adopted, the key point is that it is oriented to quite specific economic objectives. The aim is not profit maximization or economic growth in general but profit/market maximization or economic growth through promoting innovation and structural competitiveness in relatively (and increasingly) open economies. This can be achieved through re-orienting work-fare towards the reskilling of workers to compensate for the upward pressure on wages which constitute (as in the past) a cost of production in international competition rather than a source of demand for domestically produced goods.

Rounding up the regulation account

Regarding the accumulation regime, one can say that exportism is characterized by, at least in its early stages, the export of consumer goods as the motive force that permits the import of capital goods (whether in the form of investment goods proper or in the form of licensed technologies). Nonetheless, as the Ricardian workfare regime and its accumulation regime restructure through the search for new identities and governance mechanisms (e.g. regional division of knowledge and/or national systems of innovation), a new form of competition is becoming important. Spurred on by the competitive drive toward improvement and innovation, far more importance comes to be attached to the new techno-identity related to collective learning and the building of capacities for process and product innovations. In this regard, the search for a Schumpeterian niche becomes more pronounced, as are the tensions within and beyond these governance mechanisms.

Finally, regarding the social mode of economic regulation, one can briefly list the key features: (a) the wage relation is characterized by marked numerical, wage, and product flexibility and a competitive mode of regulation of labour markets; (b) the enterprise form tends to be polarized around a dualist relationship between small-and-medium-sized firms and large enterprises (which may be foreign-owned or have close links with the state), with the former being noticeable for their degree of vertical disintegration, the latter for their degree of vertical and horizontal integration; (c) competition is rooted in the capacity to exploit the flexible imitative production system to produce goods for a changeable market at low cost and high speed—later competition will come to depend on innovative capacities as well as learning capacities in relation to technology transfer; and (d) the state, as I have already argued, can be characterized as moving through two stages from a Ricardian workfare to a Schumpeterian workfare regime.

Some pointers towards a future research agenda

I would like to draw two sets of conclusions as pointers towards a future research agenda. First, in regard to the continuing debate over the relative importance of the market and the state as causal mechanisms in the East Asian miracle economies, I want to emphasize the inherent implausibility (not to mention its Enlightenment bias) of separating market and state in these terms. There is a growing body of theoretical and empirical literature on regulation and governance which reveals the poverty of this dichotomizing, polarizing approach when compared with the rich abundance of mechanisms in and through which economic and political coordination are achieved. Clans, networks, alliances, and cliques also have their role to play and, even where arms-length market relations operate, they have their own distinctive social embeddness and modes of calculation which help to stabilize them. In this sense it is imperative to move beyond the terms of the debate to show how state and economy come to be mutually implicated and mutually dependent.

Second, the stylized model of exportism presented above has been abstracted from the generic features of EANIC social formation. Exportism has been defined in stylized terms as a mode of growth which must be re-specified at more concrete-complex levels to make it more appropriate to different temporal-spatial specificities within the EANICs. It is impossible in this chapter to offer concrete case study materials (although see Sum, 1994) but it can be seen as a starting point for concrete research. It must therefore be respecified in the light of the fractions of capital and their relative dominance or hegemony within national, regional, and global circuits of capital of specific societies of the EANICs. These features are consolidated in the form of an exportist historic bloc that could be seen as a complex, contradictory and discordant unity of an accumulation regime and its social mode of economic regulation. In these terms the accumulation regime can be seen as the content and the social mode of regulation as the form; and the historic bloc in turn is the product of the constitution of accumulation regime through a dominant mode of regulation. This conception of the exportist historic bloc is mainly derived from the integral-economy mode of society-wide research. At the more concrete-complex level of country study, one has to specify the spatially-specific exportist historic bloc of each EANIC as well as the role of agency (e.g. classes, social movements), their struggles and relative capacities in realizing their objectives (Jessop, 1990; Sum, 1994).

Notes

1. Such a configuration of actions was coupled with tendencies in the periphery, e.g. the willingness and capacities of the ruling classes and the state to implement a labour-cheap strategy.
2. This corresponds to secondary import substitution industrialization (hereafter ISI) and the primary export-oriented industrialization (hereafter EOI) phases of development in the newly-industrializing countries.
3. It is worth noting here that whilst the growth dynamic of peripheral Fordism was initially extraverted, it could later be described as 'introverted' due to the internalization of the global dynamic through the structural coupling of different national economies and the strategic coordination of economic policies across them.
4. Here, I agree with de Mello (1987) that 'the periphery should not be seen as peripheral. It had to be seen as a specific capital which had reached a specific phase in its own history; it had to be seen as 'belated capitalism.' Interestingly enough, de Mello is quoted by Lipietz (1987, p. 66) who seems to use the concept of periphery, especially when related to global Fordism, loosely and ignores the historical contingency for which de Mello has called.
5. A useful reference point here is Badie and Birnbaum's distinction between a state and a political centre. They propose a fourfold typology of societies: those with a state and centre (e.g. France); those with a centre but no state (e.g. England); those with a state but no centre (e.g. Germany with its Länder); and those with no centre and no state (e.g. Switzerland). For Badie and Birnbaum, a state is characterized by a high degree of institutional differentiation of the political administration, evidenced in special channels of recruitment, a strong and independent system of administrative law, a clear hierarchy of state apparatuses, and a distinctive state ideology. In contrast one can talk of a stateless centre when civil

society is capable of self-organization through personal and institutional connections among representatives of different social systems.

6. Thus van Wolferen (1989, p. 5) writes that: 'Statecraft in Japan ...has entailed a balance between semi-autonomous groups that share power. Today, the most powerful groups include certain ministry officials, some political cliques and clusters of bureaucrat-businessmen. There are many lesser ones, such as the agricultural cooperatives, the police, the press and the gangsters. All are components of what we may call the System in order to distinguish it, for reasons to be discussed latter, from the state. No one is ultimately in charge. These semi-autonomous components, each endowed with discretionary powers that undermine the authority of the state, are not represented by any central body that rules the roost.'

7. It is worth noting at the outset that my use of the term 'extraversion' to describe exportist economies differs from Samir Amin's usage. For Amin interpreted extraversion as a mechanism which led to underdevelopment. Thus 'peripheral capitalism' differed from 'central capitalism' because its form was not 'self-centred' (autocentric) and peripheral capitalism had little chance to break out of its vicious dependence on another system (Amin, 1974). In contrast, the present author agrees with Cardoso (1973) that dependent development is possible even if the economy is extraverted and linked as an integral part to the global economy. In this sense, the term extraversion is used simply as a counterpoint to the autocentricity of Fordism; it is not intended to convey any message about the best trajectory for economic development.

8. Lipietz gives an account of the motivating force behind peripheral Fordism as domestic urban middle-class consumption. In this sense his mass-production-mass-consumption cycle privileges the centre as the site of expanded reproduction and seems to imply that urban middle-class consumption can be controlled (and varied) domestically to secure the conditions for a virtuous cycle of peripheral Fordist production-consumption within the context of global Fordism.

9. In addition to my introduction of the concept of Ricardian workfare regimes, I also prefer the term 'regime' to 'state' on the grounds that the state is not necessarily, if at all, the dominant mechanism of regulation and governance in securing the conditions for exportism as a mode of growth.

10. The phrase 'workfare shelters' is used instead of 'safety nets' because the former refers to policy areas that are related to possible forms of wage subsidies in low-cost production sites. These may include policy areas such as public housing, free education, social services and street hawking which help to absorb the surplus labour in times of unemployment, whereas safety nets are used in relation to the provision of social protection in a welfare state.

References

Aglietta, M. (1979), *A Theory of Capitalist Regulation*, NLB, London.

Aglietta, M. (1982), 'World Capitalism in the Eighties', *New Left Review*, No. 136, pp. 25-35.

Amin, S. (1974), *Accumulation on a World Scale: A Critique of the Theory of Underdevelopment*, Monthly Review Press, New York.

Amsden, A.H. (1989), *Asia's Next Giant, South Korea and Late Industrialization*, Oxford University Press, New York.

Amsden, A.H. (1990), 'Third World Industrialization, 'Global Fordism' or New Model?', *New Left Review*, No. 182, pp. 5-31.

Applebaum, R.P. and Henderson, J. (eds) (1992), *States and Development in the Asian Pacific Rim*, Sage, London.

Asheim, B.J. and Haraldsen, T. (1991), 'Methodology and Theoretical Problems in Economic Geography', *Norsk Geografisk Tidsskrift*, Vol. 45, pp. 189-200.

Balassa, B. (1986), 'The Lessons of East Asian Development: An Overview,' *Economic Development and Cultural Change*, Supplement, Vol. 36, No. 3, S273-S290.

Balassa, B. (1991), *Economic Policies in the Pacific-Area Developing Countries*, Macmillan, London.

Bhaskar, R. (1979), *A Realist Theory of Science*, Harvester, Brighton.

Bhaskar, R. (1986), *Scientific Realism and Human Emancipation*, Verso, London.

Boyer, R. (1990), *The Regulation School: A Critical Introduction*, Columbia University Press, New York.

Boyer, R. (1991), 'The Eighties: the Search for Alternatives to Fordism', in B. Jessop, et al. *The Politics of Flexibility: Restructuring State and Industry in Britain, Germany and Scandinavia*, Edward Elgar, Aldershot, pp. 106-134.

Boyer, R. (1994), 'Do Labour Institutions Matter for Economic Development? A Regulation Approach for the OECD and Latin America, with an Extension to Asia', in G. Rodgers (ed.), *Workers, Institutions and Economic Growth in Asia*, International Institute for Labour Studies, Geneva, pp. 25-112.

Bryan, R. (1987), 'The State and Internationalization of Capital: An Approach to Analysis', *Journal of Contemporary Asia*, Vol. 17, No. 3, pp. 253-275.

Camagni, R. (1995), 'The Concept of Innovative Milieu and its Relevance for Public Policies in European Lagging Regions', *Papers in Regional Science*, Vol. 74, No. 4, pp. 317-340.

Campbell, J.L., Hollingsworth, J.R. and Lindberg, L.N. (eds) (1991), *Governance of the American Economy*, Cambridge University Press, Cambridge.

Cardoso, F.H. (1973), 'Associated Dependent Development: Theoretical and Practical Implications', in Stepan, A. (ed), *Authoritarian Brazil: Origins, Policy, and Future*, Yale University Press, New Haven.

Cho, M-R. (1988), 'The State, Peripheral Fordism and the Regional Problem: A Case of South Korea', *Working Paper*, No. 62, Urban and Regional Studies, University of Sussex.

Deyo, F. (ed.) (1987), *The Political Economy of the New Asian Industrialism*, Cornell University Press, New York.

Dosi, G., Freeman, C. Silverberg, G. and Soete, L. (eds) (1988), *Technical Change and Economic Theory*, Pinter, London.

Douglass, M. (1993), 'Social, Political and Spatial Dimensions of Korean Industrial Transformation', *Journal of Contemporary Asia*, Vol. 23, No. 2, pp. 149-172.

DuBois, M. (1991), 'The Governance of the Third World: A Foucauldian Perspective on Power Relations in Development', *Alternatives*, Vol. 16, No. 1, pp. 1-30.

Dunford, M. (1988), *Capital, the State and Regional Development*, Pion, London.

Dunford, M. (1990), 'Theories of Regulation', *Environment and Planning D: Society and Space*, Vol. 8, pp. 297-321.

Ernst, D. and O'Connor, D. (eds) (1989), *Technology and Global Competition, the Challenge for Newly Industrializing Economies*, Development Centre Studies, OECD, Paris.

Escobar, A. (1984-85), 'Discourse and Power in Development: Michel Foucault and the Relevance of his Work to the Third World', *Alternatives*, Vol. 10 (Winter), pp. 377-400.

Escobar, A. (1995), *Encountering Development*, Princeton University Press, New Jersey.

Ferguson, J. (1990), *The Anti-Politics Machine: 'Development', Depoliticization, and Bureaucratic Power in Lesotho*, Cambridge University Press, Cambridge.

Gereffi, G. and Korzeniewicz, M. (eds) (1994), *Commodity Chains and Global Capitalism*, Praeger, London.

Gereffi, G. and Wyman, D. (eds) (1990), *Manufacturing Miracles: Patterns of Industrialization in Latin America and East Asia*, Princeton University Press, Princeton.

Grabher, G. (ed.) (1993), *Embedded Firms: On the Socioeconomics of Industrial Networks*, Routledge, London.

Graham, J. (1991), 'Fordism/Post-Fordism, Marxism/Post-Marxism: The Second Cultural Divide?', *Rethinking Marxism*, Vol. 4, No. 1, pp. 39-60.

Gramsci, A. (1971), *Selections from the Prison Notebooks*, Lawrence and Wishart, London.

Hamilton, G. (ed.) (1991), *Business Networks and Economic Development in East and Southeast Asia*, Centre of Asian Studies, University of Hong Kong Press, Hong Kong.

Hausler, J. and Hirsch, J. (1987), 'Regulation und Parteien im Ubergang zum Postfordismus (Regulation and parties in the transition to post-fordism)', *Das Argument*, No. 165.

Hirsch, J. (1995), 'Nation-State, International Regulation and the Question of Democracy', *Review of International Political Economy*, Vol. 2, No. 2, pp. 267-284.

Hobday, M. (1994), 'Technological Learning in Singapore: a Test Case of Leap frogging', *Journal of Development Studies*, Vol. 30, No. 3, pp. 831-858.

Hobday, M. (1995), *Innovation in East Asia*, Edward Elgar, Aldershot.

Hodgson, G.M. (1993), *Economics and Evolution: Bringing Life Back into Economics*, Polity Press, Cambridge.

Jenson, J. (1990), 'Representations in Crisis: the roots of Canadian Permeable Fordism', *Canadian Journal of Political Science*, Vol. 24, No. 3, pp. 653-683.

Jessop, B. (1989), 'Regulation Theories in Retrospect and Prospect', *Economy and Society*, Vol. 19, No. 2, pp. 7-69.

Jessop, B. (1990), *State Theory*, Polity Press, Cambridge.

Jessop, B. (1992), 'Fordism and Post-Fordism: A Critical Reformulation', in A. J. Scott and M. J. Storper (eds), *Pathways to Regionalism and Industrial Development*, Routledge, London.pp. 43-65.

Jessop, B. (1993), 'The Schumpeterian Workfare State', *Studies in Political Economy*, Vol. 40, pp. 7-40.

Kim, E.M. (1993), 'Contradictions and Limits of a Developmental State: with Illustrations from the South Korean Case', *Social Problems*, Vol. 40, No. 2, pp. 228-249.

Kooiman, J. (ed.) (1993), *Modern Governance: New Government-Society Interactions*, Sage, London.

Larrain, J. (1991), 'Classical Political Economists and Marx on Colonialism and 'Backward' Nations', *World Development*, Vol. 19, Nos 2/3, pp. 225-243.

Leborgne, D. and Lipietz, A. (1987), 'New Technologies: New Modes of Regulation, Some Spatial Implications', *Environment and Planning D: Society and Space*, Vol. 6, No. 3, pp. 263-80.

Lipietz, A. (1982), 'Towards Global Fordism?', *New Left Review*, No. 132, pp. 3-47.

Lipietz, A. (1984), 'Imperialism or the Beast of the Apocalypse', *Capital and Class*, No. 22, pp. 81-109.

Lipietz, A. (1987), *Mirages and Miracles*, Verso, London.

Lipietz, A. (1993), 'The Local and the Global: Regional Individuality or Interregionalism', *Transactions of The Institute of British Geographers*, Vol. 18, pp. 8-18.

Nielsen, K. and Pedersen, O.K. (1993), 'The negotiated economy: general features and theoretical perspectives', in J. Hausner et al. (eds), *Institutional Frameworks of Market Economies*, Avebury, Aldershot, pp. 89-112.

Noel, A. (1988), '*Action collective, partis politiques et relations industrielles: une logique politique pour l'approche de la regulation*'. Paper prepared for the 'International Conference on Regulation Theory', Barcelona, June.

Norcliffe, G.B. (1985), 'The Industrial Geography of the Third World', in M. Pacione (ed.), *Progress in Industrial Geography*, Croom Helm, London, pp. 249-283.

Page, J. (1993), *The East Asian Miracle*, Oxford University Press, Oxford.

Palloix, C. (1975), 'The Internationalization of Capital and the Circuit of Social Capital', in H. Radice (ed.), *International Firms and Modern Imperialism: Selected Readings*, Penguin, Harmondsworth, pp. 63-88.

Piore, M. and Sabel, C. (1984), *The Second Industrial Divide: Possibilities for Prosperity*, Basic Books, New York.

Poulantzas, N. (1978), *State, Power, Socialism*, NLB, London.

Salais, R. and Storper, M. (1992), 'The Four 'Worlds' of Contemporary Industry', *Cambridge Journal of Economics*, Vol. 16, pp. 169-193.

Schmitz, H. (1990), '*Flexible Specialization in Third World Industry: Prospects and Research Requirements*', Paper presented in the Workshop 'Flexible Specialization in Europe', 25-26 October, 1990, Zurich.

Sum, N-L. (1994), *Reflections on Accumulation, Regulation, the State and Societalization: A Stylized Model of East Asian Capitalism and an Integral Economic Analysis of Hong Kong* Ph.D. Thesis, Department of Sociology, Lancaster University.

Sum, N-L. (1995), 'Capitalism in East Asian NICs: a Regulation Perspective', *Occasional Paper Number 7*, Political Economy Research Centre, University of Sheffield.

Sum, N-L. (1997), ''Embeddedness' and 'Geo-Governance' of Cross-Border Regional Modes of Growth: Their Nature and Dynamics in East Asian Cases', in A. Amin and J. Hausner (eds), *Beyond Markets and Planning*, Edward Elgar, Aldershot (in press).

Teague, P. (1990), 'The Political Economy of the Regulation School and the Flexible Specialization Scenario', *Journal of Economic Studies*, Vol. 17, No. 5, pp. 32-54.

Tickell, A. and Peck, J.A. (1992), 'Accumulation, Regulation and the Geographies of Post-Fordism: Missing Links in Regulation Research', *Progress in Human Geography*, Vol. 16, pp. 190-218.

Ting, W.L. (1986), *Business and Technological Dynamics in Newly-Industrializing Asia*, Quorum Books, London.

Van Wolferan, K. (1989), *The Enigma of Japanese Power*, Macmillan, London.

Vernon, R. (1966), 'International Investment and International Trade in the Product Cycle', *Quarterly Journal of Economics*, No. 80 (May), pp. 190-207.

Wade, R. (1990), *Governing the Market: Economic Theory and the Role of Government in East Asia Industrialization*, Princeton University Press, Princeton.

White, G. (ed.) (1988), *Developmental States in East Asia*, Macmillan, London.

3 Competing for Transnational Corporations? The Regional Operations of Foreign Firms in Hong Kong and Singapore

HENRY WAI-CHUNG YEUNG

Introduction

Pacific Asia has become an increasingly important centre of gravity in the global economy (Dixon and Drakakis-Smith, 1993; Abegglen, 1994; Kawagoe and Sekiguchi, 1995; de Bettignies, 1996). There is now a surge in the influx of foreign direct investment (FDI) in the region, primarily through the activities of transnational corporations (TNCs). Several countries within Pacific Asia (e.g. China, Singapore, Malaysia and Hong Kong) are the leading destinations for FDI and TNCs among the developing countries. Together, these four Asian economies accounted for 37 per cent of the total FDI to all developing countries (US$281 billion) for the period 1981-1992 (see UNCTAD, 1994, Table I.5). Given their export orientation and small domestic economies, Hong Kong and, particularly, Singapore have relied upon foreign investment to drive their industrialization processes and economic development over the past three decades. Because of the vibrant indigenous entrepreneurship in Hong Kong, foreign investment plays a complementary role in the growth of the colonial economy (Chen, 1983; Chen et al., 1991; Ho, 1992). On the other hand, TNCs are certainly no strangers to Singapore because together with public sector programs, they have played a leading role in the economic development of the Republic and contributed to its industrialization program since Independence in 1965

(Mirza, 1986; Rodan, 1989; Ho, 1993; Low et al., 1993). Today, some 70 per cent of Singapore's exports, 40 per cent of employment and 26 per cent of gross domestic capital formation are directly or indirectly accounted for by foreign TNCs (Yeung, 1994).

If FDI and TNCs play an important role in the economic development of the twin cities, the question remains how do these TNCs organize their management and production activities in the Pacific Asian region? The establishment of regional headquarters (RHQs) and regional offices (ROs) have recently been one of the most popular strategies for global TNCs to organize their presence in the region. It should be noted that the organization of transnational operations via the concept of RHQs or ROs is not altogether new. The use of multi-domestic structures for international production was well practiced by British and American TNCs in the early part of this century (see Dunning, 1993). For example, Ford used to have its European regional headquarters located in the U.K. to coordinate its production facilities throughout Europe (Chandler, 1990; Dicken, 1992). To date, however, there are very few studies of the role of RHQs and ROs in the globalization of TNCs. Of those scant studies available (e.g. Heenan, 1979; Dunning and Norman, 1983; 1987; Daniels, 1986; 1987; Sullivan, 1992), most cases and examples of RHQs were taken from Europe, reflecting a traditional bias towards American direct investment in Europe.

This exploratory paper aims to address this imbalance and relative lack of attention to the location and nature of RHQs and ROs in Pacific Asia in view of strong recent interest of global TNCs in the region. The first objective of the chapter is therefore to provide a general overview of the regional operations of foreign TNCs in Hong Kong and Singapore.[1] There is an urgent need simply to understand more about the nature and extent of regional operations among foreign firms in these two city-states to assist the decision making of these foreign firms. Just where in Pacific Asia should a TNC locate its RHQs? Should Hong Kong or Singapore be chosen as the location for such regional operations? These are very important questions that keep the boardrooms throughout the world and local authorities in Hong Kong and Singapore busy. Hong Kong and Singapore are well known as 'twin-capitals' for the location of RHQs and ROs. Together with Tokyo, they were rated the 'Big Three' centres for RHQs in the Pacific Asian region in the 1990s (Business International, 1990). One of the major issues in this apparently difficult choice is whether the twin cities are competing or complementary with each other (e.g. Shirreff, 1995). This issue has drawn significant attention from policy makers, particularly in the context of Hong

Kong's reversion to China in July 1997 and Singapore's recent drive towards a hub for international business. There is now an ongoing debate that Singapore is 'stealing' RHQs of foreign firms from Hong Kong by capitalising on the confidence crisis in the territory. To what extent is this observation an accusation or a reality? The second objective of this chapter thus is to verify the claim that Hong Kong is competing with Singapore (and vice versa) for the regional operations of foreign firms.

On the basis of secondary data and other published materials, the chapter argues that Hong Kong is *not* competing directly with Singapore for the regional operations of foreign firms and vice versa. In fact, both city-states are *complementary* insofar as the organization of regional activities within the global structure of TNCs is concerned. First, most foreign firms in Pacific Asia either have more than one RHQs located in both Hong Kong and Singapore to take charge of different geographical areas or to divide corporate functions between two or more RHQs or ROs in the region. Second, the recent relocation of some RHQs of foreign firms from Hong Kong to Singapore should be seen as the failure of Hong Kong to keep these RHQs, rather than the result of competition from Singapore. Most of these relocated RHQs continue to keep key corporate functions in their other Hong Kong offices. Moreover, newly established RHQs and ROs of foreign firms in Hong Kong continue to out-number those relocating to Singapore by a very large margin.

This chapter is divided into three major sections. The next section starts with a discussion of the role of regional operations in the globalization of TNCs to set the context for subsequent arguments. This is followed by a descriptive analysis of the organization of regional operations by foreign firms in Hong Kong and Singapore. The main variables considered are (1) number of regional operations; (2) countries of origin; (3) business activities and (4) geography of responsibility. The penultimate section discusses the argument that Hong Kong and Singapore are competing for the RHQs of foreign firms. The general attractiveness of both cities for RHQs and ROs is presented. The role of fiscal and tax incentives offered by the Singapore Government via the Operational Headquarters (OHQs) scheme is examined to verify whether Singapore is competing with Hong Kong for RHQs. The problems and prospects of RHQs in Hong Kong and Singapore are also outlined. The concluding section sums up the arguments of the chapter and draws some important implications for strategic planners, academic researchers and corporate executives.

The Role of Regional Operations in the Globalization of Transnational Corporations

TNCs can be organized in different ways and corporate structures because cross-border operations pose additional problems of coordination and control. Standard international business texts identify at least three most commonly adopted organizational structures (Dicken, 1992; Dunning, 1993): (1) product division structure with separate international division; (2) global product division structure and (3) global geographical division structure. It is this third type of organization structure that involves the role of regional operations in co-ordinating and managing activities within specific geographic areas. Regional operations, in the forms of either regional headquarters (RHQs) or regional offices (ROs), serve specific functions within the corporate organization of TNCs. They exhibit some general characteristics unmatched by other types of foreign subsidiaries and affiliates. A RHQ and/or RO usually occupies an intermediate position of control and administration between the head office and foreign operating units within the corporate hierarchy (Dunning, 1993). It plays a dual role as (1) a co-ordinating mechanism within the TNC and (2) an important element in the TNC's intelligence gathering system (Dicken and Kirkpatrick, 1991). Its major responsibilities are:

1. To coordinate and control the activities of a specific number of corporate affiliates in a defined geographical region - in today's Triad world, the global economy is divided into three major regions comprising North America, Western Europe and Pacific Asia (Ohmae, 1985; 1995). These three regions receive over 90 per cent of global FDI.

2. To act as an intermediary between corporate headquarters and dispersed affiliates, channeling information both upwards and downwards in the corporate hierarchy.

3. To provide services to the parent company such as manpower recruitment, the search for additional investment opportunities, site selection, public relations and liaison with host governments and/or regional authorities.

Generally speaking, organizing a TNC's activities on a worldwide geographical basis is most appropriate to mature businesses with narrow product lines. The structure tends to improve the efficiency of co-ordinating all product lines within each geographic area. Operating a business on an international level requires the management of the tension of global integration and local responsiveness (Bartlett and Ghoshal, 1989; Hamel and Prahalad, 1994). Sullivan's (1992) study of American TNCs, as seen from the perspective of their European RHQs, indicates that they accomplish this task by mediating the tension between rationality prescribed by the formal structure (the head office) and the dialectic rationality enacted by the informal substructure (local subsidiaries). This task ultimately comes down to developing coherence between processes of centralization, formalization and enculturation - a task well-suited for the matrix mentality of regional management. The establishment of RHQs is therefore important in reproducing systemic advantages embedded in the multi-divisional structure of the parent company (Dunning, 1993, p. 130): (1) the benefits of centralized purchasing; (2) the use of sophisticated accounting systems; (3) the reduction of environmental risks and (4) the ability to move top personnel between subsidiaries. These potential gains emanate less from internalized transactions between the parent company and affiliates that can lead to new foreign production, but more from the common governance of value-added activities of the affiliates themselves. In a way, RHQs are virtually a separate class of organizational structures in their own right. As TNCs grow in size and spatial reach, they tend to establish RHQs and/or ROs in major markets. The propensity of a TNC establishing a RHQ elsewhere is greater (Dunning, 1988; 1993; Dicken and Kirkpatrick, 1991):

1.   The larger the number of branches operated by the TNC within a region;
2.   The more internationally integrated the firm's operations;
3.   The stronger the parent company's commitment to a regional approach to its global operations, and
4.   The more strategic and operational benefits from diversification.

Among recent developments in the organization of transnational operations, the emergence of the network or matrix structure is particularly important in the changing role of RHQs and ROs. Instead of organizing transnational operations on a product or area structure, the network structure contains elements of both and involves a whole set of dual reporting links between product and area segments of the TNC (Bartlett and Ghoshal, 1989; Dicken, 1992; Ghoshal and Bartlett, 1993; Gilroy, 1993). Some of the changes in the role of RHQs and ROs are:

1. *More flexibility in organizational choice*: Varying organizational forms between intra-firm integration (e.g. wholly-owned subsidiaries) and inter-firm cooperation (e.g. strategic alliances) allow a strategic combination of organizational forms to maximize the opportunities of the operation.

2. *Overlapping functions and responsibilities*: The locus of decision making depends on the location of particular chief executives, rather than a strict hierarchy of authority.

3. *More footloose in location*: As the chain of command and hierarchy of authority are getting increasingly blurred, TNCs may want to locate their regional operations in accordance with the preferences of key members of the corporate network. Top executives in charge of particular functions or products may choose to reside in world cities (e.g. Hong Kong or Singapore) and to coordinate the global operations from that city. For example, the purchasing services arm of Inchcape Plc., a London-based wholesale and distribution TNC, is headquartered in Hong Kong by virtue of the residence of its CEO in Hong Kong.

To sum up, these recent developments tend to favour the location of RHQs in world cities which are the geographical 'controlling points' of the global economy (Dicken, 1992). These cities offer a strategic location on the global transport and communication network, high-quality external services (e.g. financial and business services), a particular range of labour market skills (e.g. skilled labour in information processing) and rich social and cultural amenities. In this regard, Hong Kong and Singapore stand out as the top choices for RHQs in Pacific Asia.

The Organization of Regional Operations by Foreign Firms in Hong Kong and Singapore

Methodology

Before we examine the nature and extent of regional operations by foreign firms in Hong Kong and Singapore, it is necessary to introduce the sources of data employed in this chapter. There are mainly two sources of secondary data. First, the Industry Department of the Hong Kong

Government has been conducting annual surveys on regional representation by foreign firms in Hong Kong since 1990. Before that, apart from a small-scale survey conducted by the Industry Department in 1985, information on regional representation by foreign firms in Hong Kong was collected mainly through the government's working contacts and from media reports. The annual survey collects information on the number of RHQs and ROs set up by foreign firms in Hong Kong, ascertains whether any of the foreign firms covered by the survey have plans to set up new RHQs or ROs in Hong Kong and obtains views on the factors affecting the attractiveness of Hong Kong as a place for regional representation. The results of these surveys have been published in the form of an annual report since 1991 (see Hong Kong Government Industry Department, 1990; 1992-1995).

These reports contain fairly comprehensive and representative data on the nature and extent of regional representation by foreign firms in Hong Kong. This regional representation is a combination of RHQs and ROs. A RHQ is defined as an organization which has control over the operation of one or more other offices or subsidiaries in the region without the need to make frequent referrals to, or consult with, the overseas parent company or headquarters. A RO is a company which is responsible for general business activities in other countries in the region for the overseas parent company (Hong Kong Government Industry Department, 1992-1995). The number of RHQs in Hong Kong surveyed by the Industry Department increased from 572 in 1990 to 782 in 1995, whereas the number of ROs grew even faster from 283 in 1991 to 1,290 in 1995. The usable sample responses from all foreign firms also increased substantially from 2,281 in 1991 to 3,431 in 1995. The ratios of RHQs and ROs in these samples range roughly from 20 per cent to 26 per cent and 12 per cent to 38 per cent respectively. These patterns reflect the underlying structural changes in the colonial economy from a manufacturing base for foreign firms to a service centre for RHQs and ROs. The variables covered in the surveys are source countries, line of business, region of responsibility, newly established RHQs and planned RHQs, attractiveness of Hong Kong and problems encountered by RHQs in Hong Kong.

Second, the data on the RHQs of foreign firms in Singapore are much harder to come by. There is no comprehensive survey in Singapore that can match the survey by the Industry Department in Hong Kong. All published studies on this subject have to rely upon information supplied by the Economic Development Board (EDB) of the Singapore Government and media reports. Small scale surveys were conducted to obtain additional firm-level data (e.g. Dicken and Kirkpatrick, 1991; Perry, 1992; 1995). Although the EDB does not keep track of the RHQs of foreign firms in Singapore, it does publish occasionally the information pertinent to recipients of the Operational Headquarters (OHQ) incentives (see penultimate section) which can be used as the basis to ascertain the nature and extent of OHQs in Singapore (Dicken and Kirkpatrick, 1991; Perry, 1992; 1995; Kumarapathy, 1994). This chapter is no exception but it updates the database on OHQs (e.g. 3.2 below) from published sources.

It must be cautioned here that the data on Hong Kong and Singapore are not strictly comparable because they are not collected on the same sampling basis. Although the Hong Kong data for different years may contain different sample foreign firms, they do support simple time-series analysis because to a large extent, the sampling frames of the surveys are consistent over time. The Hong Kong data on RHQs, however, cannot be directly used to make inter-country comparisons with the Singapore data on OHQs because the latter are not as comprehensive and are collated from diverse secondary sources. The two different databases also offer slightly different information on the variables examined in this chapter. As far as possible, this chapter pools extra information from other secondary sources (e.g. newspaper reports and business magazines) to complement the two sets of data.

Number of Regional Operations

Table 3.1 shows the RHQs of foreign firms in Hong Kong by year of establishment from 1990 to 1995. Few observations clearly stand out. First, Hong Kong was already the home for a relatively large number of RHQs prior to 1980. There were at least 150 RHQs of foreign firms in Hong Kong in 1979 and before, indicating the prominence of Hong Kong as the destination for RHQs in Pacific Asia. Second, in a period of 10 years, the number of RHQs in Hong Kong rose to 572 in 1990 and subsequently to 782 in 1995. The growth rate in the early 1980s was relatively low at roughly 20 each year. But this growth rate was doubled in the later part of the 1980s to reach a historical record of 75 in 1994. The overall pattern is that the number of RHQs in Hong Kong has been growing continuously in the 1980s and 1990s. Studies have shown that Hong Kong was a clear leader with some 51 per cent of the RHQs market in 1990 (Wilson, 1992). Third, there are some interesting differences in the number of RHQ

Table 3.1 Regional Headquarters in Hong Kong by Year of Establishment, 1990-1995

Year	1990 Survey	1991 Survey	1992 Survey	1993 Survey	1994 Survey	1995 Survey
To 1979	178	153	151	176	163	158
1980	-	21	22	-	24	22
1981	12	17	20	17	17	17
1982	18	12	12	18	20	22
1983	24	24	18	15	18	24
1984	26	32	27	38	21	23
1985	54	45	34	41	36	40
1986	56	51	48	48	52	49
1987	68	55	42	37	37	43
1988	58	43	53	33	42	39
1989	60	65	54	58	51	51
1990	18	58	39	44	47	47
1991	-	26	44	46	40	42
1992	-	-	24	39	60	59
1993	-	-	-	14	66	59
1994	-	-	-	-	20	75
May-95	-	-	-	-	-	12
Total	572	602	588	624	714	782

Note: No comparable data are available for the regional offices of foreign firms in Hong Kong.

Source: Industry Department, Hong Kong Government (various years), *Report on the Survey of Regional Representation by Overseas Companies in Hong Kong*, Hong Kong: Industry Department.

establishments in different surveys. In the 1990 survey, for example, the number of RHQs from 1984 to 1989 is greater than that in the 1995 survey. This indicates that a number of RHQs might have been closed or excluded from the subsequent survey sample.

The lack of statistics for Singapore limits comparisons in the early 1980s. Some estimates of the annual growth of newly established RHQs of foreign

Table 3.2 Companies Awarded Operational Headquarters Status in Singapore, 1986-March 1996

Name of Company	Home Country	Major Business Activity

1. Awarded between 1986-1987

Name of Company	Home Country	Major Business Activity
ASEA Pacific	Sweden	Process automation and electronics
Brown & Root Far East	US	Marine and civil engineers
Cerebos Pacific	UK	Food
Data General International	US	Computers
SKF South East Asia	Sweden	Industrial bearings
Times Publishing	Singapore	Publishing

2. Awarded between 1987-1988

Name of Company	Home Country	Major Business Activity
ANZ Bank	Australia	Finance
Chloride Eastern Industries	UK	Industrial batteries
Deutsche Bank Asia	Germany	Finance
Foxboro Far East	US	Industrial control systems
Pico Art	Singapore	Exhibition design
Polysar Asia Pacific	Canada	Synthetic materials
Sasson	Singapore	Finance
Sony International Singapore	Japan	Consumer electronics

3. Awarded between 1988-1989

Name of Company	Home Country	Major Business Activity
Fujikura Asia	Japan	Fibre optics
Management Investment and Technology	Hong Kong	Investment
Nixdorf Computer	Germany	Computers
Omron Management Centre of Asia Pacific	Japan	Electronics

Polytek Wearnes Holdings	Hong Kong	Industrial distribution
Reuters	UK	Information services
SITA	France	Airline services

4. Awarded between 1989-1991

Asia Matsushita	Japan	Electronics
Chubb Pacific Underwriting Management	US	Insurance
Dominion Textile	Canada	Textile
Electrolux	Sweden	Consumer appliances
GP Batteries	Hong Kong	Batteries
General Electric Plastics Pacific	US	Plastics
General Electric Pacific	US	Electronics
Goodman Fielder Wattie	New Zealand	Food
Hitachi Asia	Japan	Electronics
Imperial Chemical Industries	UK	Chemicals
Molex (S) Pte Ltd	US	Electronics
NEC Business Coordination Centre (S)	Japan	Computers
Neste	Finland	Chemicals
New Zealand Milk Products	New Zealand	Dairy foods
Philips Singapore	Netherlands	Consumer appliances
Thomson Consumer Electronics	France	Consumer electronics
Toshiba Electronics Asia	Japan	Consumer electronics
Union Carbide Asia Pacific	US	Chemicals

5. Awarded between 1991-March 1996

Acer Computer International	Taiwan	Computers
Auric Pacific Food Industries	Australia	Food
BASF	Germany	Chemicals
British Gas Asia Pacific	UK	Power generation
British Petroleum	UK	Petroleum
C S First Boston (S)	US	Finance
Carnaud Metal Box Asia	France	Can maker
Caterpillar Overseas SA	US	Heavy equipment manufacturing
Compaq Computer Asia Pacific	US	Computers
Danone Asia	France	Food
Datacraft Asia	Australia	Telecommunications
Digital Equipment Asia Pacific	US	Computers
Eastman Chemical Asia Pacific	US	Chemicals
Fuji Xerox Asia Pacific	Japan	Computers
Gillette Asia Pacific	US	Consumer products
Hewlett-Packard Asia Pacific	US	Computers
IBM World Corporation	US	Computers
IBM Singapore Pte Ltd	US	Computers
Ipco International	US	Engineering and construction
Mobil Asia Pacific	US	Petroleum
Morgan Grenfell Asia Holdings	US	Finance
Motorola Electronics	US	Electronics

SGS-Thomson Microelectronics	France/Italy	Semiconductors
Schneider Southeast Asia (HQ) Pte Ltd	France	Electricity generation and supply
TNT Express Worldwide	Australia	Transport logistics
Unisys Asia Pacific	US	Computers
United Parcel Service Singapore	US	Package delivery service
Whirpool Corp Southeast Asia	US	Home appliances

Note: This is not an exhaustive list as it is compiled solely from published sources. It also may not reflect the current position of these companies in terms of their OHQ status.

Sources: Kumarapathy (1994: Exhibit 7); Perry (1995: Table 1); *The Straits Times*, various issues; *The Business Times*, various issues.

firms are provided by The Nippon Credit Bank (Quoted in *The Business Times*, 26 June 1991). In the year 1986, there were no RHQs of foreign firms established in Singapore. In the period 1987-1989, some 33 RHQs were established in Singapore. By 1994, there were over 250 RHQs in Singapore (*The Straits Times*, 6 July 1994). These statistics show that the number of RHQs in Singapore proliferated drastically in the late 1980s and early 1990s. This is not surprising given the intensive promotion of Singapore as a home for the RHQs of foreign firms since the inauguration of the OHQ scheme in 1986 (Dicken and Kirkpatrick, 1991; Perry, 1992; 1995; Kumarapathy, 1994). As shown in Table 3.2, some 67 foreign firms in Singapore had been awarded the OHQ status by March 1996. Informal discussions with the EDB indicate that today, over 80 firms in Singapore have been granted the OHQ status. In the first five years of the scheme, some 39 (58 per cent) foreign firms established in Singapore were granted the OHQ status. The process slows down over time because the EDB has become more cautious in granting the OHQ status.

Countries of Origin

Table 3.3 shows the regional operations of foreign firms in Hong Kong by source country of ultimate parent companies from 1990 to 1995. The U.S. and the U.K. have historically been the leading source countries establishing RHQs in Hong Kong. In 1990, there were some 252 RHQs by American firms and another 77 by British firms. In 1995, the number of American RHQs in Hong Kong dropped to 198. This decrease was more than compensated by the five-fold increase of Japanese RHQs in Hong Kong from 20 in 1990 to 116 in 1995. There is thus a growing penetration and influence of Japanese interests in Hong Kong. The number of British RHQs in Hong Kong also increased slightly during the same period. Another serious 'invader' into the RHQ market in Hong Kong is represented by firms from the two Chinas - the People's Republic of China (PRC) and Taiwan. These Chinese firms set up their holding companies and RHQs in Hong Kong to take advantage of incentives and preferences in China when they invest in mainland (see Chiu and Chung, 1993; Low et al., 1995; Ng and Tuan, 1996). The PRC firms in Hong Kong also take charge of the international operations of Chinese TNCs (Gang, 1992).

During the same period, many foreign firms established their regional offices in Hong Kong. One of the main reasons was to coordinate their investment activities in the emerging market of the PRC. From a meagre total number of 283 in 1991, there were some 1,290 ROs of foreign firms in Hong Kong in 1995, representing an almost five-fold jump. Unlike the patterns of RHQs, Japan has been the leading source country in setting up ROs in Hong Kong, together with the U.S. Both countries accounted for almost half of the total number of ROs in Hong Kong in 1995. Interestingly, there is a significant presence of ROs from Asian Newly Industrialized Economies (NIEs). Some 90 ROs in 1995 came from South Korea and Taiwan, reflecting the strategic advantage of co-ordinating regional operations from Hong Kong instead of home countries which are not far from Hong Kong.

The data on RHQs in Singapore by source country of ultimate parent companies are limited to those being awarded the OHQ status. Referring to the 67 recipients of the OHQ status in Table 3.2, there were 24 from the U.S., 19 from Europe and only 8 from Japan. The overall pattern does not differ much from that of Hong Kong — in the dominance of Triad countries. But in Singapore, OHQs from Japanese TNCs are significantly less than those from North America and Europe. This can be attributed to the fact that Japanese TNCs generally prefer to control and coordinate their Southeast Asian operations from the head offices in Japan. In addition, most of Japanese affiliates in Southeast Asia are low cost assembly operations that involve relatively low level of managerial expertise (Perry, 1995). The level of authority given to these local affiliates is low compared to Japanese operations in North America and Western Europe. On the other hand, TNCs from North American and Western Europe may find Singapore an attractive location for their high value-added manufacturing operations which require a substantial level of local autonomy. Firms from these countries are also more willing to decentralize decision making to their OHQs in Singapore. Geographical distance plays a role here as well. It is far longer to travel from America or Europe to Southeast Asia than from Japan. It therefore makes more sense for American and European firms to establish RHQs in Singapore.

Business Activities

Table 3.4 presents the regional operations of foreign firms in Hong Kong by major lines of business from 1991 to 1995. About 40 per cent of RHQs and ROs during the period were engaged in wholesale, retail, import and export activities. This bias towards trading activities among RHQs and ROs reinforces the industrial structure of the Hong Kong economy (Ho, 1992). The service orientation of Hong Kong is also reflected in the importance of RHQs and ROs in other business services, finance and banking and transport and related services. Contrary to the conventional wisdom that Hong Kong's manufacturing sector has been 'hollowed out' by out-sourcing and outward FDI (Tuan and Ng, 1995a; 1995b), the data show that more RHQs and ROs of foreign firms were established to manage and coordinate manufacturing activities in the region. The number of manufacturing RHQs increased from 69 in 1991 to 94 in 1995 and the number of manufacturing ROs from 36 in 1991 to 97 in 1995. This finding demonstrates that Hong Kong remains as a viable manufacturing centre, particularly for foreign TNCs.

The industrial distribution of OHQs in Singapore is quite different from the pattern in Hong Kong. It must be cautioned here, however, that Table 3.2 tends to be biased against small and medium RHQs and ROs (e.g. those in wholesale and trading activities). Manufacturing OHQs come to dominate over their service counterparts. In Table 3.2, there are over 43 manufacturing OHQs: 22 OHQs in the consumer and industrial electronics industry, 8 in the chemical and petroleum industry, 5 in the food industry and 8 in other industries (cf. Dicken and Kirkpatrick, 1991; Perry, 1992; 1995). The heavy concentration of OHQs in the manufacturing sector, particularly in the electronics and chemical industries, reflects the strategic plan of the Singapore Government towards developing a high value-added economy with capital-intensive industries and high R & D expenditure (Ministry of Trade and Industry, 1986; 1991). Because there is no detailed breakdown for manufacturing RHQs in Hong Kong, both sets of data are not strictly comparable. In the service sector, some 11 OHQs in Singapore specialize in business services whereas another 7 OHQs provide financial and insurance services. The specialization of service OHQs in these two service industries also conforms to the vision of the EDB to develop Singapore into an international business hub with world-class financial institutions (Economic Development Board, n.d.; various years).

Based on a survey of 27 recipients of the OHQ incentive awarded by the EDB in 1991, Perry (1992; 1995) identifies four major activities of OHQs in Singapore. These characteristics are summarized in Table 3.5:

1. *Bridge-head*: As the first stage of a company's expansion into the region, these OHQs are established to spearhead investment in a new region of operations.
2. *Profit collector*: The primary role of these OHQs is in determining income distribution from independent branches through the region and contributing to strategic planning.
3. *Technical support centre*: These OHQs provide engineering, testing or design skills and other expertise in service industries.
4. *Regional integrator*: These OHQs are responsible for co-ordinating regional operations, disseminating policies and decisions from the ultimate corporate headquarters and monitoring the performance of branches for reporting to the corporate head office.

Geography of Responsibility

Figure 3.1 shows the regional operations of foreign firms in Hong Kong by region of responsibility from 1990 to 1995. Two trends clearly emerge: First, managing operations in Hong Kong and China has become the dominant influence in the decision of foreign firms to set up their RHQs and ROs in Hong Kong. From merely 47 RHQs focusing exclusively on

Table 3.3 Regional Operations in Hong Kong by Source Country of Ultimate Parent Companies, 1990-1995

Country	1990 Survey RHQs	1991 Survey RHQs	1991 Survey ROs	1992 Survey RHQs	1992 Survey ROs	1993 Survey RHQs	1993 Survey ROs	1994 Survey RHQs	1994 Survey ROs	1995 Survey RHQs	1995 Survey ROs
Canada	-	-	6	10	22	14	-	-	-	-	-
USA	252	258	62	206	178	182	183	178	193	198	228
France	29	25	7	25	22	21	20	26	-	28	-
Germany	-	30	12	28	35	26	35	35	52	33	48
Italy	-	11	11	10	24	-	25	-	-	-	-
Netherlands	31	31	16	24	24	26	22	22	46	28	42
Sweden	-	14	12	-	25	11	17	13	26	-	-
Switzerland	34	31	18	33	39	25	38	34	38	23	57
UK	77	75	25	73	79	81	102	91	107	94	132

Country	1990 Survey RHQs	1991 Survey		1992 Survey		1993 Survey		1994 Survey		1995 Survey	
		RHQs	ROs	RHQs	ROs	RHQs	ROs	RHQs	ROs	RHQs	ROs
China	-	-	-	-	-	67	42	62	69	71	81
Japan	20	44	61	74	193	88	185	91	257	116	303
South Korea	-	-	-	-	-	-	-	-	45	16	60
Taiwan	-	-	-	-	-	-	-	14	39	22	30
Australia	-	9	5	9	20	-	35	14	31	-	33
Others	129	78	48	104	104	88	145	137	240	164	276
Total	572	606	283	596	765	629	849	717	1143	793	1290

Note: Some companies are joint ventures between two or more foreign firms. The total in this Table is therefore greater than the number of regional headquarters/offices identified in the survey.

Source: Industry Department, Hong Kong Government (various years), *Report on the Survey of Regional Representation by Overseas Companies in Hong Kong.*

Table 3.4 Regional Operations in Hong Kong by Major Line of Business, 1991-1995

Line of Business	1991 RHQs	Survey ROs	1992 RHQs	Survey ROs	1993 RHQs	Survey ROs	1994 RHQs	Survey ROs	1995 RHQs	Survey ROs
Manufacturing	69	36	82	61	76	91	93	102	94	97
Construction, Architectural & Civil Engineering	36	13	43	56	44	59	58	68	44	69
Wholesale/Retail, Import/Export	311	128	281	375	277	347	332	531	366	606
Restaurants and Hotels	12	0	17	11	10	8	13	13	10	12
Transport and Related Services	60	17	62	45	80	72	78	87	66	88
Communication Services	26	9	20	22	20	22	18	40	24	30

Line of Business	1991 RHQs	Survey ROs	1992 RHQs	Survey ROs	1993 RHQs	Survey ROs	1994 RHQs	Survey ROs	1995 RHQs	Survey ROs
Finance and Banking	57	32	63	108	64	122	86	151	84	160
Insurance	24	13	21	30	29	35	27	31	25	25
Real Estate and Other Business Services	77	10	113	133	22	7	17	18	30	14
Other Business Services	-	-	-	-	122	149	131	187	153	272
Others	22	58	7	9	8	7	22	33	11	11
Total	694	316	709	850	752	919	875	1261	907	1384

Note: Some companies had more than one line of business. The total in this Table is therefore greater than the number of regional headquarters/offices identified in the survey.

Source: Industry Department, Hong Kong Government (various years), *Report on the Survey of Regional Representation by Overseas Companies in Hong Kong.*

Table 3.5   Characteristics of Operational Headquarters in Singapore by Type of Operations, 1991

	Bridge-head	Profit Collector	Technical Support	Regional Integrator
1. Number	5	4	7	11
2. Employment				
OHQ	18	12	90	160
Affiliates	115	2,400	630	6,380
3. OHQ expenditure S$M	1.5	2.5	12.5	25.0
4. Share of global income by regional affiliates	2.0	55.0	12.0	5.5

Source: Perry (1995: Table 2).

operations in Hong Kong and China in the 1990 survey, there were 269 RHQs in 1995 primarily responsible for operations in Hong Kong and China only. This reflects not only a more than five-fold increase in the number of such RHQs, but also a rapid increase of their lion share in the total number of RHQs from 8 per cent in 1990 to 34 per cent in 1995. Another indicator of this focus on Hong Kong and China comes from the substantial decline of RHQs responsible for East Asia for which Hong Kong is ideally located. As argued later, the exclusive focus of these RHQs on business in Hong Kong and China has made it even more difficult for Singapore to lure them away by offering them incentives. These RHQs basically have to live with the fortune of Hong Kong and China. It is possible that Hong Kong and Singapore host RHQs having *different* geographical responsibilities. This argument can also be supported by the relative stability in the proportion of

RHQs responsible for Southeast Asia (excluding China) at 20-23 per cent during the period 1990-1995.

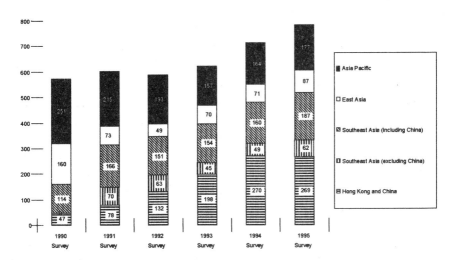

Figure 3.1 Regional Headquarters in Hong Kong by Region of Responsibility, 1990-1995

Note: Southeast Asia (excluding China) refers to Hong Kong, Taiwan, the Philippines, Indonesia, Thailand, Malaysia and Singapore. East Asia refers to Southeast Asia plus Japan and Korea; Asia-Pacific refers to East Asia plus Australia, New Zealand, India and Pakistan.

Source: Industry Department, Hong Kong Government (various years), *Report on the Survey of Regional Representation by Overseas Companies in Hong Kong*, Hong Kong: Industry Department.

Second, the rapid decrease of RHQs in Hong Kong that are responsible for the Pacific Asian region illustrates the trend towards multiple RHQs even within the same region. Almost half of the RHQs of foreign firms in Hong Kong in 1990 were managing their Pacific Asian operations. But by 1995, only 23 per cent did so (n = 177). During the same period, the Pacific Asian countries in East and Southeast Asia had experienced rapid economic growth. A plausible explanation for such a pattern is that global TNCs are establishing more than one RHQs in the Pacific Asian region. For example, fewer RHQs in Hong Kong are responsible for East Asia now. Their corporate functions for other East Asian countries may well be transferred to other RHQs in the region (e.g. Tokyo and Singapore). This trend towards multiple RHQs within Pacific Asia further strengthens the complementarity of Hong Kong and Singapore as the 'twin capitals' for the RHQs and ROs of foreign firms.

In the case of Singapore, there are no comprehensive published data on the geographical responsibility of OHQs. But small scale surveys conducted by Dicken and Kirkpatrick (1991) and Perry (1992; 1995) provide some scattered information. For example, Dicken and Kirkpatrick (1991) found that among the five OHQs interviewed, each OHQ was responsible for co-ordinating a small number of regional affiliates. But the actual geographical extent of the OHQ's responsibilities varied considerably. Three of the five OHQs were responsible for operations in Southeast Asia only. This is rather expected because of the dominant role of Hong Kong as the location for RHQs responsible for operations in East Asia. Another OHQ's geographical scope extended throughout East and Southeast Asia, whereas the last OHQ even had responsibility for co-ordinating operations in India. They conclude, however, that 'such geographical boundaries are by no means fixed. As a company increases the complexity and diversity of its operations it tends to re-evaluate the geographical organization of its activities and to redefine the geographical span of control of its regional headquarters offices' (Dicken and Kirkpatrick, 1991, p. 180). Similar broad patterns were also observed in Perry's (1995) study of 27 OHQs in Singapore. He found that large regional integrators tended to serve affiliates concentrated in Singapore, Malaysia and Thailand. Smaller regional offices were linked to affiliates throughout Southeast Asia and, in some cases, their area of responsibility stretched to the whole of the Pacific Asian region from Pakistan to New Zealand.

Competing for Transnational Corporations? Regional Headquarters and Offices in Hong Kong and Singapore

After the above analysis of the nature and extent of the regional operations of foreign firms in Hong Kong and Singapore, this section is concerned with the second objective of the paper. In order to examine the validity of the argument that Hong Kong is competing with Singapore for the RHQs and ROs of foreign firms and vice versa, this section first outlines some general factors that account for the success of Hong Kong and Singapore in attracting RHQs and ROs. It then looks into one specific policy through which Singapore is seen as competing with Hong Kong for RHQs. Some problems and prospects of existing regional operations in Hong Kong and Singapore are also discussed.

General Attractiveness of Hong Kong and Singapore for Regional Operations

There are many general factors that can account for the attractiveness of Hong Kong and Singapore as a location for RHQs and/or ROs (see Dicken and Kirkpatrick, 1991; Kumarapathy, 1994; Wu and Duk, 1995). Two points should be noted here: First, some of these factors are relevant to both city-states. Their impact on the choice of location for RHQs is rather ambiguous and depends on the specific needs of individual firms. A purely 'profit collector', to use Perry's (1992; 1995) typology, tends to prefer Hong Kong because the corporate income tax rate is significantly lower in Hong Kong than in Singapore. Second, while at the general level these factors seem to be relevant, they often do not enter into the calculus of key decision makers in their choice of location for RHQs. In fact, these key executives are more likely to choose a particularly location according to their personal preferences. To these executives, the questions are which location is a better place to live in, which place has better shopping, food and entertainment and so on. The relevance of these general factors in the decision to locate in a particular city therefore depends very much on the decision making process of individual foreign firms. These factors have become 'symbolic commodities' that make an impact only in their absence. In other words, they are the necessary, but not sufficient, conditions for the choice of RHQ locations. Both economies are attractive to foreign firms because of:

1. *Their role as an international financial centre*: Both city-states offer high liquidity, a strong presence of international financial institutions, the absence of exchange controls and the presence of sophisticated and discreet private banking industries. These facilities are important to fund seeking RHQs which are independent profit centres within the overall corporate structure. Table 3.6 shows that banking and financial facilities are consistently the most important factor affecting Hong Kong as a regional centre for TNCs. In Singapore, Ho (1993) found that a Japanese OHQ used

the relatively developed Singapore financial market to source funds on behalf of affiliates and to manage treasury activities.

2. *Excellent transport and communication infrastructure*: Both cities have free ports and excellent airports. The provision of excellent infrastructure has made Hong Kong very appealing to TNCs (see Table 3.6). Similarly, Ho (1993) found that several Japanese TNCs located their OHQs in Singapore to focus their regional efforts on the sourcing of electrical components, mechanical and precision parts and semiconductor devices from suppliers to Southeast and East Asia for affiliated factories in the region. These OHQs were also handling warehousing and forwarding activities. One company estimated that such procurement activities through Singapore resulted in a 10-20 per cent saving.

3. *Political neutrality*: TNCs will examine the reliability of the legal system and the consistency of host government action. Although both city-states welcome foreign firms and their investment flows, Hong Kong has an advantage over Singapore because of its relatively less restrictive operating environment. As shown in Table 3.6, a favourable government economic policy is highly valued by foreign firms in their decision to locate RHQs in Hong Kong.

4. *Effective legal environment*: The public administrations of both city-states have a pro-business attitude and effective law enforcement and low corruption. Wu and Duk (1995) note particularly that the Western legal and accounting systems are well established and transparent in Hong Kong and Singapore. They tend to facilitate corporate activities and allow easy adaptation of existing corporate practices.

5. *Strategic location*: Both cities offer good proximity to customers, suppliers and principal markets of global TNCs in East and Southeast Asia. Their RHQs may eventually be situated close to the largest market, a problem market or the largest potential market (Maddox, 1990). The geographical location of both economies therefore favours the regionalization of TNC corporate strategy and operations. Perry (1995, p. 185), for example, argues that '[the] regional focus in corporate strategy allied with the ASEAN division of labour has given Singapore the opportunity of developing a new role as a centre for coordination, logistics support, product development and service support'. He refers particularly to

Japanese TNCs and the regional division of labour in their electronics assembly operations throughout Southeast Asia. Both economies also serve as beachheads for entering into new markets in Pacific Asia. Hong Kong performs its role as the conduit for getting plugged into the Overseas Chinese networks of capital and for penetrating into China, potentially the largest market in the world. Singapore serves as a beachhead to take advantage of extensive presence of the Overseas Chinese business networks in Southeast Asia (see Yeung, 1996a; 1997a).

6.   *Favourable tax regimes and/or fiscal incentives*: In 1996, the corporate income tax is 16.5 per cent in Hong Kong and 27 per cent in Singapore, compared to over 30 per cent in other East and Southeast Asian countries. But Singapore was quick to inaugurate the OHQ incentive in 1986 to neutralize the tax advantage in Hong Kong. The tax code in Hong Kong is also clearer than Singapore and this tends to minimize the indirect costs of taxation on corporate income by RHQs. It gives Hong Kong an added advantage over Singapore in attracting 'profit collectors'.

7.   *Cosmopolitan business hubs*: Both city-states have been subject to strong British influence. They have become westernized and cosmopolitan in outlook and strategic orientation.

Competing with Hong Kong? The Role of Government Incentives in Singapore

If Hong Kong is not directly competing with Singapore for the RHQs and ROs of foreign firms, is it perhaps Singapore that is competing explicitly with Hong Kong for the regional operations of TNCs? This is a tricky question but it remains to be answered convincingly. In this paper, Singapore is seen more as an alternative if anything goes wrong with Hong Kong in the count down to 1997. But Hong Kong remains as the first choice to the regional operations of most TNCs. This argument can be supported by the earlier analysis that the number of RHQs in Hong Kong continues to growth at a phenomenal rate even in the 1990s. Similarly, an industry commentator in Hong Kong noted that:

Table 3.6 Importance and Favourability of Factors Affecting Hong Kong as a Regional Centre for Transnational Corporations, 1991-1995

Factor	1991 Survey	1992 Survey	1993 Survey	1994 Survey	1995 Survey
Banking and financial facilities	3	1	1	1	1
Infrastructure	1	2	2	2	2
Government economic policy	4	3	3	3	3
Availability of managerial/professional skill	2	5	5	4	4
Political climate	5	4	4	5	5
Cost/rental of office/factory space	6	7	7	6	6
Wage level	8	9	9	8	7
Regional location	9	6	6	7	8
Labour productivity	-	8	8	9	9
Availability of suitable office/factory space	-	-	-	-	10
Local market potential	-	10	10	10	11
Support of linkage industries	-	11	11	11	12

Source: Industry Department, Hong Kong Government (various years), *Report on the Survey of Regional Representation by Overseas Companies in Hong Kong*, Hong Kong: Industry Department.

There is certainly a partial shifting perhaps, and a re-orientation toward that region, but it's not a massive exodus as people would imagine. Most of the big names are already well-established here in Hongkong and I don't believe relocation is a big worry at this time.
(Quoted in *South China Morning Post*, 9 August, 1990)

The Hong Kong Government practises an economic policy of 'positive non-intervention' and does not provide fiscal or tax incentives to RHQs of foreign firms. The launching of various incentive schemes in Singapore since 1986 has therefore been seen as the main policy instrument for Singapore to compete with Hong Kong for RHQs. The first policy instrument was initiated in late 1986 under the broad umbrella of the Operational Headquarters (OHQ) scheme coordinated by the Economic Development Board of Singapore (Dicken and Kirkpatrick, 1991; Perry, 1992; 1995; Low et al., 1993; Kumarapathy, 1994).[2] The OHQ scheme was promulgated to secure a greater share of the 'regional office pie' through tax incentives. As shown in Table 3.2, 33 OHQs had been awarded by February 1991 and this number increased further to over 45 by 1992, over 50 by 1994 and over 80 by 1995. The second incentive program was launched under the Business Headquarters (BHQ) scheme in February 1994 to extend existing EDB tax and investment incentives to companies engaged in providing business, technical and professional services to their affiliates out of Singapore (*The Business Times*, 18 February 1994). The BHQ status was awarded to 3 Singapore companies and 2 foreign companies during its launch in February 1994. By April 1995, the number of BHQs in Singapore had grown to 12, including Siemens Components, Volex Asia and Van der Horst Technologies.

This chapter argues that whether the OHQ or BHQ schemes are seen as competing for RHQs from Hong Kong, they fail to achieve policy objectives. At most, they have brought some goodwill to Singapore in terms of showing the keen interest of the Singapore Government in attracting RHQs that contribute significantly to the local economy. At their worst, as noted by Perry (1992), the incentive scheme was ill-founded and, indeed, 'the scheme has not attracted a greater share of regional offices to Singapore' (p. 292). In fact, as early as 1990, a survey of 50 American and European TNCs in the *Fortune* 500 league by Business International (1990) found that some 70 per cent of the respondents did not regard tax or investment incentives as a major factor in their decision to choose Singapore as the top alternative location to Hong Kong (Cited in *The Straits Times*, 3 April 1990). Even so, Singapore was chosen more as an alternative location for a sub-regional office, not a location for RHQs. Many TNCs continued to retain their offices in Hong Kong to serve affiliates in East Asia.

In the Business International (1990) survey, most TNCs did not come under pressure from their head offices to move out of Hong Kong. For those RHQs in Hong Kong relocating to Singapore, four reasons were found to be most influential in the choice of Singapore as the top *alternative* location to Hong Kong:

1. *The effects of 'brain-drain' in Hong Kong*: The expected emigration of over 55,000 Hong Kong people each year has pushed up costs of senior staff sharply. Business International remarked that 'Hong Kong's political uncertainty is not an immediate problem. It is the cost factor and the availability of staff which everyone is bothered about' (Cited in *The Straits Times*, 3 April 1990).

2. *A shift in business interests from East Asia to the ASEAN countries*: It becomes more difficult for TNCs to control and coordinate their Asian operations from just one regional office. Many of them are looking into the possibility of setting up a second or sub-regional office elsewhere in the region. A number of Hong Kong firms have set up their RHQs in Singapore to manage their Southeast Asian operations, e.g. Wong's Industrial (Holdings) and Stellux Holdings (*The Straits Times*, 7 December 1994). Another example is the relocation of Mountain Rose's RHQ, the buying arm of Ralph Lauren, from Hong Kong to Singapore in 1990 (*South China Morning Post*, 12 June 1990). The main reason given was the location of its main production in Singapore and Malaysia, not so much because of other competitive advantage possessed by Singapore over Hong Kong.

3. *Diversification of businesses across the region*: One of the best opportunities to diversify business away from Hong Kong is the higher price-earning ratios from a listing on the Stock Exchange of Singapore (SES). Some Hong Kong firms have sought primary and secondary listing in the SES to obtain extra funds for further expansionary activities in the region, e.g. IMC Holdings (listed in Singapore in December 1989) and Gold Peak Industries (listed in Singapore in March 1991).

4. *Protection from bilateral investment pacts*: Singapore has an investment pact with China which many Taiwanese firms would like to take advantage. Singapore has become the bridgehead for this group of foreign firms. In 1992, for example, Acer Inc. of Taiwan established its Singapore subsidiary, Acer Computer International (ACI), as the RHQ responsible for sales, marketing, service and assembly of the company's computers in the Asia Pacific region, Africa, Latin America, the Middle East and the Commonwealth (*Far Eastern Economic Review*, 12 October 1995, pp. 62-3). It

was awarded the OHQ status in December 1993 and subsequently listed in the SES in 1995.

To illustrate how these factors work for Singapore vis-à-vis Hong Kong, the case of Imperial Chemical Industries (ICI) is instructive here. In August 1990, ICI was awarded the OHQ status by the EDB of Singapore (Maddox, 1990, p. 94). ICI is a truly global company with diversified chemical manufacturing operations throughout 150 countries. In Asia, the group's basic strategy is to manufacture chemicals, particularly industrial chemicals, in a particular country for local consumption. ICI Asia Pacific, its Singapore OHQ, covers operations in 15 countries: Brunei, Cambodia, China, Hong Kong, Indonesia, Japan, South Korea, Laos, Malaysia, Myanmar, the Philippines, Singapore, Taiwan, Thailand and Vietnam. Locating a RHQ in Singapore is part of ICI's long term strategy to boost its presence in the Asia Pacific region.

Singapore was selected over Tokyo and Hong Kong as the location of its RHQ because ICI was mainly concerned over Hong Kong's political uncertainty that might disadvantage British companies such as ICI. The decision to locate the RHQ in Singapore was therefore more political than economic. The CEO of ICI Asia Pacific, Dr. William F. Madden, noted that 'Hong Kong we thought about long and hard. From a geographic point of view, it's ideally placed. But, in practical terms, there are quite a few negatives — the 1997 issue, which is likely to disadvantage UK companies as we get closer to 1997; the worker turnover issue, the high costs and the logistics, which aren't great' (Quoted in Maddox, 1990, p. 94). It is apparent that ICI chose Singapore as the second best. Hong Kong was its best choice had it not been confronted with the 1997 uncertainty. There is thus no direct competition between Hong Kong and Singapore for RHQs. Rather, Singapore is chosen by foreign firms which are eager to move out of Hong Kong because of its political uncertainty. Instead of eyeing the tax benefits conferred by the OHQ status, ICI considered political reasons as the most strategic in its location of OHQ in Singapore. Dr. Madden again added that 'OHQ status is recognition that you are setting up a significant operation that is a long-term commitment' (Quoted in Maddox, 1990, p. 94).

Despite the above reasons, most RHQs and ROs of foreign firms in Hong Kong choose to remain in Hong Kong for a variety of other reasons. Table 3.7 shows, for example, that more than 93 per cent of RHQs and ROs in Hong Kong planned to remain in Hong Kong during the surveys conducted between 1992-1995. It must be emphasized that their

Table 3.7 Future Plan of Regional Headquarters/Offices of Foreign Firms in Hong Kong, 1992-1995

Problem	1992 Survey	1993 Survey	1994 Survey	1995 Survey
Remain in Hong Kong	275 (94%)	289 (94%)	298 (95%)	330 (93%)
Relocate to other places	19 (6%)	17 (6%)	16 (5%)	24 (7%)
Total responses	294 (100%)	306 (100%)	314 (100%)	354 (100%)

Source: Industry Department, Hong Kong Government (various years), *Report on the Survey of Regional Representation by Overseas Companies in Hong Kong*, Hong Kong: Industry Department.

reasons for relocation can be very idiosyncratic and hence are not subject to universal generalization. From an official standpoint, the Singapore Government denied that it was cashing in Hong Kong's confidence crisis. Even during the post-Tiananmen Square period from 1989 onwards, How Peck Huat, Director of the Services Promotion Division and Asian Operations of the EDB, made it clear that:

> Hongkong and Singapore are fundamentally different in their business environments. The two can complement each other. While regional headquarters are set up here, businessmen can continue to have their products manufactured in Hongkong. Shifting business to Singapore gives employers the advantage of being able to transfer their staff here instead of seeing them drained to the West. Operation in Singapore differs greatly from Hongkong. It's the cross-fertilization of the two places that will further strengthen the two cities.
> (Quoted in *Hong Kong Standard*, 23 October 1989)

His view was later echoed by Shum Sze Keong, a director of the EDB office in Hong Kong, who dismissed suggestions that Singapore was competing with Hong Kong for RHQs. He argued that Singapore and Hong Kong complemented each other — whereas Hong Kong's sphere of influence is in North Asia, Singapore is in South Asia. To him, 'The growing pie in the Asia-Pacific region is big enough to go round' (Quoted in *The Straits Times*, 14 October 1992).

What then are the reasons accounting for the failure of the incentive schemes to attract RHQs from Hong Kong? As shown in earlier analyses, few RHQs or ROs seek to relocate from Hong Kong to Singapore. In 1992, a survey of 45 RHQs in Hong Kong found that although Singapore would be chosen by 42 per cent of the respondents if they moved out of Hong Kong, most companies (84 per cent) did not feel any pressure from the home office to move out of Hong Kong (*The Straits Times*, 8 May 1992). Their reasons for not moving out of Hong Kong were:

1. *Its proximity to major markets and suppliers*: It would make more sense for TNCs to locate their regional operations in Hong Kong if their primary activities are concentrated in China and other North Asian countries (e.g. South Korea and Taiwan) (see Sung, 1991; Ng and Tuan, 1996). Industry observers noted that 'aside from Hong Kong's strength as a financial centre and corporate inertia, there are very good reasons for why Hongkong will retain and attract further regional HQs. International companies have found Hongkong a convenient base for China-related business — a factor that will not change due to cyclical cost considerations' (Quoted in *The Straits Times*, 27 July 1994). In order to stay really close to the market, a growing number of foreign companies are recently moving not only their China headquarters but even regional head offices out of Hong Kong to Beijing or Shanghai, e.g. ABB, Fluor Daniels, PepsiCo and General Electric (*Business Asia*, 18 December 1995, pp. 1-3).

2. *A recent trend towards multiple RHQs*: This is particularly common among TNCs with extensive operations in Asia. The location and scope of each RHQ reflects the extent of the company's market and the nature of its operations (Maddox, 1990). For example, Molex, the world's fourth largest maker of electronic connectors, has a North Asian regional headquarters in Japan to cover Japan, Taiwan and South Korea. It also has a Singapore OHQ to oversee manufacturing subsidiaries in ASEAN, India and China. On the other hand, Datacraft keeps its RHQ in Hong Kong

after opening a second OHQ in Singapore (*The Straits Times*, 7 December 1994).

3. *The spatial division of corporate functions*: There is also an increasing tendency for TNCs to split their corporate functions between Hong Kong and Singapore, with the former taking on financial, marketing and sales functions and the latter, manufacturing and R & D tasks (*The Straits Times*, 8 May 1992).

4. *Compensation of property costs by lower tax rates in Hong Kong*: Although property costs are an issue in Hong Kong, it is estimated that these account for only 15-20 per cent of operating costs and are more than offset by the lower rate of corporate taxation in Hong Kong (16.5 per cent) than that prevails in Singapore (27 per cent) (*The Straits Times*, 27 July 1994; 14 January 1996).

For those five out of 27 OHQ recipients surveyed in Perry's (1992; 1995) study which had relocated from Hong Kong to Singapore, the reasons for their relocation were not specifically related to Singapore *per se*, but to changing conditions in Hong Kong: First, their locational decision was largely influenced by the political uncertainty of Hong Kong. For example, in the immediate aftermath of the Tiananmen Square incidence in June 1989, some 30 companies in Hong Kong either applied or planned to apply to move their regional operations to Singapore (*Hong Kong Standard*, 23 October 1989). These companies were more prompted by the political uncertainty of Hong Kong than by the inherent attraction of Singapore *per se*. On the other hand, there were 22 new RHQs established during the second half of 1989 and another 18 in the first three months of 1990 (*Da Gong Bao*, 28 August 1990), indicating that Hong Kong remained attractive to TNCs in their Pacific Asian operations. Second, they suffered from the indirect impact of political uncertainty in Hong Kong, e.g. a tight labour market for professional and managerial expertise and the reluctance of head offices to invest in new property and/or projects. Third, three out of these five regional offices moved prior to commencing capital projects, thereby reducing sunk costs or inertia in relocation.

There are also other reasons accounting for the failure of the OHQ scheme to accomplish its expectations and thereby adding to its inability to attract RHQs relocated from Hong Kong to Singapore:

1. *Misplaced expectations*: Perry (1992) argues that the OHQ scheme has overestimated the geographical mobility of the regional

operations of TNCs. Most TNCs divide Pacific Asia into several subregions and the RHQs in Singapore serve primarily only Southeast Asia.

2. *The design of the incentive*: It may cause reaction from tax authorities in affiliate locations. Many countries (e.g. India and Sri Lanka) do not permit the payment of management fees by subsidiaries to their RHQs which may find tax incentives in Singapore less useful.

3. *The rigidity of the scheme*: A company's management flexibility may be curtailed by the commitments that are made to obtain the OHQ status, e.g. 'lock-in' effects on spending and staffing levels (Maddox, 1990). A few OHQs have been forced to go back to the EDB to renegotiate the level and scope of activities specified in the original commitments.

4. *No necessity for RHQs*: Many global TNCs today still adopt a multi-domestic structure of transnational operations in which the individual country managers report directly to the home office (e.g. Nestlé from Switzerland and Bayer from Germany). In this situation, each country subsidiary is able to operate relatively independently, obviating the need for a RHQ.

Regional Operations in Hong Kong and Singapore: Problems and Prospects

Table 3.8 ranks the main problems encountered by the RHQs and ROs of foreign firms in Hong Kong between 1991-1995. High rental and staff costs have become the foremost important consideration. Both problems have aggravated over the period 1991-1995. In the 1991 survey, only 70 per cent and 55 per cent respondents cited high rental and staff costs as key problems. But in the 1995 survey, the percentages went up to 78 per cent and 63 per cent respectively. Hong Kong has now one of the highest rental costs for offices in the world and the trend is that it will continue to be one of the most expensive locations to operate (*The Straits Times*, 14 January 1996). But contrary to the conventional wisdom, the 'brain drain' effects of executive emigration are better absorbed by responding RHQs and ROs. While Hong Kong salaries have always been higher than those offered by comparable positions in Singapore, the 'brain drain' has widened the salary differential to 25-30 per cent in some cases. The recent return of former Hong Kong residents from their new countries by nationality has eased the acute shortage of the skilled and qualified labour market (Findlay et al., 1996). In Table 3.8, high staff turnover rate and the shortage of qualified personnel were less a problem in 1995 than in 1991. Another problem cropping up in the survey is the 'limited prospects' to companies that attach little importance to doing business with China (*The Straits Times*, 28 May 1990). Reducing business in the region, particularly in China, was cited by some 22 per cent of respondents in the 1995 survey, compared to only 5 per

Table 3.8 Problems Encountered by Regional Headquarters/Offices of Foreign Firms in Hong Kong, 1991-1995

Problem	1991 Survey	1992 Survey	1993 Survey	1994 Survey	1995 Survey
High rental cost	90	203	227	258	275
	(70%)	(70%)	(74%)	(82%)	(78%)
High staff cost	70	176	194	209	219
	(55%)	(60%)	(63%)	(67%)	(63%)
Political uncertainty	-	-	-	-	155
					(44%)
High staff turnover rate	63	109	110	127	99
	(50%)	(37%)	(36%)	(40%)	(28%)
Shortage of qualified personnel	54	91	86	108	88
	(42%)	(31%)	(28%)	(34%)	(25%)
Reducing business in the region	6	45	46	35	76
	(5%)	(15%)	(15%)	(11%)	(22%)
Inadequate supporting services	7	12	11	16	21
	(6%)	(4%)	(4%)	(5%)	(6%)
Others	-	21	18	14	14
		(7%)	(6%)	(5%)	(4%)
Total number of responses	128	294	306	314	352
	(100%)	(100%)	(100%)	(100%)	(100%)

Source: Industry Department, Hong Kong Government (various years), *Report on the Survey of Regional Representation by Overseas Companies in Hong Kong*, Hong Kong: Industry Department.

cent in the 1991 survey. Some of these foreign or local companies in Hong Kong are relocating to or considering to relocate elsewhere because Hong Kong is no longer important in their organization of transnational operations.

In Singapore, Perry (1995, p. 194) recently notes that 'considerable inertia exists within the development of regional headquarters in Singapore' for two reasons: First, major reorganization with the overall corporate hierarchy is required for establishing new RHQs in Singapore. This process may suffer from resistance from existing centres of control and power with the corporate hierarchy. For example, one Japanese OHQ recipient was still preparing for the organization of an OHQ, although in public it claimed to have control and coordination power over regional subsidiaries. Second, a further problem emanates from the absence of a pool of prospective regional managers. It is difficult to find regional managers in their Southeast Asian operations which tend to be mostly joint ventures as required by host government regulations (Yeung, 1996a; 1997b). In other words, many of these Southeast Asian affiliates rely on local managers to take charge of local operations, reducing the opportunity to rotate their own staff and making it difficult to exercise cross-subsidiary learning.

Conclusion and Implications

Hong Kong and Singapore, as 'twin capitals' in the Pacific Asian region, have captured their fair shares in the battle for foreign investment and in the dynamism of regional economic growth. In this process, both city-states appear to be complementary rather than competitive insofar as the location of regional headquarters and regional offices of transnational corporations is concerned. Based on an analysis of secondary data, this chapter lends some support to the complementary role of Hong Kong and Singapore as the twin cities in Pacific Asia. Instead of competing against each other for RHQs and thereby entering into a 'zero-sum game', Hong Kong and Singapore continue to attract a large number of RHQs and ROs of foreign firms. This pattern reflects their success in promoting a more service-oriented economy in which high value-added activities are carried out. These RHQs and ROs not only incur more expenditure on business services, but also create more knowledge-intensive and higher paid employment. Their operations in Hong Kong and Singapore carry out more decision making activities and corporate management functions. By virtue of their success in attracting these RHQs and ROs, Hong Kong and Singapore have secured a central place in the global maps of TNCs.

One of the main implications of this chapter is that fiscal incentives are less important in attracting RHQs and ROs of foreign firms because transnational operations are less responsive to investment incentives than firm strategies and other structural forces (see Yeung, 1996b). Hong Kong has traditionally been very successful in attracting RHQs and ROs without any fiscal and tax incentives from the colonial government (Wilson, 1992). It has been capitalising on its geographical proximity to other Asian countries and its relatively free operating environments. Viewed in this context, the provision of the OHQ and BHQ incentives in Singapore has not been successful if one of its objectives is to attract RHQs to relocate from Hong Kong to Singapore. In order to make it more effective, there is a need to be more focused in the two schemes. Perry (1992) suggests that more assistance should be given on an office's direct sources of income to avoid attracting 'shell' operations and more focus should be placed on indirect advantages (e.g. priority in dealing with public authorities) to make the incentive more attractive to foreign firms. Second, the schemes should be seen as attracting regional offices that have strategic power rather than those that are merely established to provide operational support. Perry (1995, p. 195) found that among the 27 OHQ recipients in Singapore, most of them serve a role complementary to, rather than in competition with, established tiers of control.

Another clear implication of this chapter is that we still know very little of the nature and organization of regional headquarters and/or regional offices. Like any other form of corporate organization, they are subject to constant pressure to change and adapt. It becomes very difficult to generalize on their behaviour and spatial organization which depend so much on country characteristics and industry characteristics. For example, our traditional concept of RHQs may be readily applicable to the globalization of some high tech global TNCs (e.g. electronics TNCs). They may also adopt a multiple RHQ structure to manage their diversified operations worldwide to achieve simultaneously global integration and local responsiveness (Bartlett and Ghoshal, 1989; Hamel and Prahalad, 1994). Most of today's TNCs, however, are still small and their main markets are still in their home countries. They are mostly national firms with international operations (Hu, 1992; Hirst and Thompson, 1996). They tend to coordinate and manage their international operations in their home countries and therefore they do not conform to the RHQ model of organizing international production. We need much more research before arriving at a conclusive picture of the role and organization of regional headquarters in the globalization of economic activities.

Notes

1. In recent years, there are several small scale studies of RHQs in Hong Kong (Wilson, 1992) and in Singapore (Dicken and Kirkpatrick, 1991; Perry, 1992; 1995; Kumarapathy, 1994) which provide some background information to this comparative analysis.
2. The details of this OHQ scheme are not given in this chapter because they can be found in other studies (see references). Instead, the chapter concentrates on evaluating the success or failure of the scheme in 'competing' for RHQs from Hong Kong.

References

Abegglen, J. C. (1994), *Sea Change: Pacific Asia as the New World Industrial Center*, Macmillan, New York.

Bartlett, C. A. and Ghoshal, Sumantra (1989), *Managing Across Borders: The Transnational Solution*, Century Business, London.

Business Asia, 18 December 1995, pp. 1-3.

Business International (1990), *Organizing For Asia/Pacific: Structuring And Locating Your Regional Management*, Business International Asia/Pacific, Hong Kong.

Chandler, A. D., Jr. (1990), *Scale and Scope: The Dynamics of Industrial Capitalism*, Harvard University Press, Cambridge, Mass.

Chen, E. K.Y. (1983), *Multinational Corporations, Technology and Employment*, Macmillan, London.

Chen, E. K.Y., Nyaw, Mee-Kau, Wong, T. Y.C. (eds) (1991), *Industrial and Trade Development in Hong Kong*, Centre Of Asian Studies, University Of Hong Kong, Hong Kong.

Chiu, Lee-In Chen and Chung, Chin (1993), 'An Assessment of Taiwan' S Indirect Investment Towards Mainland China', *Asian Economic Journal*, Vol. 7, No. 1, pp. 41-70.

Da Gong Bao, in Chinese, Hong Kong, Various Issues.

Daniels, J.D. (1986), 'Approaches to European Management by the Large US Multinational Firm', *Management International Review*, Vol. 2, pp. 27-42.

Daniels, J.D. (1987), 'Bridging National and Global Marketing Strategies Through Regional Operations', *International Marketing Review*, Vol. 4, Autumn, pp. 29-44.

De Bettignies, H.-C. (ed.) (1996), *Trade and Investment in the Asia-Pacific Region*, Routledge, London.

Dicken, P. (1992), *Global Shift: The Internationalization of Economic Activity*, Second Edition, Paul Chapman, London.

Dicken, P. and Kirkpatrick, C. (1991), 'Services-Led Development in ASEAN: Transnational Regional Headquarters in Singapore', *The Pacific Review*, Vol. 4, No. 2, pp. 174-84.

Dixon, C. and Drakakis-Smith, D. (eds) (1993), *Economic and Social Development in Pacific Asia*, Routledge, London.

Dunning, J. H. (1988), *Explaining International Production*, Unwin Hyman, London.

Dunning, J. H. (1993), *Multinational Enterprises and the Global Economy*, Addison Wesley, Reading, Mass.

Dunning, J. H. and Norman, G. (1983), 'The Theory of the Multinational Enterprise: An Application to Multinational Office Location', *Environment and Planning A*, Vol. 15, pp. 675-92.

Dunning, J. H. and Norman, G. (1987), 'The Location Choice of Offices of International Companies', *Environment And Planning A*, Vol. 19, pp. 613-31.

Economic Development Board, Singapore (n.d.), *Singapore: The Business Architect with Global Connections*, EDB, Singapore.

Economic Development Board, Singapore (Various Years), *Economic Development Board Yearbook*, EDB, Singapore.

Far Eastern Economic Review, 12 October 1995, pp. 62-3.

Findlay, A .J., Li, F. L. N., Jowett, A. M. and Skeldon, R. (1996), 'Skilled International Migration and the Global City: A Study of Expatriates in Hong Kong', *Transactions of the Institute of British Geographers*, Vol. 21, No. 1, pp. 49-61.

Gang, Ye (1992), 'Chinese Transnational Corporations', *Transnational Corporations*, Vol. 1, No. 2, pp. 125-33.

Ghoshal, Sumantra and Bartlett, C. A. (1993), 'The Multinational Corporation as an Interorganizational Network', in Sumantra Ghoshal and Westney, D.E. (eds), *Organization Theory and the Multinational Corporation*, St. Martin's Press, New York, pp. 77-104.

Gilroy, B. M. (1993), *Networking in Multinational Enterprises: The Importance of Strategic Alliances*, University Of South Carolina Press, South Carolina.

Hamel, G. and Prahalad, C.K. (1994), *Competing for the Future: Breakthrough Strategies for Seizing Control of Your Industry and Creating the Markets of Tomorrow*, Harvard Business School Press, Boston.

Heenan, D. A. (1979), 'The Regional Headquarters Decision: A Comparative Analysis' , *Academy Of Management Journal*, Vol. 22, No. 2, pp. 410-5.

Hirst, P. and Thompson, G. (1996), *Globalization in Question: The International Economy and the Possibilities of Governance*, Polity, Cambridge.

Ho, Kong Chong (1993), 'Industrial Restructuring and the Dynamics of City-State Adjustments', *Environment And Planning A*, Vol. 25, No. 1, pp. 47-62.

Ho, Yin-Ping (1992), *Trade, Industrial Restructuring and Development in Hong Kong*, Macmillan, London.

Hong Kong Government Industry Department (1990), *Survey on Regional Headquarters of Overseas Companies in Hong Kong*, Industry Department, Hong Kong.

Hong Kong Government Industry Department (1992-1995), *Survey of Regional Representation by Overseas Companies in Hong Kong*, Industry Department, Hong Kong.

Hong Kong Standard, Hong Kong, Various Issues.

Hu, Yao-Su (1992), 'Global Firms are National Firms with International Operations', *California Management Review*, Vol. 34, No. 2, pp. 107-26.

Kawagoe, Toshihiko and Sekiguchi, Sueo (eds) (1995), *East Asian Economies: Transformation and Challenges*, Institute Of Southeast Asian Studies, Singapore.

Kumarapathy, Suchitra L. (1994), *'Singapore: A Base For MNCs'*, Regional Headquarters In Asia, Research Paper No.43, DBS Bank, Singapore.

Low, L., Ramstetter, E. D. and Yeung, Wai-Chung H. (1995), *Accounting for Outward Direct Investment from Hong Kong and Singapore: Who Controls What?*, Paper Presented at the Annual Conference of the National Bureau of Economic Research, Washington D.C., 19-20 May 1995.

Low, L., Toh, Mun Heng, Soon, Teck Wong, Tan, Kong Yam and Hughes, H. (1993), *Challenge and Response: Thirty Years of The Economic Development Board*, Times Academic Press, Singapore.

Maddox, Marvin (1990), 'Getting Closer To The Markets', *Singapore Business*, November, pp. 89-95.

Ministry of Trade and Industry, Singapore (1986), *The Singapore Economy: New Directions*, Report of the Economic Committee, MTI, Singapore.

Ministry of Trade and Industry, Singapore (1991), *Strategic Economic Plan*, MTI, Singapore.

Mirza, Hafiz (1986), *Multinationals and the Growth of the Singapore Economy*, Croom Helm, London.

Ng, Linda Fung-Yee and Tuan, Chyau (eds) (1996), *Three Chinese Economies - China, Hong Kong and Taiwan: Challenges and Opportunities*, Chinese University Press, Hong Kong.

Ohmae, Kenichi (1985), *Triad Power: The Coming Shape of Global Competition*, The Free Press, New York.

Ohmae, Kenichi (1995), *The End of the Nation State: The Rise of Regional Economies*, Harpercollins, London.

Perry, M. (1992), 'Promoting Corporate Control In Singapore', *Regional Studies*, Vol. 26, No. 3, pp. 289-94.

Perry, M. (1995), 'New Corporate Structures, Regional Offices and Singapore's New Economic Directions', *Singapore Journal of Tropical Geography*, Vol. 16, No. 2, pp. 181-96.

Rodan, G. (1989), *The Political Economy of Singapore's Industralization: National State and International Capital*, Macmillan, London.

Shirreff, D. (1995), 'A Hub to Replace Hong Kong?', *Euromoney*, February, pp. 80-2.

South China Morning Post, Hong Kong, Various Issues.

Sullivan, D. (1992), 'Organization in American MNCs: The Perspective of the European Regional Headquarters', *Management International Review*, Vol. 32, No. 3, pp. 237-50.

Sung, Yun-Wing (1991), *The China-Hong Kong Connection: The Key To China's Open-Door Policy*, Cambridge University Press, Cambridge.

The Business Times, Singapore, Various Issues.

The Straits Times, Singapore, Various Issues.

Tuan, Chyau and Ng, Linda Fung-Yee (1995a), 'Manufacturing Evolution Under Passive Industrial Policy and Cross-Border Operations in China: The Case of Hong Kong', *Journal of Asian Economics*, Vol. 6, No. 1, pp. 71-88.

Tuan, Chyau And Ng, Linda Fung-Yee (1995b), 'The Turning Point of the Hong Kong Manufacturing Sector: Impact of Outward Investment to Pearl River Delta', *Journal of International Trade and Economic Development*, Vol. 4, No. 2, pp. 153-70.

UNCTAD (1994), *World Investment Report 1994: Transnational Corporations, Employment and the Workplace*, United Nations, New York.

Wilson, J. C. (1992), *Hong Kong as Regional Headquarters*, Paper Presented at the ASEAN-China Hong Kong Forum 1992 on Hong Kong's Role in the Asian Pacific Region in the 21st Century, Centre For Asian Pacific Studies, Lingnan College, Hong Kong, 28-29 February 1992.

Wu, Friedrich and Duk, Sin Yue (1995), 'Hong Kong and Singapore: 'Twin Capitals' for Overseas Chinese Capital', *Business & The Contemporary World*, Vol. 7, No. 3, pp. 21-33.

Yeung, Wai-Chung Henry (1994), 'Hong Kong Firms in the ASEAN Region: Transnational Corporations and Foreign Direct Investment' , *Environment and Planning A*, Vol. 26, No. 12, pp. 1931-56.

Yeung, Wai-Chung Henry (1996a), 'Business Networks and Transnational Corporations: A Study of Hong Kong Firms in the ASEAN Region', *Economic Geography*, Vol.72.

Yeung, Wai-Chung Henry (1996b), 'Attracting Foreign Investment? The Role Of Investment Incentives in the ASEAN Operations of Transnational Corporations', *The Pacific Review*, Vol. 9, No. 4.

Yeung, Wai-Chung Henry (1997), 'Cooperative Strategies and Chinese Business Networks: A Study of Hong Kong Transnational Corporations in the ASEAN Region', In Paul W. Beamish And J. Peter Killing (Eds.), *Cooperative Strategies: Asia-Pacific Perspectives*, The New Lexington Press, San Francisco, CA.

Yeung, Wai-Chung Henry (Forthcoming), *Transnational Corporations And Business Networks: Hong Kong Firms in the ASEAN Region*, Routledge, London.

4 The Problems of Doing Business in Pacific Asia: An Overview

GEOFFREY MURRAY

Introduction

In some respects, it has never been easier for foreigners to do business in Pacific Asia. Countries once closed have flung open their doors to foreign direct investment (FDI) and have attempted to create an attractive environment for international business. They have done this because they consider FDI the quickest route to economic development in catching up with the industrialized world. The advantages for foreign companies of establishing a trading and/or manufacturing presence in the region have also been well documented. Even if one excludes China, with a quarter of the world's population, the region still offers a potential market at least equal in size to that of the current European Union (EU) — although there are still large disparities in the potential demand for foreign products and services. But overall, this is a region of rapid economic growth that seems likely to continue well into the 21st Century and one that offers foreign companies the opportunity for sustained and significant profit. The advantages of doing business in Pacific Asia are fairly well known, so that I do not intent to dwell on them for long. Rather it is my intention to concentrate on the negative side, looking at why an increasing number of foreign companies who rushed into the market with great enthusiasm have found themselves somewhat disappointed, with some even going so far as to withdraw. In due course, I will analyse why the initial optimism of the foreign business community has proved ill-founded in specific cases. The purpose is not to castigate the countries concerned or to provide any sort of hit list of places where 'no white man should tread'. Rather, the intention is to demonstrate that those wishing to do business in the region, and those who are providing

120

the opportunity, sometimes have conflicting motives and ideas that can lead to frustrations and disillusionment, and thus both sides need to re-examine their thinking and seek to bridge the understanding gap. What follows is based on almost 30 years of analysing economic and business trends throughout Asia, and, in more recent years, research for a series of business-related books which are listed in the reference notes for this chapter. This has resulted in the opportunity to talk to many senior government officials, analysts and businessmen. The evidence that will be presented is largely anecdotal rather than empirical, but I believe there are several common themes which occur to a greater or less degree right across the region. I do not intend to discuss each country in the region, which would be a mammoth task far beyond the scope of a single chapter. Instead, I have chosen to deal at length with only a few countries which I consider are representative of the theme, especially China, Vietnam, Indonesia and Singapore.

At this point, the key elements to be discussed can be summarized as:

- Investment that runs ahead of adequate infrastructure provision.

- Problems created by an inadequate legal structure.

- Frustrations caused by lack of basic information.

- Difficulties caused by conflicting policy goals or sudden changes in direction.

- The threat of growing labour problems.

The problem of an inadequate infrastructure

In some countries, the enthusiasm for foreign investment has moved far ahead of the two key supporting elements — the physical and the legal infrastructure. Many businessmen have recounted to me their horror stories about frequent power failures or brownouts (significant reduction in power), hours spent trying to make a telephone call or send a vital fax, days lost with goods stalled in railway sidings, on docksides or on the back of a lorry struggling through traffic jams.

In 1994, I spent considerable time investigating the investment advantages offered by the economic development zones on which the Chinese Government places such high hopes. I happened to be in Chengdu, capital of Sichuan Province, and was sitting in the management office of one such zone being promoted as one on the cutting edge of high technology. As usual, I asked the standard question: how is the power supply? No problem was the instant response; 24 hour-a-day guaranteed supply. Right on cue, of course, the lights went out![1]

In the rush to get economic development programmes off the ground, countries sometimes get ahead of themselves. In mid-1995, a very high profile project being built by South Korea's Daewoo Corporation in the Vietnamese capital Hanoi, virtually ground to a halt because it was suddenly realised that three things were lacking — water, power and adequate telecommunications. It is hard to understand how a high profile international company like Daewoo could have neglected to ensure such basic utilities were in place before making a multi-million dollar commitment, but the Koreans seemed to have got carried away with a desire to get in on the ground floor as a leading player in Vietnam's dash from a command to a market economy.

One cannot under-estimate the size of the problem facing many countries in Asia as they seek to create the necessary basic infrastructure in order to attract foreign industrial investment. Acute peak hour power shortages, long delays at the ports, and a waiting list for a new telephone that can run into years are a way of life in India, for example, and it has been estimated that in order to overcome *some* of the deficiencies, it needs to find US$30 billion for the power sector, $12 billion for telecommunications and $40 billion for road improvements.[2] Vietnam has presented the World Bank with an infrastructure shopping list currently costed at $50 billion.[3] China, which has poured many billions into overcoming infrastructural deficiencies in the first half of the 1990s, estimates it needs $500 billion more in the second half of the decade to complete the job.[4] Much of this will have to come from overseas sources. Indonesia has estimated it needs about $16 billion to improvements in transport infrastructure alone up to the end of the century in order to keep pace with economic growth. Of this, 14 per cent is likely to come from the government, 21 per cent from foreign loans, while state-owned companies and the private sector will be encouraged to find the rest any way they can. A total of 149 separate road, rail and port development projects have been identified, but by early 1996 only five had definitely received fund commitments.[5] Between 1994 and 2000, Malaysia expected it would have to spend some $28 billion on new infrastructure to keep up with its rapid economic development. For a start, with electricity demand growing at 14 per cent a year, power shortages have become common.[6]

Some countries are now trying to slow down the inflow of foreign capital to the manufacturing sector, and channel it into basic infrastructure development. Experiments with Build, Operate, Transfer (BOT) arrangements are being tried out in areas such as road construction, power stations and water treatment facilities. Malaysia has been an enthusiastic exponent of the concept, and others, such as China and Vietnam, are gingerly following the same route. Investors in China, however, have so far been slow to take up such opportunities, partly out of concern about the lack of guarantees of an adequate return on capital over the operating period, as well as the inadequacies of the legal framework for such schemes. Hong Kong companies who rushed into the neighbouring Chinese province of Guangdong to build and operate toll roads, for example, have already expressed concern at the low profits, mainly because the traffic volumes have proved less than expected.[7]

Infrastructure problems tend to surface when governments decide that it would be a good idea to concentrate foreign investment in designated areas offering preferential policies — export processing zones (EPZs), industrial and high-tech science parks etc. In 1991, the Vietnamese government decided to create six export processing zones around the country in the hope they would become magnets for foreign investment. Two were to be located in Ho Chi Minh City, and one each in Can Tho, Da Nang, Hanoi and Haiphong. But only the zone in Ho Chi Minh City has actually got off the ground and had any success. The rest have sunk under the weight of their own ambitions. A consortium of Malaysian companies was formed and combined with provincial authorities to develop the Da Nang zone which was licensed on October 1.1993. Two years later, there was only one tenant on the site — which lacks both water and electricity supply. That brave pioneer only soldiered on because it had installed its own generator and sunk its own well. Da Nang province eventually decided the zone should now be incorporated into a larger and supposedly more flexible 'industrial zone'. Can Tho suffered the same problem with only one factory completed — for a Thai manufacturer of fishing nets (Murray, 1997).

One problem could be that the authorities do not have a clear idea of what export processing zones or industrial estates really are and what they need in order to function well; nor is there a clearly defined industrial policy. The United Nations Industrial Development Organ' has studied the problem and concluded that inappropriate choice of locations and expensive infrastructure costs made export processing zones in Vietnam a rather impractical choice at this stage in the country's development. What were really wanted, it suggested, were simple industrial zones close to the main population centres that could tap into the growing domestic market for basic products. The EPZs failed to prosper because the developers waited for tenants to arrive to contribute towards the cost of infrastructure development. The tenants failed to arrive partly because of this very lack of infrastructure.[8] The same situation has arisen in Indonesia where attempts to create industrial parks on the island of Batam, close to Singapore, have been hampered by inadequate utility provision, where the provision has been left to private developers who do not necessarily have the capital for such investments (Murray and Perera, 1995, p. 59).

Some of these problems have also surfaced in the 'Growth Triangle' promoted by Singapore and designed to take advantage of perceived synergies between the island republic and its larger neighbours on either side, with Singapore providing the ideal environment for the administrative and financial sides of a manufacturing operation, while the actual factories were located in contiguous areas of Johor State in Malaysia and the Riau Archipelago of Indonesia, which had the two things Singapore lacked — land and labour. On the Indonesian side, Batam island, in particular, was promoted as a low cost site for manufacturing and, as such, did quite well in attracting Singaporean and foreign manufacturers forced to move out of the republic by high costs. These were then channeled into several industrial zones built from scratch (ibid, pp. 153-4).

But costs on Batam have proved to be higher than expected, due to the fact that it is a small island with no native population nor agricultural base to support its growing migrant population working in factories. According to one British executive who has a factory on Batam: 'Food has to be imported. So it's not as low cost as other places and it is rising fast and that is a concern. We no longer see it as a low cost plant. With our products we are having to move up the technology, quality and added value ladder far more quickly than we anticipated. Increasingly, Batam would be one of the less competitive new sites that is vying for inward investment in the region' (ibid, p. 63).

This executive complained about the high freight costs of shipping his products from Batam to Europe via Singapore, with between a quarter and a third of the cost coming in the very short inter-island journey — US$700 to go 12 miles, out of a total cost to Europe of US$2,500. Ideally, Batam needs a roll on-roll off operation enabling cargo to be shipped direct to its final destination, which would make the Port of Singapore unhappy due to the loss of business. As a result, at present, a container is loaded onto a truck at the Batam factory, unloaded and placed on a barge for the short journey to Singapore, where it is offloaded onto a lorry to be carried a short distance to a storage area in the port to await reloading on a lorry for movement onto the ship bound for Europe or elsewhere. Added to this is the fact that the Batam electricity rate is four times higher than average elsewhere; and the water rate is 10 times higher. Batam might be more attractive for some foreign investors if it was the gateway to the rest of Indonesia. But, given its duty-free status, that would be difficult while the government in Jakarta remains concerned to protect some of its fledgling local industries from the competition of foreign products (ibid, p. 64).

An Australian businessman involved in establishing one of the first companies on Batam commented that:

> in 1990, when we began, there wasn't really anywhere else to go, but it was the correct move because we were producing very labour intensive. low skill stuff. But now, with the range of China, Vietnam, Cambodia, it is getting less and less competitive and very quickly uncompetitive. It may still have a niche, because the higher and higher tech businesses in Singapore are going over there. So in comparison with Singapore, although it is getting uncompetitive on the very labour intensive stuff which is easy to move to Vietnam (making components for televisions etc.) for a higher tech firm it might be the thing to do, using a slightly more skilled Indonesian work force, but which is still a tenth of the cost of a Singaporean work force. And you have the added advantage of Singapore's infrastructure, finance, shipping etc. on the doorstep.
> So, for Singapore the Growth Triangle still makes sense, and for Indonesia it makes sense, because, with a population of 190 million, it's got to create two million jobs a year to stand still. But for Malaysia, it doesn't make sense really. I know this well because I have a factory in Johor now, and because I can't get labour for love nor money. I'm having to bring in Bangladeshis.
> Johor is worse than Batam, bureaucratically, racially, administratively. Batam is designated as a free trade zone and things can go in and out; it's isolated in a sense from the rest of Indonesia so it's a dedicated business island and you can overcome all the nonsense that you might have to go through if you are anywhere in Indonesia. In essence it is becoming an Indonesian microcosm of Singapore, which is fine. But Johor is still part of mainland Malaysia. It has all the rules and

regulations — racial quotas on the work force and equity holdings (to safeguard the interests of the Malay population vis-à-vis the Chinese minority); duties to take stuff in, duties to take stuff out; various other payments to take stuff in and out, and so forth.
(ibid, pp. 65-6)

Creating an investor-friendly legal environment

Infrastructure problems can be overcome. You can provide your own stand-by power generator to guard against blackouts; you can sink your own well for water; you can overcome some of the telecommunications problems perhaps with a satellite dish. But one of the most worrying and less easily solvable problems for businessmen is the somewhat hazy legal environment under which they may have to operate.

One of the biggest areas of concern currently is land ownership. In Indonesia, all the land belongs to the people via the government — which has also been the system in China under communist rule. What you end up getting as an investor in some instances are an assortment of land use rights over a specified period, with the possibility but not a guarantee of a further extension. But who can foresee that far into the future and plan with any certitude? In Vietnam, land rights used to be synonymous with land ownership. Now, foreign investors or their local partners must lease land directly through a handful of State-owned companies. New rules defining land use rights were introduced in January 1995, in a bid to curb speculation and erratic escalation of land prices. In fact, all this has done is create total confusion. In particularly, the new rules have made it much more difficult to organize joint ventures and calculate their equity value, especially as land is virtually the only thing a local partner has to offer to set against the injection of capital and technology from the foreign side.

If an investor is getting land from a local developer, which is the case in some countries, the legal right to use that land can depend heavily on the financial integrity, strength and longevity of the developer. Often, investors discover the fragility of their legal hold on their so-called investment and pull out

Leases can be and often are a minefield. For example, an American company launched a fast food venture with a local partner in the northern Chinese city of Dalian, based on a 20-year guaranteed occupancy on the ground floor of a building in a key location. Within three months it was ordered to quit, because the building was to be demolished to make way for a 38-storey office and apartment complex to be built with a big injection of Hong Kong capital. More than 120 families and 28 enterprises in the vicinity were relocated until the fast food venture was the sole occupant. And it refused to move.

A confrontational tone quickly set in. City officials cut off the electricity, gas and water. The foreign partner claimed that a conflict of interest was involved because one of the three partners in the skyscraper project was a subsidiary of the city government office which had ordered the company to vacate. After complaining to the US Embassy, the Chinese embassy in Washington, several American congressmen and the local mayor, the food company succeeded in little more than having its utilities restored.

Negotiations then began over the amount of compensation to be paid for the forced relocation, but the two sides were far apart on the amount. While these negotiations were underway, the builders of the office tower filed a damages suit against the Americans for 'long-term, unreasonable refusal to move'. Soon after, the local civil court notified the food company its accounts were to be sealed and that the building had to be vacated in five days. Only then did it accede to the pressure, and within hours the building had been demolished (Murray, 1994, pp. 161-2).

In 1992, Western Australian beach sands miner, Westralian Sands became the first foreign resources company to secure a mining license in Vietnam. Part of the license condition was that the company form a joint venture with a local partner — the Ha Tinh Provincial Government — and that the Australian company, with a 60 per cent stake in the venture, retained sole marketing rights to ilmenite mined in the province. But in November 1994, the company discovered that the joint venture's Vietnamese chief executive, also a senior cadre in the Ha Tinh People's Committee, was selling ilmenite from the joint venture mine to a Japanese buyer.

After the Australian side protested about this, five 'investigations' were conducted by the Ha Tinh authorities, the joint venture had its bank accounts frozen, an attempt was made to stop executives from leaving Vietnam and some were temporarily placed under house arrest by the local authorities. Added to this, $3.3 million worth Westralian Sands' mining equipment was held up by Vietnamese customs because its local partner claimed it was trying to smuggle it into the country — even though all the necessary Australian and Vietnamese paperwork was in order. As a result, the Central Government's Department of Internal Affairs has become involved in the 'investigation' process. If that was not bad enough, the Ha Tinh Government has accused the Australian company of withholding financial information and urged Prime Minister Vo Van Kiet to revoke the joint venture license. In the end, the venture collapsed with millions of dollars in debts (Murray, 1997).

Of course, if partners fall out they can always go to court. But can they? In some countries, the legal process takes for ever and it is expensive. The only beneficiaries are the lawyers. And while you are battling through the court, new locks might be installed at the office to prevent you getting in; your investments are frozen; money sits idly in a bank account to which you no longer have access; production grinds to a halt, and everyone ends up the loser. Each country has a different legal system.

The 1995 World Bank country report on Indonesia, for example, cited lack of confidence in the legal system as one of the factors holding back foreign investment. It said the court system was perceived by investors as being inadequate; procedures were slow with the result that cases often took a long time to resolve. The Indonesian Supreme Court has a backlog of some 60,000 civil cases, so that it can take up to five years for a major commercial case to move through the legal system from district to supreme courts.

The courts are said to be understaffed and overburdened. There is little specialization so that all types of cases have to go to the general courts; this makes it difficult when the case is a complicated one involving enforcement of credit security or protection of copyright interests. There is an alternative through the National Arbitration Board (BANI), but as yet it does not have sufficient staff or good overseas links, nor does it have an ability to have its awards legally enforced. There would seem to be a strong case for the creation, at the very least, of a specialized commercial court.

It is sometimes difficult to find a lawyer who understands your needs and the legal environment from which you have come. Take Vietnam: deluged with foreign businessmen since it opened up its economy in the late 1980s, it is preparing rules to bar foreign law firms from advising clients on Vietnamese law and representing them in local courts. They will not be able to hire Vietnamese lawyers, except as cadets, who will then have to leave them after training. Foreign law firms, apparently, will be restricted to advising clients on foreign or international law and nothing else. In addition, they will be restricted to only one branch in the country. So, you will have to decide whether you want to be close to the law-making centre, Hanoi, or close to the business action, which probably means Ho Chi Minh City. The foreign firms will have to work through Vietnamese law firms to advise and assist international clients — which is fine, except that Vietnam has very few lawyers experienced in Western ways of working or of drafting documents in English.

Throughout Indochina, in fact, there are constant legal uncertainties. The legislative framework is still incomplete. There is an ad hoc, experimental approach, with the rules frequently changing. Ask three different officials for an interpretation of the rules, and you will get three different answers. Even when laws are in place, they are not always obeyed by the departments supposed to administer them.

The judicial systems are administered by people with little legal experience, or perhaps even more important, no commercial experience. The development of competent and independent court systems able to handle complex international civil litigation and to enforce judgements in a difficult political climate may be years away.

Case study: changing the rules in Vietnam

There is great concern among manufacturers, and indeed investors of any description, about the legal protection they can expect. Sudden changes of regulations can catch investors in a legal limbo, creating frustrating delays and costing them money which do nothing for the host country's reputation as a safe haven for foreign capital.

A high technology zone in Vietnam where South Korea's Daewoo Corporation was building a television and video components site, ran into legal problems within weeks of its scheduled opening because of a sudden change in regulations which nobody had predicted. The result was that, with its first factory almost complete, Daewoo had to reapply for permission to use the land at the site for its allotted purpose. Reports about construction in Vietnam, in fact, usually start off with an anecdote about a building getting approved and built, only to be revisited by a fickle committee which requests the top five floors — or 15 — be lopped off. Or taking three years to get basic approval only to learn it will cost another $500,000 to relocate residents who moved into the structure slated for demolition once they learned a foreign company was involved. Everyone has got a story and they are all true (Murray, 1997).

There may well be foreign investment laws in place in most if not all countries. But there are so many grey areas, so many ambiguities, to confuse the local bureaucrat, in the absence of specific bylaws or guidelines on specific questions. What this means is that either the potential investor faces months of working through the bureaucratic maze, getting a chop from this agency, a chop from that agency.

Nowhere have rule changes been more apparent, and disruptive, than in Vietnam's minuscule automobile manufacturing industry.[9] Early in 1996, Japan's Mitsubishi Motors Corp. decided on a drastic cut in its projected vehicle output from Vina Star Motors Corp., its joint venture with the state-run Vietranscimex. The Figures are somewhat startling. Output was to be reduced from the earlier target of 2,000-3,000 vehicles to 600-800 units — the sort of production Figures one might have expected for the hand-built vehicles from the earliest days of the automobile. Mitsubishi's Tokyo headquarters said the decision had been taken because the joint venture only sold 500 small buses and trucks in 1995, mostly to state-run enterprises. Edgar Chiongban, vice-president of Vietnam Motors Corp. (VMC), assembler of various German, Japanese and Korean models, has similar problems. Although VMC got the biggest share of the government's 1996 assembly quota, the allotted number of vehicles had all been built by the middle of April. What, he asked, 'are we going to do for the rest of the year?'

These experiences are fairly typical of the Vietnamese automotive market at present. Yet, most of the well known foreign automobile and truck makers remain keen to assemble automobiles and trucks in Vietnam. This is optimism indeed, considering the fact that much of the country's road network remains in tatters, the result of war damage and poor upkeep. In the two main cities, Hanoi and Ho Chi Minh City, taxis fight a constant battle for road space with waves of bicycles and motor cycles, and travel between virtually any two places throughout the country is a time-consuming and nightmarish experience.

Never in the history of the automotive industry can such a poor country [where the average annual income at the time of writing wouldn't even buy a set of tyres] with such a small market have attracted such intense interest from investors. The government has issued 12 vehicle assembly licenses in an effort to jump start the fledgling industry. But at the same time, a series of measures designed to build up a domestic components sector is actually stalling the industry just when it should be moving into second gear. The assembly quotas issued by the Ministry of Trade, necessitated by its ban on import of semi-knockdown units (SKDs) and strict controls on complete-knockdown (CKD) kits, are so restrictive that one assembler says the 'ministry is our biggest competitor'.

To illustrate the way the government is keeping its foot on the brake, one only had to look at the ministry's 1996 import quota for vehicles with under 12 seats. Completely built-up units (CBUs), whether new or used, were restricted to 1,500. CKD kits were pegged at 3,500. Of this total, VMC received an allocation of 750 units. To put that into some sort of perspective, South Korea produces two million automobiles a year, and its factories could cope with Vietnam's entire CKD quota in one eight-hour shift. In desperation, mainly to keep the plant open and to avoid massive layoffs, VMC in 1995 decided to keep producing its Korean KIA trucks even though there were few buyers. These ended up packed into its warehouses for months on end.

So why is Vietnam so irresistible? The Americans, it seems, want to avoid losing another Southeast Asian market to Japan. The Japanese are moving aggressively because they have had good experiences in other Southeast Asian markets and would like to block the competition out of the region completely which dominance in Vietnam would certainly accomplish. The Japanese are also keenly aware of their failure to recognize the early potential of the Chinese market, where their late arrival has put them at something of a disadvantage against their European and American rivals. The Europeans and South Koreans, meanwhile, are also seeking gains from getting in on the ground floor.

Given the size of the market — conservative sales projections of 40,000 vehicles a year by the turn of the century from the government, and 60,000-80,000 units among more optimistic market analysts — an eventual shakedown will be necessary in which a number of businesses will either have to merge or retire from the fray. If all the proposed projects are built, by the year 2007, foreign joint ventures will be assembling more than 120,000 automobiles, trucks and buses each year. This worries some investors. 'The government is issuing too many licenses for this small market', said Naoko Tatebe, general director of Mekong Corp., which has been assembling four-wheel drive vehicles since 1992. 'One or two is enough', agreed Wann Lee, former general director of Vidamco, owned partly by Daewoo Corp. Some of the automobiles assembled in Vietnam hopefully will be sold to neighbouring countries. In fact, Vidamco's operating license requires it to export one-fifth of its output to earn hard currency. But most companies are counting on Vietnam's 72 million people for the bulk of demand.

There is considerable frustration among investors at what they see as Hanoi's erratic policies. State planners originally said they would allow only four firms to set up in the sector, but then threw the door open to all-comers when Japanese manufacturers complained about the restrictions. Chrysler, for one, said its decision to enter the Vietnamese market was based on what it considered a government guarantee that no more than six assembly licenses would be issued.

Import duties and assembly licensing requirements have been altered several times since 1992. In a policy designed to shift demand in favour of domestically assembled vehicles, a July 1994 directive raised the import duty on passenger automobiles by 200 per cent and banned imports of used automobiles. Six months later the government reversed part of the directive and authorized the import of used automobiles. As the used automobile imports were counted as part of total imports, this had the effect of drastically lowering the quota on CKD kits for vehicles with 12 seats of less to 2000 in 1995 [as already noted this was raised to 3,500 in 1996].

The two major domestic manufacturers, Vietnam Motor Corp. and Mekong Corp. petitioned the Ministry of Trade to reconsider as they had already fulfilled their allocation for the year. VMC, the biggest player in the market with 850 passenger automobiles sold domestically last year, compared with 400 for Mekong, pointed out that it had received a quota of only 600 kits when it had an annual production capacity of 20,000 vehicles. As a result, the company said it would have to lay off at least 500 workers at its Hanoi plant.

The decision to limit imports of kits apparently was aimed at building up a components industry in Vietnam. What officials did not seem to realize was that parts production of the quality insisted upon by foreign manufacturers would require massive investment that could not be offset by returns from the limited vehicle market. Nevertheless, existing and would-be investors have had to agree to a government demand that five per cent of vehicle parts they use be locally made within five years, rising to 40 per cent after — a move clearly designed to weed out companies that are not deemed serious about technology transfer. Privately, however, some foreign executives say that finding the right sort of local parts is likely to be tough in a country where even the indigenous bicycle industry has difficulty surviving with outmoded technology.

Reference was made earlier to the problems suffered by Westralian Sands in its ilmenite project. It was not alone. Portman Mining, for example, opted out of a $8 million silica sand operations in the central coastal region of Da Nang. The official line from Portman is that its Da Nang venture was not financially viable, but reports from Vietnam claim the miner also had serious problems with its joint venture partner. Portman abandoned the project only six months after receiving its joint venture license. Originally, the license had been for 30 years, but when the paperwork returned from the authorities, the contract period had been reduced to 20 years, the area to be mined had been greatly reduced and a guarantee to allow Portman to mine a second substantial adjacent site had been scrapped. The company later discovered its local partner was negotiating with a Taiwanese company to mine the second site.

Kleenheat Gas, a subsidiary of another Western Australian company, Wesfarmers, decided to pull out of Vietnam after struggling for three years to obtain a joint venture license to distribute Australian liquefied petroleum gas (LPG) in the country. According to reports in the Australian press, the Kleenheat project collapsed because the central government had increased the project's tax rate from 15 to 25 per cent and raised the import tax on LPG from one to 30 per cent after the joint venture agreement had been signed.

Many of the problems appear to stem from the Vietnamese Government's 1994 decision to only deal with large investors and to hand over responsibility of small and medium-sized foreign investment projects to provincial authorities. This leads to claims that provincial authorities are unable to handle even the basic business and legal issues and responsibilities, and are run by officials more concerned with personal gain than contractual obligation. Another reason cited is the wording of the 1987 foreign investment legislation, which gives the Vietnamese partner the most power in a joint venture, irrespective of the size of its shareholding.

Problems with different perceptions and insufficient information

One important element which foreign investors in the region sometimes fail to understand is that, all the talk of an 'open door' notwithstanding, they are actually in a country as a guest, because the host government has decided to allow them in for one reason or another. The two sides do not always have the same motives. This is typified, perhaps, by the attitudes of the United States and Vietnam when they finally normalized relations in 1995, putting an end to the hostility generated by the Vietnam War. When the Clinton Administration lifted a long-standing trade embargo and allowed American firms to do business with Vietnam again, this was seen as bestowing great benefits on the latter — 'at last, those poor benighted souls in Hanoi can finally enjoy the delights of Coca Cola'. Vietnam saw it differently — 'at last, those poor benighted souls in American can enjoy the opportunities and benefits of dealing with an extremely important market of 72 million people'. America thought it was doing Vietnam a favour, while Vietnam saw the situation in reverse. Neither side is entirely correct, but it is well for any investor to be aware of the implications behind such thinking.

One experienced business consultant has observed in regard to China that,

> the foreign company may decide to come because they feel there is a market. But they must take a step back and realize that when they enter China, actually the Chinese have semi-engineered that — putting the idea in your head previously, by, for example, shutting the door so that you couldn't come in with a certain product. Now, they have opened the door they have given you that opportunity. So you say: 'I see a market and I'm going to go for it'. But it only exists because the Chinese have decided it is beneficial to China that it should exist — the implication being that they could at any time decide that it is not beneficial to China. And then your opportunity is out the window and you're out the door and that's the end of your company.
> (Murray, 1994, pp. 152-3).

It is all too easy to waste much time and money in pursuing projects that have little or no chance of approval — and discover this only at the end after, perhaps, years of fruitless negotiations. It is important, therefore, to ascertain at the beginning whether a proposed project is approved or in the local, provincial or central government plan, or merely represents the ambition of the Chinese party, where approval is far from certain — especially if the project is perceived as financial wasteful or not in the public interest.

Many parts of China, particularly those distant from Beijing, have been trying to go their own way and achieve more autonomy in the decision-making process especially in attracting foreign investment. Every city had its industrial development zone, for both high and low-tech industries, all offering a wonderful package of incentives to persuade manufacturers to set up shop. The conflicting claims became rather bewildering. In Chengdu, for example, I was once briefed on an economic development zone that sold itself on the fact it was approved by the central government and had direct links into the State Council in Beijing. This ensured that projects would get rapid top-level approval, and one did not have to go through the frustrating, time-consuming bureaucratic maze of having to first get city, then provincial and finally central government approval. Just down the road, another zone sold itself on the basis that it was under local government control, with close links with the provincial governor, and therefore one could bypass the incredibly time-consuming, frustrating bureaucratic maze required to get central government approval for a project. Here, I was told, we can have everything processed within 10 days without bothering about Beijing. Officials even quoted that old maxim of 'the mountains are high and the Emperor is far away'. Could they both be right?

There is a lot of wishful thinking on both sides of the fence. If foreign businessmen have had inflated ideas of the benefits of breaking into China, local companies have been equally guilty — especially in seeing foreign investment as the solution to all their problems of poor products, outdated technology, lack of marketing techniques, an unmotivated work force and mountains of debt. Enter the foreign white knight in shining armour ready to come to the rescue. The same comment can be made of most countries in Pacific Asia.

Where does one start to find a good local partner for a manufacturing joint venture? A Japanese company was interested in establishing a manufacturing presence in the automotive sector of a certain country. It was inundated with offers. Some were from single component suppliers who thought they would like to expand into entire vehicle manufacture. Some were companies just starting up. In some cases they did not even have a factory, and had nothing to show but a piece of paper from the local government giving them permission to start operating. They would come to the Japanese company waving this bit of paper and couldn't understand why they were turned down. They had no track record, nothing to show that they had the business acumen to be a good partner.

A big problem in finding a suitable partner can often be the general lack of criteria on which to judge a local company's abilities or viability. With the concept of stock markets only in the fledgling stage in some countries — and even if they exist, there are very few firms listed — there are no annual reports to be perused for key performance-related Figures such as turnover and profits. Foreign companies I have spoken to repeat the same litany: better auditing of accounts, more information please on the performance of potential local partners. Someone must have this, they argue, otherwise how could these firms operate — especially those in countries where the government is likely to be the factory owner.

Figures, if any are available, have to be treated with considerable caution, especially in areas where accountancy principles don't yet conform to internationally-accepted standards. One problem I have encountered is that of treating loans, say from banks, as part of the company's assets or even profit for the year, when they are, in fact, liabilities because they need to be repaid. Then there is the problem of double book-keeping — the real set and the one that is presented to the taxman. Which set are you seeing?

Some countries, especially those newly converted to the market economy, still have a hangover from the old days of 'need-to-know' mentality about the handling of information. Everything tends to be treated as a State property not to be divulged unless there are very good reasons — reasons which are hard to establish.

In July 1995, for example, Vietnam decided to classify trade and customs statistics as state secrets and banned their publication. Reliable statistics on Vietnam's economy have never been easy to obtain. The Trade Ministry routinely has required businessmen and journalists to pay for data on imports and exports — statistics now freely available in most countries. If the report is correct, it seems odd that at a time when Vietnam is courting foreign investors, basic data which they need to make a decision — for instance, in analyzing market trends — will not be available. Economic and business data, particularly details of corporate performance, are going to have to become more readily available. In some countries this will mean starting almost from scratch in creating the necessary data base and also developing proper accountancy procedures.

The great need is to find a local partner with whom there is some correspondence of eventual goals. They may not necessarily be exactly the same, but they certainly shouldn't be so conflicting as to destroy any hope of mutual cooperation. An investor needs to be satisfied that success of the venture is as important to its partner as it is to itself, and that the two sides agree on the means to achieve it. A cautionary tale is provided by the now defunct American Motor Company (AMC), now owned by Chrysler, which set up a joint venture in the Chinese capital known as Beijing Jeep. When AMC and the Beijing Automotive Works (BAW) — formerly the 'East Is Red' plant — signed their historic deal in May 1983, press coverage contained several false assumptions and misunderstandings. First, the agreement was seen as the way forward for American companies who could team up with China, with its low labour costs, to create a base within Asia to compete on equal terms with the highly-successful Japanese. For AMC in particular it was a chance to overcome some of its financial weaknesses that relegated it to a poor fourth in its own market. Yet although the two sides had been talking to each other for almost five years when their new venture

Beijing Jeep finally opened for business in 1984, neither had yet decided what sort of vehicle they were going to produce. The Chinese essentially were producing the same jeep they had introduced with Russian help in the 1950s, and what they wanted from AMC was its technology and input to help design and manufacture a completely new Chinese product (influenced largely by the Peoples Liberation Army (PLA) which was undergoing a determined modern' drive after its embarrassments in Vietnam five years earlier). The Americans, however, weren't particularly interested in this idea. Development of an entirely new vehicle probably would have cost in the vicinity of a billion dollars, and neither side had that sort of cash available. What AMC wanted was a Chinese jeep which would be as close as possible to those it was producing in America, and with the primitive Chinese automobile industry hardly likely to be able to produce world-standard parts, this, in essence, meant the Beijing factory would have to produce a CKD jeep from parts made in the US. When the idea was first raised, the Chinese had reacted angrily, accusing the Americans of treating China as a backwater colony and of trying to find a way to control the local market. So, the idea was allowed to drift. At the same time, AMC executives knew that if they rejected outright the idea of designing a completely new Chinese jeep, the chances of concluding any deal would have been virtually nil.

The sort of vehicle Chinese officials wanted could not be made from any of AMC's existing jeeps. But in signing the contract, the two sides glossed over this point. The Chinese intended to persuade the Americans to invest the effort and money necessary to build a completely new jeep in China. The Americans hoped to persuade the Chinese to abandon the idea of having its own unique new jeep and accept one based largely, or, better yet, based entirely on the American model. Finally, in October 1984, the two sides agreed that from the following year Beijing Jeep would begin to build the AMC-developed Cherokee from American parts (although the joint venture would gradually replace these with Chinese-made components as justified). To the Americans this seemed the only alternative to scrapping the joint venture entirely. The Chinese side thought that it was going along with a short-term expedient, and certainly did not give up the idea of a new jeep for the PLA. What they did not realize at the time was that their acquiescence shaped AMC's attitude towards the Chinese market. AMC would be making money by selling kits of Cherokee parts to Beijing Jeep, and inevitably it would want to sell as many kits as possible. The Americans, on their side, were also guilty of a fundamental misunderstanding.

Although Beijing Jeep officials had given their reluctant blessing to the change in strategy, written approval had not been obtained from any higher authority (in this case, the State Planning Commission and State Economic Commission), even though the import of the CKD kits would require significant amounts of rare foreign exchange. It was a big risk and it rebounded on the venture when the money was not forthcoming, leaving thousands on ordered kits sitting on warehouses in the United States, and Beijing Jeep unable to pay its bills — including workers' salaries. The result was anguished representations in Beijing and Washington that eventually reached the highest levels in both governments before AMC got its way — in a deal which had to kept secret because the Chinese had no intention of allowing other foreign enterprises similar generous treatment (especially a provision permitting the joint venture to convert Yuan earned from continued sales of the old Chinese jeep into dollars). Beijing Jeep was getting this treatment only because of its high profile as a 'model' for Sino-foreign joint ventures.

There were further problems when American Motors officials, observing a sudden upsurge in the number of Japanese vehicles being sold in China, hurriedly tried to get into the action. The Americans told their partners they were willing to ship completed AMC jeeps to China immediately and offer the joint venture a handsome commission for one each. But it was to no avail.

China wanted American Motors for a different purpose: to give China the sort of technology and expertise necessary for it to develop a modern automobile industry of its own. That was, after all, what the two sides had been talking about for the previous five years. AMC had happily accepted the idea, believing it would gain, in exchange for its technology, not only entree into the Chinese market, but also a low-cost labour base from which to export to the rest of Asia.

The differences over thwarted ambitions outlined here caused serious rifts in the joint management, with the repercussions being felt for a number of years. And all because the two sides had decided to skate around fundamental differences in approach in their pre-agreement discussions. Wishful thinking prevailed instead. Beijing Jeep is now one of the most successful vehicle joint ventures in China. But it took almost a decade to achieve its targeted production Figures and the achieve the sort of profit levels the American side first dreamt off in the early 1980s.[10]

This problem is not unique to the Beijing Jeep project as far as China is concerned, nor, I would contend, is it even unique to China; throughout the region, every day partners in a joint venture will be struggling to overcome differences caused by insufficient attention to creating an understanding on common goals and common ways of doing business. It could also be argued that the Beijing Jeep example is rather old and that, *surely*, the situation is different now? Not necessarily; it is my contention that there is still a lot to learn from the Beijing Jeep example in conducting negotiations for a joint venture in the late 1990s whether in China or anywhere else.

The crucial role of labour relations

Many of the investments which are being made in manufacturing in the Asia-Pacific region in recent years have been in labour-intensive operations. One of the prime motivations of the Growth Triangle concept promoted heavily by Singapore, for example, has been the need to cope with a labour shortage — shifting labour-intensive operations to Johor and Indonesia's Riau province, notably the islands of Batam and Bintan.

Inevitably, however, no matter where a company locates its operation, costs are going to go up. The question then is whether to move on or upgrade. There are certainly signs of growing mobility of capital across Asia. One can see this trend happening around the region. Labour-intensive operations moved out of Singapore into Malaysia, for example. Now, those labour intensive operations are moving out of Malaysia as that country follows the high-tech, capital; intensive road, motivated like Singapore by a worker shortage. Some will find a home in Indonesia, where many of Singapore's former processing plants have been relocated. Others will look further afield — Vietnam, Burma, Bangladesh etc.— where labour costs remain low and the manufacturing potential has not been fully tapped.

But cheap labour cannot be the long-term solution. Each country has its ambitions to move up the chain; all want to be one of Asia's new tigers. Governments are forced to balance economic development needs with a requirement, at least partially, to keep the populace happy. Unrest, either on the streets or in the factories, has led to the gradual introduction of stronger labour laws, stricter regulations on healthy and safety and environmental protection, and other measures to meet rising worker expectations. The additional costs this incurs tends to end up on the profit and loss accounts of the foreign investor.

In Indonesia, minimum labour rates have increased drastically under the initiative of the government in Jakarta and this has particularly hit the labour-intensive operations on the island of Batam referred to earlier. In 1991, one of the early arrivals was paying 2,400 Rupiahs a month, which was the minimum wage, and by early 1995 it was paying 6,750 Rupiahs. The rising cost of labour, therefore, has become a matter of concern, even though the Rupiah has been devaluing at around seven per cent per annum against the US dollar. As a result, some of the labour-intensive operations are considering moving on to cheaper sites elsewhere (Murray and Perera, 1995, p. 237).

For many companies, savings have not been what they projected. Items cited as costly in comparison to other low-cost production centres like China were food, which has to be brought in from outside, freight, utilities, medical care and rents. The extra costs of recruitment and taking care of Indonesian workers and expatriate staff add to the burden. One of the biggest problems is worker turnover. A large proportion of the people at the end of their two year work contract go back to their home village. Companies can anticipate a 25 per cent turnover per annum.

Because of this rapid turnover, recruitment remains a real problem. One of the complaints is that companies cannot get quantity and quality that they want. First, they can never get quantity. Some of the companies want to recruit 500 workers at a time, but what they find is that they might only get 380 candidates. The Indonesian side scours high schools for potential migrants to Batam, but find it hard to obtain enough people of the requisite quality. By the time the employer on Batam has undertaken a screening process and probably rejected some of the limited number on offer, then the problem is obvious. Eventually, it seems the answer is going to be moving up the high tech ladder and letting the basic labour-intensive operations migrate somewhere else (ibid, pp. 61-2).

China is an obvious possibility given its large labour pool. But China too has ambitions to move upmarket. The problem then becomes a lack of skilled labour. The shortage of skilled labour, in fact, is a common worry across the region. In 1995, Malaysia reduced its tertiary education courses by a year to get young educated people into the workplace quicker to overcome a chronic shortage, although whether this would compensate for the loss of a year acquiring further skills in the classroom remains unclear. In Indonesia, meanwhile, 60 per cent of private company workers only have elementary school education, prompting the Finance Ministry to lament that the country was one of the least competitive in the region. In addition, more than 13 per cent of those employed work less than 15 hours a week, illustrating the twin problems of too many workers, but not enough skilled ones. Singapore has had to cope with a chronic labour shortage by getting rid of its basic industries and trying to upgrade its worker profile as one of high-tech excellence. Nevertheless, it still has to rely on imported labour to a worrying extent.

Two 1995 surveys highlighted the fact that a key worry for foreign investors in China was a shortage of skilled labour and local management expertise.[11] According to official estimates, there are currently some 80 million people under the age of 35 in the Chinese work force. Of these, at least 80 per cent are rated by the government as having only 'elementary-level skills'. Most of the remainder have 'medium-level skills', while only one per cent are regarded as having reached an 'advanced level'. The State Statistics Bureau says only 1.87 per cent of the current work force have received college education. As a result, labour efficiency is estimated at one-tenth of that in developed countries. There is fierce competition for a small pool of talent which cannot hope to meet current demands either for domestic companies or there foreign counterparts. Foreign investors complain bitterly about the high rate of worker turnover, as their skilled staff are lured away by higher pay offers from rival firms. Despite this, China continues to send out signals that it no longer wants to be a home for the cheap labour-intensive manufacturing operations of countries like Japan and South Korea, but desires a high percentage of investment at the high-tech end of the spectrum.

Of equal concern to investors in a number of countries are a spate of new labour laws designed to give workers more rights and greater protection in such areas as wages and other benefits, working environment, health and safety. China has, for example, suddenly shifted to a five-day working week. Even some Chinese experts have warned that this is premature, in what is still a developing country, and rising labour costs can only place it at a disadvantage in the current heated competition for foreign investment. It was only in March 1994, that the maximum working week was set at 44 hours, with no more than eight hours worked each day. On May 1, 1996, however, a further reduction to 40 hours was introduced. The government insisted that this would help reduce the pressure of rising unemployment while also raising labour productivity.

The move certainly caught many investors by surprise. They had only just begun to absorb the impact of the 44-hour week and were upset at not being consulted over the latest change which they regarded as 'hasty and ill-advised'. There was a feeling that the government should have concentrated on getting a worker commitment to raising productivity before introducing such a radical new work schedule. Inevitably, this is going to influence labour-intensive operations, which comprise the bulk of foreign investments in China at present.

The argument put forward by Chinese officials is that 'we cannot sacrifice the interests of Chinese labourers to please certain foreign investors'. A front page report in the *Workers' Daily* about a dispute at a South Korean clothing factory made no bones about the point being made — 'If you make money on Chinese land by using Chinese labour, you must abide by Chinese law', the large headline declared.

Considerable unrest has been reported in the southern province of Guangdong, where a lot of labour-intensive, low-tech operations have been set up, mainly by Hong Kong and Taiwanese interests. A survey by the provincial branch of the All-China Federation of Trade Unions reported that almost 90 per cent of workers worked without any safety protection; eight out of 10 said they had been forced to work overtime or even work without pay to meet company output quotas; 18.9 per cent reported they had suffered beatings or other forms of physical abuse for complaining about conditions.[12]

The Labour Ministry says that most disputes occur in the small and medium-sized enterprises, 'mainly those which send materials, designs and samples to be processed in China''. According to one official: 'these investors didn't bring much capital to China. They didn't bring any advanced management experiences or technology. They were merely workshops, and not the main target for China in seeking to attract foreign investment.' Despite these seemingly disparaging remarks about 'workshop' operations, these are exactly the type of investments which are likely to be attracted by the prospect of cheap, unskilled labour which is what China has in abundance and which has been an important consideration in many of the investment decisions made since the country was again opened up to foreign capital. And these investments are still needed: unemployment is rising steadily, and the Chinese work force increases by 10 million a year.

So, we have a government which is on the one hand trying to soak up high unemployment among a predominantly unskilled or, at best, semi-skilled labour pool — which means labour-intensive industries that need to be extremely cost-effective by controlling wages — and, on the other hand, trying to move rapidly upmarket by attracting high-technology investments, which tend to be capital-intensive and which require a small pool of highly skilled labour. And, this is exactly the commodity which is in short supply, and will continue to be so, unless the government can come up with a wide-ranging national skills development programme. And who is going to pay for this? The government — or the foreign investor?

Many foreign companies in China are beginning to complain about what they call the 'hidden costs' of doing business. They are finding that having calculated the monthly wage bill is no indication of how much the production side is going to cost. Many of the extra charges are labour-related and involve such areas as the provision of housing, medical care and welfare facilities. When the State was virtually the only employer, wages were kept down by factories providing cheap, heavily subsidized housing, food, medical care and virtually everything else from the cradle to the grave (the so-called iron rice bowl). This virtually bankrupted the State, and recent economic reforms have dictated the disappearance of many of the perks and, thus, a consistent need for higher wages. Foreign companies, particularly multinational manufacturing corporations assumed to have lots of spare cash, have come under pressure to take over the role of nanny from the state. They have resisted such pressure and this has caused further tension.

And China is not alone: 'workers in Vietnam's foreign joint ventures are facing growing insecurity', the state press has warned, in a signal that overseas investors may face a new trade union drive for more laws, higher wages and better conditions. Many workers face little more than three months' job security, with few contracts, minimal safety and health insurance, as applicants queue to take their jobs, according to reports following a recent national trade union review meeting..

The official *Vietnam News* was quoted as saying that the government should create more detailed and strict regulations for joint venture owners, covering outline contracts, training and union formation nationwide. 'It is easy to fire employees who want to try their luck in these joint ventures. Most trainees who want to join work very hard at first. After a while their productivity declines, because of low salary. Applications pile high on employers' tables, enabling them to dismiss the previous trainees. Shop unions, where they existed, were said to be hampered by lack of contracts, meaning any attempt to strike would lead to workers losing their jobs', the agency added.[13]

Only about 100 strikes were reported in Vietnam between 1990 and 1995 and most of those were illegal. The 1995 Figure was 46, against 28 the previous year, all but eight involving foreign companies. But this would seem to be a serious underestimate, ignoring the numerous wildcat strikes and disputes of short duration that did not attract official attention through the arbitration process. Low wages appears to be the main cause. Other reasons cited include strict working regimes, long hours without overtime pay, management refusal to grant medical and other social benefits as stipulated by law, and direct physical abuse by employers.

The worst offenders were not identified by the government, but union officials have previously singled out South Korean and Taiwanese investors in particular for having bad relations with workers. Certainly, 11 of the 1994 strikes occurred in South Korean factories, according to various official sources. Of eight industrial disputes recorded in the first quarter of 1996, six were in South Korean-owned firms. Among these, about 970 workers at a footwear factory in Ho Chi Minh City walked out after a Korean technician allegedly beat 15 employees around the head and face with unfinished shoes. Two of the employees required hospital treatment. Negative press treatment of various problems at Korean enterprises became such a source of concern that the country's ambassador to Hanoi warned the government this might result in less Korean investment in future.[14]

A Labour code went into operation on January 1,1995, giving workers the right to form trade unions and to strike for the first time. It also provided for the formation of labour courts, a mechanism for tripartite arbitration involving business, unions and government.

'The operation of trade unions and the inspection of and management of labour problems in enterprises, especially in the private sector, is still too weak to force employers to follow the regulations', complained Hoang Minh Chuc, deputy president of the Vietnam General Confederation of Labour. In the state-run sector, these were often a legacy of decades of bureaucracy and the inability, in some cases, of companies to pay their work force. 'But as many state-run enterprises are becoming more stable and profitable, the number of strikes is likely to decrease'. He also admitted, however, that on occasions disputes could be solved through negotiations, if Vietnamese workers were 'not so hasty in over-reacting to what they see as violations of their rights'.

To push for more regulation, trade unionists cited recent trouble at a Taiwanese garment joint venture, Da Nang Valley View, with more than 1,000 employees. The Vietnam News said staff petitioned the government with complaints of unfair dismissals, low pay and 'high-handed' management — a move followed by a stiff Confederation of Labour report demanding unions and changes at the company. But just days after a union was created, the company announced that half the staff would have to leave because of 'production cutbacks'. The newspaper said: 'This is seen as a trick that the management board played on those who wanted to protect their own legal rights'.[15]

The Ministry of Labour estimates that around 90,000 Vietnamese are now directly employed by foreign-invested joint ventures or wholly-owned companies, not to mention several hundred thousand labourers who find temporary employment especially in the construction industry. But while around 90 per cent of state enterprises are said to have trade unions, the Figure in the private sector and for foreign companies is only about 30 per cent.[16]

In the industrial zones of Dong Nai on the northern outskirts of Ho Chi Minh City, one of the fastest growing areas for foreign investment, there have been a number of major disputes, prompting the provincial labour organ' to step up its efforts to persuade employers to sign labour contracts with their work force. But it admitted it did not have the resources to monitor all labour violations nor the muscle to overcome management resistance. The Vietnam General Confederation of Labour submitted proposals to the National Assembly calling for harsh punishment for those who violated the labour laws, including having their operating license revoked. A watchdog body should be set up with powers to bring to court foreign investors who repeatedly violated the laws, and after being punished the specific managers should be expelled, it argued. It also called on the government to only license those foreign investments projects that agreed to recognize an in-house union. Whether these far-reaching steps would be accepted remains unclear, especially as Vietnam needs to balance the protection of workers' rights without discouraging foreign investment (Murray, 1997).

Conclusion

These, then, are some of the concerns faced by foreign businessmen as they consider whether to invest in Pacific Asia. This is by no means an exhaustive list. There is, for example, the frustration of widespread corruption and bureaucratic red tape that in some countries in the region can tie up a project for months if not years, until sometimes the investor walks away disgusted. There are also political considerations. In the socialist countries such as China and Vietnam, there is an ongoing debate within the power structure over the pace of economic reform, with some more conservative elements worried that the door has been opened too wide to foreign influences which could undermine the dominant role of the communist party — not to mention the fear that sectors of the economy considered of strategic importance (telecommunications, for example) might come under foreign control, posing a long-term security threat. There is also the need for foreign businessmen to tread lightly to avoid upsetting hyper-sensitive governments who don't like to hear any criticism, particularly from the West. Financial analysts in certain countries, for example, have expressed concern that they are unable to provide their clients with the best possible advice because they fear that forthright comments on government economic policies might rebound on them (resulting in their company perhaps losing an operating license in the country concerned).[17] Finally, there is the issue of whether a business should be investing in a country whose human rights record is deemed less than perfect. The issue has come up on a number of occasions with regard to China and Vietnam, while Myanmar is currently the hot issue over whether by investing one is 'helping to keep an unacceptably authoritarian regime in power' or is 'helping to reintegrate the country into the world economy and mitigating some of the worst excesses of government power.' That is beyond the scope of this particular work. But it is certainly an issue, along with all the others discussed in this chapter, which any businessman needs to examine before committing a single pence or cent of corporate capital.

The other issue I wish to raise in conclusion stems from the fact that many of the examples of problems cited in this chapter relate to Western businesses. This might suggest that many of the problems stem simply from ethnocentrism, even racism, or at least Western ignorance of local culture and customs. Many Western business executives I have spoken to agree that a good knowledge of Asia and its customs can only be helpful in doing business in the region. So, if having Asian experience is helpful, does that mean Asian enterprises have an inherent advantage over Western ones?

I raised this question with a number of people on a visit to Vietnam in 1996. On the surface, said a Foreign Ministry official, Asians would seem to have an advantage when engaged in business in other parts of their own region. 'At the very least [an Asian] is eating rice and using chopsticks'. But this ignores the fact that many Westerners are now thoroughly familiar with using chopsticks and rice is often just as much a fixture on Western dining tables as those in Asia. But if you scratch beneath this surface, will you find a deeper understanding of Vietnam among, say, Japanese, Koreans or Taiwanese? Asian countries may share a long list of traits, but in the end they are still different cultures. The Vietnamese press, for example, often carry articles criticizing certain Asian companies, in particular joint ventures and 100 per cent foreign-invested manufacturers accused of abusing Vietnamese labourers. Charges of bribery, false invoicing and tax evasion are routine. The same applies in China where Japan and Korean enterprises are often castigated for their bad attitude.

Confucian values may be shared by many Asians, but this can be a double-edged sword. A Japanese diplomat says, for example, that while there may be a common understanding of how to behave and how Confucian societies work, there are different interpretations. Confucianism, he argues, can imply authoritarianism or at the very least a hierarchical structure. This could lead to the Asian business executive looking down on the local partner during business negotiations. This is especially relevant in Vietnam — and to a varying extent elsewhere — where in almost every joint venture, the local partner is in a substantially weaker financial position.

What it comes down to is that on a certain level, Asian business executives may understand their fellow Asians, better and instinctively know some of the rules by which the business game is played. But Western businessmen also have their strengths, and if they take an effort to learn about the local culture and demonstrate their understanding, suppressing any temptation to sink into ethnocentrism or to show impatience, they can be just as successful. In China, for example, I have found Japanese businessmen just as frustrated and expressing exactly the same sort of irritation at the slow pace of negotiations or the complex maze of regulatory channels to be negotiated, as their Western counterparts. The issues discussed above, therefore, apply to foreign businesses regardless of nationality.

Notes

1. Suspicions were further heightened by a tour of the zone which revealed a number of companies taking the precaution of installing their own stand-by generating facility.
2. *Asia Infrastructure Monthly, Asia-Pacific Telecommunications Analyst.*
3. Figure given to author during meetings with government officials in Hanoi May 1996.
4. Author's research.
5. 'Tailback of woes feeds congestion in Indonesia,' *South China Morning Post International Weekly*, Jan.20,1996.

6. 'Malaysian planners ride the fast lane,' *Financial Times*, Sept.9,1994.
7. The newsletter *Asian Infrastructure Monthly* carried considerable analysis of this problem in its first three issues of 1996.
8. The other major reason was Vietnamese insistence that none of the manufacturers in the zone could have any access to the domestic market. Producing purely for export simply wasn't attractive enough or technically feasible in most cases — especially when the raw materials had to be imported.
9. This section on the Vietnamese automobile industry has been prepared from personal investigation, as well as from material published in 1995 and 1996 by a variety of publications — the Associated Press, *Bangkok Post*, *Financial Times*, *Saigon Times*, *South China Morning Post International Weekly Edition*, *Vietnam Business Journal*, *Vietnam Economic Times* and *Vietnam Investment Review*.
10. A full account of the Beijing Jeep saga is contained in Mann, J. *Beijing Jeep: The short, unhappy romance of American business in China*, 1989, Simon and Schuster, Simon and Schuster. This is a classic cautionary tale which should be read by every businessman wishing to invest in Asia.
11. These were conducted by the Bank of East Asia, covering 50 joint ventures and three wholly-owned foreign enterprises and the Information Centre of the Chinese Chamber of Commerce, involving more than 1,400 firms.
12. *China Daily*, February 3,1996.
13. Agence France Presse report from Hanoi, August 2,1995.
14. *The Nation*, Bangkok, May 3,1996.
15. *Vietnam Investment Review*, Jan.29, Feb.4,1996.
16. Estimate of Pham Gia Thieu, deputy director of the Vietnam General Confederation of Labour's Foreign Department in conversation with the author, Hanoi, May 1996.
17. For example, British investment bank Kleinwort Benson had to scrap a report and apologise to the Malaysian Government after a scathing reference to its economic policies as 'Noddynomics'. Brokerages in Singapore, Thailand and South Korea have also faced problems with sensitive governments. See 'Falling victim to anti-fun police', *South China Morning Post International Weekly*, February 3,1996.

References

Mann, J. (1989), *Beijing Jeep: The Short, Unhappy Romance of American Business in China*, Simon and Schuster, New York.

Murray, G. (1993), *The Rampant Dragon*, Minerva Press, London.

Murray, G. (1994), *China: The Last Great Market*, China Library, London.
Murray, G. and Perera, A. (1995), *Singapore: The Global City State*, China Library, London.
Murray, G. (1997), *Vietnam: Dawn of a New Market*, China Library, London.
World Bank Country Report: Indonesia, 1995, World Bank.

Other sources:

Agence France Presse
Asia Infrastructure Monthly
Asia Pacific Telecommunications Analyst
Associated Press
Bangkok Post
Financial Times
Saigon Times
South China Morning Post International Weekly Edition
Straits Times, Singapore
The Nation, Bangkok
Vietnam Business Journal
Vietnam Economic Times
Vietnam Investment Review

5 The Malaysian Manufacturing Industry: Key to Sustainable Economic Development

HOCK B. TAN

Introduction

The purpose of this chapter is to analyse the structure of the Malaysian manufacturing industry. Under the Seventh Malaysia Plan, covering the period 1996-2000, the Malaysian manufacturing industry will play a crucial role in sustaining economic development in Malaysia (Malaysia, 1996, p. 2). According to the Second Outline Perspective Plan (OPP2), covering the period 1991-2000, manufacturing industry has been targeted to grow by over 10 per cent per annum (Malaysia, 1991b, p. 4). Therefore manufacturing industry will continue to be the largest contributor to value-added growth. It has been estimated that between 1990 and 1995, manufacturing industry alone would contribute to over 40 per cent of the increase in the gross domestic product (GDP) (Malaysia, 1991c, p. 3).

Based on the analysis of the industry structure the chapter examines how active support measures and facilities could be instituted and reinforced to make the manufacturing industry more dynamic, modern and internationally competitive. The question of creating a conducive investment environment will also be discussed.

The chapter first briefly examines the changes in the structure of the Malaysian economy since the 1970s, and Malaysia's development path. The role of the manufacturing industry in the economy and the hostile environment in which it operates are discussed. Then, an analysis of the Malaysian manufacturing industry is carried out, highlighting its main weaknesses. Subsequently, the chapter examines the ways in which the competitiveness of the manufacturing industry could be enhanced via consideration of such issues as the efficiency of infrastructure facilities, finance and third factor development. Finally, this is followed by a brief analysis of the social and environmental issues which are critical in maintaining political stability in a multi-racial society like Malaysia, since political stability is crucial in attracting foreign direct investment.

Malaysia's economic structure

The structure of the Malaysian economy principally changed since the 1970s. This is when agriculture fell from a third to 14.5 per cent by 1994, and manufacturing rose from 14 to 32.5 per cent of the total GDP in 1994 (*Financial Times*, 19 September 1995). The export of manufactures started to rise during the 1970s, rising from 19 to over 75 per cent by 1995. This development is expected to continue, but at a declining rate, with manufacturing reaching 37 per cent of output by 2000 (*Bank Negara Malaysia Annual Report 1992*, p. 2).

The main industrial country market is the US, which takes in 25 per cent of Malaysia's manufacture, the EU taking 18 per cent and Japan only 9 per cent. When all goods are taken into account, the imports of these three areas are more equal, with the US importing about 17 per cent, Japan 16 per cent and the EU slightly less. However, it is interesting to note that 58 per cent of Malaysia's trade is with East Asia, i.e. ASEAN, Japan, South Korea, China, Taiwan, Hong Kong and Vietnam (Page, 1994, p. 140).

Malaysia continues to head the Asian growth league. Target growth is 7 per cent until 2020. Output in the first half of 1995 was 9.5 per cent, accelerating from the previous year's 8.7 per cent. Despite a rapid population growth, the GNP per head increased to US$3750, the sixth highest in Asia after Japan, Hong Kong, Singapore, Taiwan and Korea. Manufacturing, the engine of growth for the last 10 years, still recorded 14.6 per cent growth in the second quarter of 1995 (Baker, 1995a, p. 3).

More than US$80 billion of private investment, about 65 per cent of it from overseas, was ploughed into Malaysia between 1991 and 1995. If growth plans are to be realized, it is calculated that another US$150 billion of funds from the private sector will be needed before the end of the century. Whether or not these funds are forthcoming will depend largely on Malaysia's ability to enter a new phase of industrialization. This could be helped by Malaysia's external debt, which is relatively small, equivalent to under 5 per cent of gross exports and Malaysia's saving rate, a healthy 34 per cent of GNP (Cooke, 1995, p. 1).

Malaysia's development path

Westerners still often refer to Malaysia as 'Japan's backyard' or part of the 'yen block'. Yet to regard the booming economy of Malaysia simply as the success of pupils in a Japanese masterclass is to miss the point (*The Economist*, 24 June 1995, p. 16). Malaysia has followed a distinctive path to development. There are broadly three ways in which Malaysia's capitalism is different from the Japanese and Korean varieties. It is much more open to foreign direct investment. It is much less prone to try to second-guess the market through a government-directed industrial policy. And it has been much quicker to allow financial markets to develop.

The distinction is clearest over attitudes to foreign direct investment. The Japanese and the South Koreans have been determined to build up national champions and have made it difficult for foreign-owned companies to set up shop. By contrast, the 'tigers' of Southeast Asia have built their booms by welcoming foreigners. The export industries of Malaysia are heavily reliant on foreign firms. Secondly, Malaysia has tried nurturing winners, e.g. automobiles, but such efforts remain peripheral. Malaysia's state-backed automobile industry has yet to prove itself commercially viable in the long term. Malaysia has concentrated on macroeconomic stability and opposed subsidy. Thirdly, Malaysia has been much quicker to let financial markets flourish. In the early stages of South Korean and Japanese industrialization, businesses in search of credit had little option but to go to the banks, whose lending decisions were, in turn, heavily influenced by the government. By contrast, the stockmarkets of Malaysia were cleared for take-off early on the path to economic development, allowing companies to raise more money without heavy borrowings (*The Economist*, 24 June 1995, p. 17).

The Malaysian manufacturing industry

Manufacturing industry will continue to play a crucial role in the economic development of Malaysia. Until the year 2000 the manufacturing industry is expected to grow at the rate of 11.5 per cent per year, making up 45.8 per cent of the country's GDP (Malaysia, 1996, p. 4). Its share of GDP increased from 27 per cent in 1990 to 32.5 per cent in 1994. Between 1995 and 2000, growth of the manufacturing industry is forecast to generate an additional 410,000 new job vacancies, which will represent one third of the total of jobs created. In order to achieve this rate of growth from 1995 to 2000 the amount of investment required is in the region of US$32 billion. It is expected that US$19 billion will come from foreign direct investment and the remaining US$13 billion from domestic investment (Malaysia, 1991b, p. 10). The manufacturing industry will continue to be the largest contributor to the value-added growth of Malaysia. Therefore, it is critical that besides creating a conducive investment climate, sufficient support measures and facilities should be instituted and reinforced to make the manufacturing industry more dynamic and competitive.

The competitive environment of the manufacturing industry

Malaysia has an economic structure that is open and exposed to the complex and dynamic environment of global trade. This is evident because external trade plays an important role in the growth and development of the economy, with exports accounting for 89 per cent of the GNP in 1994 and imports in the region of 91 per cent of the GNP (*Financial Times*, 19 September 1995). Bearing in mind the speed of change in the international environment, the external trade of Malaysia is often unstable, caused by substantial fluctuations in external demand and prices which are linked to the economic conditions of the industrialized countries. Therefore a strong and resilient economy which can cope with external economic shocks needs to be created in order to sustain the progress of the manufacturing industry.

The manufacturing industry will have to cope with dynamic competition. Customers are increasing their demand for higher quality goods and bespoke products at competitive prices, which accelerates the competition in the manufacturing industry sector. This forces the manufacturer to adopt differentiation strategies, focusing on product customization, rapid product changes, a shorter and more reliable delivery time at a competitive price. As 'borderless' world trade increases, multinational corporations are prepared to locate manufacturing facilities anywhere in order to harvest the synergistic benefits (Bartlett, 1989, p. 12). The formation of strategic alliances, merger and acquisition of organizations are common in order to gain a competitive advantage for organizations (Elek, 1996, pp. 249-257).

With the advancement of technology, particularly in the area of materials technology and biotechnology, manufacturing processes and product development are becoming more multi-dimensional, providing for a higher degree of flexibility. As a result, time-based competitiveness has become a key element of competitive advantage. The ability to cope with the shorter product life cycle and quick obsolescence has become the key to maintaining or improving one's market share (Joynt, 1991, p. 78).

A further challenge is improving the investment climate. Countries like South Africa, with emerging political stability and larger domestic markets, will provide alternative investment opportunities for foreign investors. Major economic activities, such as the cost of the reunification programme of Germany, will significantly increase the world's demand for financial resources, consequently resulting in a strain on the world's credit availability (World Bank, 1995, p. 47).

Finally, the manufacturing industry has to be aware that customer's demand for compliance with the preservation of the environment will become more intense. The association between trade and environmental issues will therefore become more pronounced (McGrath, 1992, p. 96).

Analysis of the Malaysian manufacturing industry

Further major structural adjustments took place in the Malaysian economy in the 1980s which allowed manufacturing industry to take on new dimensions. These adjustments were more radical than those in the 1970s for they happened at a time when private investment in the manufacturing industry was decreasing due to global recession. The government made major policy changes to encourage private investment. An industrialization policy was adopted which aimed at diversifying the manufacturing industry into two broad categories, resource based and non-resource based industries. Nevertheless, weaknesses such as an imbalanced manufacturing base still characterize the manufacturing industry.

The imbalanced manufacturing base

One of the weaknesses which still characterize the manufacturing industry is an imbalanced manufacturing base. Although several subsectors, such as wood/cork and rubber products industries, registered double-digit annual production growth rates from 1990-1994 (see Table 5.1), they each accounted for less than 4 per cent of the average annual gross exports of manufactures. The two traditional subsectors of electrical/electronics and the textiles/apparel industries, on the other hand, continued to be the leading contributors in terms of average annual gross exports of manufactures: These two main subsectors together contributed to 38 per cent hereof, as shown in Table 5.1, while recording an average annual growth of 26.8 per cent and 11.5 per cent, respectively, between 1990 and 1994.

Table 5.1 Average Annual Growth Rate and Gross Exports of the Manufacturing Sector 1990-1994

Subsectors	Average annual growth (%)	Average share of annual gross exports of manufacture (%)
Electrical machinery, apparatus, appliances and supplies	26.8	29.8
Textiles and apparel	11.5	8.2
Oils and fats	9.1	4.1
Wood and cork products	11.5	3.0
Rubber products	29.3	2.9

Source: *The Sixth Malaysia Plan*, p. 8.

Judging from the trend of a sample of approved projects in 1994, these two subsectors continue to be dominant, constituting 23.5 per cent and 13.7 per cent, respectively, of the total of new projects approved, compared to the other subsectors, which registered a share of below 10 per cent each, as shown in Table 5.2 (*MIDA Annual Report*, 1994, p. 10).

The analysis shows that the manufacturing base is imbalanced and narrow and therefore the incentives granted by the government ought to be more targeted in order to broaden and deepen the manufacturing base.

Most of the projects approved are, in general, non-capital intensive, except within the basic metal products, petroleum and chemical industries. For example, although the textiles industry had a 13.7 per cent share of the total number of projects approved during 1990, its capital investment share was only 4.2 per cent compared to the basic metal products industry, which recorded only 2.9 per cent of new projects approved but had a 32.1 per cent share of the total capital investment, as shown in Table 5.3. This imbalance has not been properly addressed as shown by Table 5.4, where, with the exception of chemicals, both the electronics and textiles industries attracted the most investment. For example, in 1994, electronics and textiles attracted foreign direct investment (FDI) totalling US$712 million and US$171.2 million respectively.

Table 5.2 Projects Granted Approval by Industry Subsectors in 1994

Industry subsectors	Number of projects approved	% Breakdown of all projects approved
Electrical & electronic products	213	23.5
Textiles and apparels	124	13.7
Wood and cork products	85	9.3
Oils and fats	36	4.0
Rubber products	34	3.9
Basic metal products	26	2.9

Source: MIDA Annual Report, 1994, p. 1.

Table 5.3 Capital Investments by Industry Subsectors in 1990

Industry subsectors	Capital investment (US$ million)	% Share of total capital investment
Electrical & electronic products	1680	15.2
Textiles and apparels	480	4.2
Wood and cork	680	6.0
Oil and fats	228	2.0
Rubber products	56	0.5
Basic metal products	3620	32.1
Others	4496	40.0
Total capital investment	11240	100

Source: MIDA Annual Report, 1994, p. 1.

Table 5.4 Utilized FDI by Industry for 1993 and 1994

Industry / Year	1993 (US$ million)	1994 (US$ million)
Electronics	252.4	712
Textiles	85.2	171.2
Rubber	5.6	14.8
Basic metals	128.8	58.4
Chemicals	250.8	120
Transport equipment	46.8	39.6
Food processing	27.2	26.8

Source: Saiwa Bank Annual Investment Report, 1995, p. 11.

The government would therefore need to seek ways of targeting incentives to help to address the imbalanced industrial base. The obvious step to take is to lay less emphasis on labour-intensive industries. For example, this could be done by accelerating the growth of the Northern Growth Triangle (NGT), which consists of Northern Malaysia, Southern Thailand and Northern Sumatra, and is based upon an earlier version based around Singapore (Seiji and Karen, 1996, p. 125). Through NGT, labour-intensive operations could be channelled out of Penang (in Northern Malaysia) and into Northern Sumatra or Southern Thailand; meanwhile Penang could become a regional centre for business services, research and development and high value-added production (Goodhart, 1994, p. 2). Malaysia can no longer rely on low labour costs as a source of economic strength. The economy is approaching full employment and factory owners are complaining of labour shortages. Other Asian countries, including Vietnam, Indonesia and India, can supply cheaper workers. Malaysia will soon be too rich to qualify for the tariff exemptions offered by industrialized countries to poor nations, under the General Agreement on Tariffs and Trade (GATT) generalized system of preferences (*The Economist*, 16 July 1994, p. 31).

The emphasis ought to be on high value-added and high technology industries which are inclusive of the manufacturing of downstream resource-based products such as rubber, wood, palm oil and petrochemical products. The manufacturing of capital goods such as light machinery, automotive products and machine tools should also be encouraged.

Over-dependence on FDI

Between 1985 and 1990 alone, foreign direct investment in approved manufacturing projects amounted to US$13.6 billion. This constituted 60 per cent of the total approved investment of US$23.4 billion. The major proportion of foreign investments in 1993 and 1994 came from Taiwan, Japan, Hong Kong, Singapore and the USA, as shown in Table 5.5. The principal investors were the Taiwanese and Japanese. In the last three years, the two countries have provided over US$19.6 billion in direct investment, more than a third of inward flows (Baker, 1995d). The Japanese have found Malaysia one of the most welcoming and productive overseas locations. The total value of Japanese investment since 1985 is over US$2.8 billion, and by the end of March 1995, there were more than 1000 Japanese companies with operations in the country. For example, Matsushita alone has a turnover of more than US$3.52 billion, an unparalleled 5 per cent of the country's entire GDP (Baker, 1995c).

Though Japanese money remains the largest single component of foreign direct investment, the value has been falling. It peaked in 1990 and has dropped by more than 50 per cent since then. The emphasis these days is on smaller companies, suppliers to the great multinational names (Baker, 1995d).

Table 5.5 Utilized FDI by Country (US$ million)

Country / Year	1993	1994
Japan	278.4	280.8
Taiwan	137.2	407.2
US	220.4	225.2
Singapore	78	144.4
Hong Kong	25.2	119.2
Others	238	467.2
Total	977.2	1644

Source: Saiwa Bank Annual Investment Report, 1995, p. 12.

Whilst recognizing that foreign investment has the advantage of bringing in technical know-how, creating new employment, and promoting exports, the costs of such investment in the long term cannot be ignored. The discouragement of foreign direct investment is not an issue here, but rather creating ways to increase domestic investment, in order for domestic investment to play a more important role in the building of the Malaysian manufacturing base. Furthermore, one cannot ignore the competition for foreign investment in countries like Vietnam, Mexico, India and China, which would decrease the investment flow into Malaysia, and therefore the growth rate in foreign investment would not be as strong.

In 1995 the central bank forecast a 14 per cent increase in private investment, compared with an 18 per cent growth rate last year. It is estimated that between 1995 and 2000 domestic investment will account for 59 per cent or US$18.8 billion of the total private investment of US$32 billion (Baker, 1995a, p. 3). In order to achieve this target, the government would have to encourage domestic investment. Therefore, domestic investors should not be treated less favourably than foreign investors. Small and Medium Enterprises (SMEs) could be encouraged to diversify and seek listing on the Second Board of the Kuala Lumpur Stock Exchange (KLSE). Support measures such as venture capital, accessibility to technology and long-term soft loans should be made available. Linkages between SMEs and manufacturing enterprises ought to be strengthened to address the imbalanced manufacturing base.

Narrow export markets

Manufactured exports increased substantially from US$2.52 billion in 1980 to US$18.88 billion in 1994, i.e. there was a ninefold increase. The significant gains in manufactured exports during this period raised its share of total export receipts from 22.4 per cent in 1989 to 65 per cent in 1994. However, Malaysia's manufactured exports are heavily concentrated in two exceptionally large subsectors, namely, electrical and electronics, and textiles. Together they constituted 64.3 per cent of Malaysia's total manufactured exports in 1994 (MIDA, 1995, p. 18). Not only are the manufactured exports narrowly based in terms of products, they are also limited to a few major export markets such as Singapore, the US, Japan and the UK as shown in Table 5.6 below. Malaysia has not been too successful in diluting the market concentration of its exports from the traditional major export partners.

Malaysia's growth in the export of manufactured goods may, therefore, be adversely affected in the future because of the slowing down in the economies of major industrialized countries, the recent developments in Eastern Europe, and the trend towards regional blocs such as the creation of a unified internal market in European Union (EU) and North American Free Trade Agreement (NAFTA).

Table 5.6 The Main Trading Partners of Malaysia (1994)

Countries	Percentage share of Malaysia's exports
US	21.2
Singapore	20.7
Japan	11.9
UK	3.8
Germany	3.3

Source: Financial Times, 19 September 1995, p. 3

Malaysia would need to widen its export markets by accelerating the intra-ASEAN trade through the development of growth triangles such as the NGT and the Asean Free Trade Area (AFTA). Exports to Newly Industrialized Countries (NICs) in East Asia, such as Taiwan and South Korea, should be encouraged. In order to promote trade with less developed countries, business transactions should be facilitated by promoting counter-trade, bilateral payment arrangements and improved shipping and transportation.

Strengthening the role of Small and Medium Enterprises (SMEs)

The SMEs in Malaysia are not cohesive and their contribution to value-added is low. Most SME products have a high import content: it amounts to more than 50 per cent in the electronic sector. The SMEs lack the ability to differentiate their products. Their production processes are inflexible and they lack skilled manpower and appropriate technology (Cooke, 1995).

Nevertheless, some linkages between SMEs and multinational companies have been made. In Penang, for example, some local SMEs have benefited from the technology transfer, especially for the manufacture of printed circuit boards. SMEs in Penang now provide a growing proportion of the inputs of the foreign manufacturers (Baker, 1995, p. 6). To further develop these linkages, specific investment incentives such as those given to encourage companies to use local components could be increased. The policy to increase the local content should be continued to encourage the sourcing of raw materials and components from domestic industries.

To further strengthen the role of SMEs, large corporations could be encouraged to implement an effective local vendor development programme. The procurement policy of the government could continue to provide business opportunities to the SMEs. Special industrial zones equipped with common facilities such as Research and Development, design and testing, and toxic waste disposal could be established to facilitate the SMEs.

Sustaining competitiveness

Incentives on their own will not be able to attract the necessary investments. Other factors such as human resource development, R&D, and non-tax incentives such as the provision of better infrastructures and other supporting facilities play an important role in sustaining the competitiveness of the manufacturing industry and attracting investments. This is because the ultimate decision of investors to set up plants in Malaysia will not be based on incentives alone, but also on a conducive environment which enhances competitiveness.

Human resource development

With rapid changes in technology and demand patterns, continuous training and retraining are required to equip workers with the most up-dated skills. For manufacturing enterprises to remain competitive to meet the challenges of the international environment, the implementation of employment restructuring must be flexible, and not enforced to the extent of destroying the conducive corporate culture so painstakingly created. It is imperative that the criteria of meritocracy, excellence and hard work must prevail in the human resource development programmes of the manufacturing sector: With the shortage of labour and the likelihood of manufacturers moving to more automation to improve productivity, the creation of a more disciplined and technically oriented workforce is becoming more crucial (Clifford, 1996, p. 106).

Malaysia is already experiencing a shortage of labour, which has caused labour costs to rise dramatically over the years. Wage settlements in 1995 were running at between 10 to 15 per cent. But productivity was not climbing as fast, and according to official estimates, unit labour costs were rising at over 3% per year. This growing disparity between wage rate increases and productivity is worrying. Wages in the manufacturing sector have been going up by between 10 and 15 per cent a year; wage rises in the services sector have been considerably steeper. This wage inflation could reduce the country's attractiveness to inward investors, especially as the less developed Asian economies, with much lower labour costs, start to gear up for rapid growth (Baker, 1995b, p. 3).

Labour shortage is so acute that Japanese companies looking for more than a few hundred employees locally find it impossible to set up business. Only smaller companies, many of them requiring a higher proportion of skilled workers, can find the labour to cope with their production targets. Across all industrial sectors, companies now face a severe labour shortage that is pushing up costs and undermining the economy's potential. With unemployment at a historic low of just 2.8%, vast numbers of immigrant workers from neighbouring countries are moving onto the factory floors and building sites. But even these are not enough to reduce pay pressures. It is estimated that there are 1.5 million illegal immigrant workers now in Malaysia, out of a total workforce of 8 million. Most of these are unskilled labourers from Indonesia or Bangladesh. But a growing number of engineers and technicians are having to be recruited from overseas. The government is aware that the influx of such large numbers of immigrant workers could result in long-term social problems and upset the country's delicate racial and religious balance (Baker, 1995d, p. 2).

The human resource development programme for the manufacturing sector should, therefore, aim at producing workers possessing a 'strive for excellence' attitude with a strong desire for continual self-improvement, an awareness of the importance of quality, and the ability to communicate effectively in both written and spoken international languages, especially English. The versatility to adapt to changes and the orientation towards technical subjects, particularly in science and maths are also critical. For a successful implementation of a human resource development programme, one should pay sufficient attention to:

The basic education system Although over the last 10 years Malaysia has consistently been among the five fastest-growing countries in the world, Malaysians fear that a barrier may stand between them and the big economic league. A well-schooled population, and thus easily available educated labour, has been common to all East Asia's successes. Malaysia's secondary-school enrolment levels are respectable. Most of Malaysia's electronic industry, which accounts for over half of manufactured exports, has already made the transition from the labour-intensive operations of the

1970s to the capital- and technology-intensive industry of today. In-house training by companies has helped to make up for the shortcomings of the educational system. Nevertheless, some critics say that Malaysia's educational system suffers from being used as a social engineering tool. The number of students and the medium of instruction are higher priorities than quality. However, of late the Malaysian government has been turning against preferment for Malays in favour of merit, and against the Malay language in favour of English (*The Economist*, 13 August 1994, p. 32). The basic education system would need to keep pace with the country's growth, to deal with the chronic lack of skills in the workforce. A sound basic education, emphasizing languages, sciences and mathematics, is needed to enable school leavers to acquire skills through training. A continuous review and modification of the education policy must be undertaken to adapt the system to the changing business environment.

Higher education   The reputation of Malaysian universities needs to be enhanced and more graduates should be funneled into industry rather than into jobs in the public sector. A recent World Bank study concluded: 'At all levels the trend is clear: Malaysia is spending more on education than countries like Korea and Taiwan and getting relatively less out of it' (World Bank, 1995, p. 69).

In order to address some of the weaknesses of the higher education system, the government has in recent months devised a series of measures to make Malaysia's education system more efficient and channel its graduates more quickly into the workforce. Critics decry the ad hoc nature of many of the measures, and the absence of a coherent, long-term educational policy independent of the immediate demands of the economy. One such move which raised the eyebrows in academic circles was the recent announcement by the education minister to shorten all degree courses at local universities, except medical studies, to three years. The idea was to increase the output of graduates to help the acute shortage of skilled manpower. Some fear that academic standards are being sacrificed to economic necessity (Middelmann, 1995a, p. 3).

Meanwhile the government is trying to stem the flow of students to foreign universities, either for full degree courses or one-year stints as part of twinning programmes with private colleges in Malaysia. Malaysia is one of the world's biggest exporters of students, with an estimated 50,000 Malaysians studying abroad at any given time. Not only does this deplete the country's foreign reserves by more than US$1.2 billion per year, it also bears the risk of losing some of the country's brightest graduates to foreign shores. A survey of

Malaysians studying in Australia, conducted in 1992-94 by the Bureau of Immigration Research, showed that some 43 per cent of respondents considered staying permanently in Australia (Middelmann, 1995a, p. 3).

One way of encouraging students to stay at home is to bring foreign educational expertise to Malaysia. This also fits into the government's overall plan to make Malaysia a 'centre of educational excellence', attracting not only local students but also those of neighbouring countries. The University of London, for example, is involved in discussions about setting up a campus in Malaysia, and other institutions may follow once a planned change in Malaysia's Universities and Colleges Act allows the establishment of off-shore campuses.

Private educational institutions have begun to play an important role. These institutions have provided an important alternative for meeting increasing demand for higher education in the last five years. Such institutions should be given greater recognition such as the government recognition of certificates issued by these institutions, and the provision of financial incentives to encourage further development of such institutions. The open university concept should also be explored further.

Meanwhile, the government, keen to share the country's growing education cost with the private sector, which is the biggest consumer of skilled labour, recently announced that state universities, which currently receive the bulk of their funding from the government, are to 'corporatize'. Under this plan, universities are to remain non-profit organizations under the control of the education ministry, but will be managed as commercial entities exploring alternative ways to raise funds, such as via tuition fees or consultancy projects. Although some corporatization may stem the drain of teaching staff to higher-paying private colleges, some academics are concerned over the impact of corporatization on the intellectual climate of the country's universities, warning that they could go the way of for-profit private colleges which cater mainly to market demand for lawyers, engineers and accountants at the expense of liberal arts teaching (Awang, 1994, p. 25).

Incentives for training and co-ordination   A recent annual Federation of Malaysian Manufacturers (FMM) manufacturing survey showed that a high percentage, 43 per cent of respondents, did not incur any training expenditure (MIDA, 1995, p. 25). To encourage greater private sector investment in training, the government has set up a Human Resource Development Fund and is expected to provide incentive grants to enterprises undertaking the training of their workforce in basic, enterprise-based and new emerging skills, as well as retraining in higher skills. This fund could be a useful mechanism to promote private sector training, such as the Penang Skills Development Centre, a partnership between the public and private sectors which is often cited as a model of successful vocational training. The FMM has further established the FMM Entrepreneur and Skills Development Centre, which aims to contribute towards producing a pool of entrepreneurs, as well as skilled workers required by various industries.

It is also important to encourage early vocational and technical training to the less academically inclined. Incentives could be given to technical and vocational training which should form the basis of Malaysia's long term education policy. In encouraging more vocational training, financial and other resources must be made available for the construction of new buildings, classrooms and workshops, the purchase of equipment and training aids, the training and retraining of teachers and the recruitment of more technical teachers. The existing polytechnics and vocational schools could be expanded to meet the future demand for technicians and professional engineers.

With several ministries and agencies having direct involvement in human resource development, there is a need for better co-ordination. It is suggested that there should be a Co-ordination Council for professional, vocational and technical education to bring together all ministries and agencies involved in human resource development. This council would consist of the Minister of Education, the Minister of Human Resources, the Minister of International Trade and Industry, the Chairman of the Malaysian Industrial Development Authority (MIDA) and other relevant representatives from the universities and the private sector. The main goal of the council would be to plan for the adequate provision of trained professionals, technical and skilled manpower for the need of the labour market. In view of the long gestation time needed to generate a pool of skilled manpower, the establishment of such a co-ordinating body is of the utmost priority (MIDA, 1995, p. 34).

Encouraging R&D

The FMM manufacturing survey also showed that more than half the respondents did not incur expenditure on R&D. This lack of private sector R&D investment can hamper the industrialization process as R&D and the ability to innovate are the key factors to enhancing competitiveness. By the year 2000 the government hopes to double the nation's R&D expenditure from 1 to 2 per cent of the GNP, with the private sector contributing at least 40 per cent of the total expenditure. In order to achieve this target and to enable Malaysia to move towards high value-added industries, the science and technology policy of the country could encourage the diffusion of technology and increasing quality and design competence of companies. The science base would need to be strengthened. The emphasis on strategic research could be concentrated on enabling technologies and the exploitation of R&D. These recommendations, which have already been suggested by a government plan, would improve the scientific and technical infrastructure for the economy (Malaysian Ministry of Science and Technology, 1992, p. 35).

The main issue of concern is how to increase the private sector role in R&D to complement the government's efforts. Some private companies such as Otis, which is part of the American United Technologies group, have set up their own R&D centre in Penang for testing and modifying their products. Another example is Matsushita: anticipating labour shortages in the future, Matsushita has increased its capital investment to improve productivity. Part of that process can be seen in the creation of the company's own R&D centre, refining models designed in Japan for other Asian markets. Although the advanced work is still done in Japan, an increasing proportion of development is now taking place in Malaysia. But in this respect, Matsushita is exceptional: most Japanese companies have not transferred high technology R&D to Malaysia, about which the Malaysian government is unhappy. Japanese companies are reluctant to shift technology abroad, train local employees in the use of technology and then see them move to another company. On the other hand, the Japanese companies also point to the increasing speed with which they need to respond to demands of their customers. They have to develop a technological base if they are to respond quickly. Companies need to be able to react to those changes without referring to the research people in Japan (Baker, 1995d, p. 3).

To increase the involvement of the private sector the government could consider matching grants given to R&D undertaken by locally owned companies. The setting up of 100 per cent foreign-owned R&D centres could be encouraged as well as the employing of foreign researchers to facilitate technology transfer. There is also a specific need to promote the greater use of CAD/CAM through, for example, the granting of soft loans. This would give the companies a competitive edge through the improvement of productivity and enhancement of competitiveness of Malaysian-made products. There is also a strong need to forge closer links between universities, industry and government research centres, to coordinate the selection and exploitation of research. Intellectual property rights have to be protected to encourage private sector investment in R&D. To encourage the exploitation of research the setting up of a venture capital fund could be considered.

Improving infrastructure facilities

Serious infrastructural and other strains are increasingly evident in Malaysia, raising doubts about the government's growth management policies. Kuala Lumpur's traffic jams are rapidly becoming as bad as those in Bangkok. There are growing power shortages and supply disruptions. A power failure in September 1992, for example, blacked out most of peninsular Malaysia for several hours. Another power failure occurred in May 1996. A fire at Kuala Lumpur airport in 1992 disrupted air traffic for more than two weeks.

Industries are currently facing inadequate transport facilities, such as a lack of trucks, containers and rail wagons, to match demand, as well as a high cost of transportation, lack of suitable industrial land at reasonable rates, unavailability of housing for workers, inadequate water supply for industries and interruptions in electricity supply. In addition, telecommunication facilities and services are lagging behind demand and urgent steps must be taken to upgrade these services essential for the efficient running of businesses and industries. With a significant expansion in industrial production and the coming on stream of investment projects, there has been feedback that the power supply has been subject to frequent interruptions and voltage dips. For example, Komag, a US disk maker, reported a monthly loss of US$100,000 due to power cuts (Goodhart, 1994b, p. 13).

The range of projects to be undertaken in the coming years is extremely ambitious. Between US$3.2 and 4.8 billion will be spent on a new international airport outside Kuala Lumpur. MAS, which is more than 50 per cent owned by the government, is purchasing US$4.24 billion worth of new aircraft. Infrastructural facilities are being built in preparation for the Commonwealth Games to be held in Kuala Lumpur in 1998. The second Malaysian automobile project, Perodua, has started production. To meet the projected economic growth set at 7 per cent in each year up to 2020, there are plans to increase power supplies fourfold at an estimated cost of US$16 billion over the next 10 years. The government realizes it cannot bear the cost of all these projects. Financial backing from the private sector, both domestic and foreign, is vital (Goodhart, 1994b, p. 13).

The government does recognize the importance of reliable and efficient infrastructural facilities and utilities to support the industrial sector. The government's policy on privatization is a move in the right direction as it will bring forth the elements of dynamism and efficiency in the provision of public utilities that have been privatized, with minimum additional cost to the government. Nevertheless, there is a need to have an independent mechanism to monitor and supervise the performance of the privatized entities and disseminate indices of their productivity, efficiency and quality.

Privatization programme

Unlike other governments that have privatized only a few of their more obvious businesses, such as energy and telecommunications, Malaysia has given the private sector considerable responsibility for building infrastructure. The Malaysian capital market is readily providing the cash. OSK Research, a local investment firm, estimated that in 1995 alone private investors put US$10.4 billion into infrastructure projects. The national bank's estimate for the Figure over the next 25 years is US$2.52 trillion. In contrast, the Fifth Malaysia Plan, which runs from 1990-1995, allocated only US$3.76 billion of government money to infrastructure. One can ask what will happen in 1998 when most of these infrastructure projects are due for completion? These projects are largely responsible for keeping the economic balloon flying. The import of capital goods associated with various infrastructure projects is partly to blame for a current account deficit which increased to US$4.64 billion in 1995, or 6.6 per cent of the GNP (*The Economist*, 22 October 1994c, p. 82).

Free marketeers around the world have heaped praise on Malaysia's ambitious privatization programme, which is credited with spurring economic growth and efficiency gains without wrenching dislocation of workers. Nevertheless, some would argue that economic growth and efficiency gains could well have been achieved without privatization, and warn that shifting responsibility from the public to the private sector should not be the magic cure. 'Efficiency gains are usually a result of improved management, but that can be achieved without a significant change in ownership', says Prof. Jomo of the economics faculty at the University of Malaya (Middelmann, 1995b).

The privatization programme, which was launched more than 10 years ago, has helped to generate proceeds by the sale of government assets, as well as saved the state about US$2 billion in salaries and pension payments for 93,000 former state employees, which now come from the private sector. Moreover, the government has been able to pass the cost of much of the country's infrastructure development over to the private sector. Malaysia's privatization does not only mean the sale of state assets, but also involves awarding licences to private companies, often joint ventures between domestic and foreign firms, to build new projects such as toll roads or power plants on a build-operate-transfer (BOT) basis. Since the launch of the privatization programme in 1983, the government would have had to provide some US$16 billion for infrastructure projects had it not been for privatization. Instead it has put up only US$0.8 billion on soft loans and land costs, according to data published by the Economic Planning Unit of the prime minister's office in May 1995. By then, some 131 projects had been privatized, of which 96 were existing projects taken over by the private sector and the rest new projects, involving the construction of infrastructure and utility operations. As a result of hiving off the huge costs of infrastructure development to the private sector, the government now enjoys a budget surplus and a low level of external debt, unlike during the mid 1980s when the government accounted for half of the country's total investment, and ran a substantial budget deficit amid worrying levels of foreign indebtedness. The programme has also helped develop Malaysia's capital markets: Privatized companies account for more than a third of the Kuala Lumpur Stock Exchange's capitalization of about US$224 billion (Montagnon, 1996, p. 17).

However, critics say that in some industries, notably power and telecommunications, the government has shot itself in the foot. By deregulating the sectors too quickly, they say, it forced the former state monopolies to compete head-on with leaner newcomers before they were ready to do so. For example, power company Tenaga, in which the state still holds a 70 per cent stake, is locked in fierce competition with five independent power producers (IPPs) which were rushed out after 1992 when the country suffered from acute power shortages. The telecoms sector is experiencing a similar problem, with partially privatized Telekom having to compete with eight telecoms operators and 40 paging services for a market of fewer than 20 million people (Montagnon, 1996, p. 17).

Appropriate financial policy

As private investment activity is likely to rise in the coming years, there will be strong demands for credit from the private sector. Moreover, with the shortage of capital from international sources, the Malaysian government is expected to rely more on domestic borrowings to finance its development expenditure. Strong competition for funds could lead to higher interest rates at the expense of the private sector, particularly the manufacturing sector. The manufacturing sector, now poized for rapid expansion with higher technology involving more capital-intensive processes, could be squeezed for capital at competitive rates.

Malaysia has stepped up the pace of capital market liberalization by several gears to meet the growing costs of the country's drive to become a fully industrialized nation by the year 2020. The country also hopes to upgrade its financial services industry to boost Malaysia's standing as a regional financial centre, attracting business and capital from neighbouring Hong Kong and Singapore. Malaysia's capital markets have lagged behind the dramatic transformation of its economy and will need to catch up quickly if growth is to remain on track. Up to the year 2000 alone, capital investment of US$152 billion is to come from the private sector, which will finance at least 40 per cent of its requirements through the capital markets. Despite the country's saving rate of 34 per cent, those sums surpass domestic capacity. As a result, the government in 1994 announced sweeping reforms aimed at opening up the country's sheltered capital market to foreign players and harnessing local savings more efficiently. Under the reforms, Malaysia plans to allow full ownership of fund management companies investing non-Malaysian-sourced funds, and foreigners — albeit in obligatory joint ventures with local fund management companies — will be considered for management of domestic funds such as the Employee's Provident Fund (EPF), a government-run compulsory savings scheme which totals US$40 billion. Furthermore, the EPF's ceiling on equity investment has been raised to 15 per cent from 9 per cent, individual EPF fund holders will be able to withdraw portions of their savings to invest in funds managed by approved fund managers, and share dealing costs have been cut. These and other changes are expected to suck an extra US$9.2 billion into the stock market, spurring demand for new share listings, which in turn should propel the country's privatization programme that relies heavily on private sector finance. This should further increase the market's regional structure, which is already impressive, capitalized at US$224 billion. Malaysia's stock market is the biggest in Southeast Asia and 14th largest globally (Middelmann, 1995c).

Given that manufactured exports account for 59 per cent of total exports, the management of the exchange rate policy is vital to Malaysia's industrialization programme and future growth. The policy should promote exports, check superfluous spending on imported goods, and improve the competitive position of industries both in the domestic as well as overseas markets. In the light of more manufacturers undertaking exports, the regulation on export proceeds that must be repatriated to Malaysia within the period of payment specified in the export contract could be relaxed. Malaysian manufacturers could be encouraged to invest overseas and to penetrate the global market by adopting such strategies as off-shore operations, purchasing of distribution networks or trading houses, or establishing strategic alliances with foreign companies which have the technological expertise necessary to strengthen their competitive position. At the moment, the Bank Negara of Malaysia imposes strict regulations in cases where manufacturers have utilized domestic borrowings. There is a need for foreign exchange controls to be relaxed in order to allow remittance of funds overseas for the purpose of 'reverse' investments (Middelmann, 1995c, p. 4).

Liberalization of regulations and procedures

As Malaysia's economy continues to expand at near-geometric rates, the need for an efficient and mature financial system to facilitate this expansion grows with it. Yet in spite of the improving performance of the nation's banks and recent government moves to liberalize the system, the official policy remains tightly protective of the financial sector (Baker, 1995c). If the country is to realize its twin goals of full industrialization by 2020 and the establishment of Kuala Lumpur as a leading financial centre, it will have to move faster down the road towards complete financial liberalization.

The government's commitment to maintaining and further liberalizing regulations and procedures to assist the efficient implementation of private sector projects will go a long way towards reducing the cost of operating for the investor's business. In this regard, there is a need to regularly review all the licensing requirements, to improve administrative efficiency and eliminate regulations that tend to retard growth and competitiveness. That efforts are under way to open up parts of the market is undeniable. In 1995 the Finance Ministry announced a series of measures aimed at improving access to securities markets for foreigners, allowing fund managers to open subsidiaries in the country and expanding opportunities for overseas brokers. The government has introduced two new financial future exchanges, the Kuala Lumpur International Options and Future Exchange and the Malaysian Monetary Exchange. In 1996 the Kuala Lumpur Stock Exchange will introduce scriptless trading, a move that seems certain to enhance the market's operating efficiency. One of the main goals is to attract international financial institutions from Hong Kong to Kuala Lumpur after 1997. The country's stock market is capitalized at over US$220 billion, the fifth largest in Asia, twice the size of Singapore's and only 25 per cent smaller than Hong Kong's. But the banking sector remains largely protected behind closed doors. In spite of the enormous inward investment by foreign corporations in the last 20 years, no new banking licence has been granted to a foreign bank since 1973 (Baker, 1995c, p. 4).

Controlling inflation and wage rises

Private consumption is accelerating, growing at an annual rate of 9 per cent so far in 1995. The pace of growth is now creating its own constraints. Investment cannot be met from Malaysia's domestic savings pool alone. Nor can consumption be satisfied from domestic industrial capacity. Signs of overheating have begun to emerge in the form of inflation and balance of payments difficulties. Inflation is running at around 4 per cent and monetary measures which included high interest rates have driven up the value of the ringgit. Malaysia's competitiveness as a manufacturing base could be eroded by both further increases in the ringgit's value and wage rises. Wages in the manufacturing sector rose by 9.6 per cent in the first half of 1994 against 6 per cent a year earlier. In the public sector wages are rising by between 8 and 10 per cent in 1994. Senior bankers are concerned about a seriously overblown property sector. Consumer spending is charging ahead: in the first six months of 1995 vehicle sales went up by more than 50 per cent (Cooke, 1995, p. 1).

Consumer price inflation is put at 3.7 per cent in 1995 and rising. But that Figure is not regarded as very reliable for it does not include housing costs, for example; with rentals rising at 20 per cent a year in some parts of the country, that represents a serious omission. An anti-inflation drive is under way. The government is gradually encouraging more imports in an effort to put downward pressure on producer prices. And the central bank has recently increased the interest rates and with them the ringgit. Struggling to stop the ringgit rising, the government has raised another spectre, inflation. To most outsiders, a 3.7 per cent inflation rate for last year might not seem too alarming for an economy growing at almost 9 per cent a year. The inflation rate for 1996 is unlikely to be much above 5 per cent. But some suggest that Malaysia's inflation is actually higher than the official measures suggest, and it is true that grumbles about rising costs have become a staple of Malaysian life (*The Economist*, 1994a, p. 32).

But the external pressure that can be applied on costs is limited by the other main constraint on Malaysia's performance, the balance of payments. The current account deficit is growing rapidly. Despite an export increase of 22 per cent in 1995, the country recorded its largest trade deficit for four years in the first quarter of 1996, though the authorities attributed the unexpected dip into the red to 'lumpy' trade flows. With a persistently large services deficit the current account is expected to widen to US$6.4 billion in 1995, 8 per cent of the GDP (*The Economist*, 1996). Some economists argue that the rise in imports was due to a higher demand for investment and intermediate goods. The large increase in the import of capital goods is expected not only to raise the productive capacity of the economy but also to generate future foreign exchange earnings. Others would suggest that many of the capital imports are not now of the variety that will directly expand the country's export capacity. The general trend of capital imports has shifted more towards infrastructure-related goods, telecommunications and construction materials, which will not directly produce higher exports. There could be another structural concern about the deficit. In the past it has been more than accounted for by inflows of direct investment. But last year, according to analysts, foreign direct investment was lower than the current account deficit, and is likely to stay that way for the next few years. That will leave the country dependent more on volatile short term capital inflows (Montagnon, 1996, p. 17).

Social and environmental issues

One of the socio-economic goals of Malaysia is to create a viable Bumiputera Commercial and Industrial Community (BCIC). A great effort is made by the government to nurture the entrepreneurial skills among the Bumiputeras and to increase their equity participation in the manufacturing sector. Programmes have been launched to encourage joint ventures between Bumiputeras and non-Bumiputeras or foreign investors. Public enterprises and trust agencies could continue to play the lead role by providing linkages through product sourcing and marketing to Bumiputera enterprises. The development of rural industries, especially resource-based industries, can be further encouraged to produce spin-offs to the predominantly Bumiputera rural population (World Bank, 1991).

As the business of manufacturing is more complex, involving various facets of management, subject to international exposure and requires a more long-term perspective, a sustainable participation of the BCIC in manufacturing can only be achieved through the creation of Bumiputera entrepreneurs who are prepared to compete in and adjust to an open market economy. This becomes more essential if Malaysia's heavy dependence on the export of manufactured goods to sustain economic growth is taken into account.

The location and geographical spread of industries should be left to be determined by market forces. Nonetheless, the provision of infrastructure facilities to less developed areas could provide incentives for industries to locate in such areas. One way of encouraging the development of industrial estates both in developed and less developed areas is to allow the private sector to develop and manage the industrial estates. Common facilities required by industry, like the treatment of water effluents and R&D facilities, could be developed in specialized industrial estates.

There is a greater awareness now of the negative consequences of industrialization on the environment, therefore industrial development must take this into account. Among the environmental issues the Malaysian manufacturing industry has to address are the lack of efficient on or off site waste disposal facilities, the pollution caused by unorganized disposal of consumer products and the continued international campaign against Malaysia's export of natural resource-based products such as timber-based products. To address these issues there is a need for strict enforcement of existing laws which require industrial establishments to control the production of pollutants. Future approvals of investment proposals should give due consideration to the technology to be used to ensure that the negative impact on the environment is minimized. The public R&D research establishments could devote a greater part of their research to disposal systems, and the feasibility of using wastes for productive purposes. Industries should be encouraged to shift to the production of biodegradable as well as recyclable products. The rehabilitation of over-logged areas should be ensured, making sure that effective reforestation is carried out properly (Ho, 1991, p. 25).

Conclusion

Under the pressure of rising costs, Malaysia is developing new ways to remain competitive. Its principal aim is to create a highly-skilled workforce producing quality high-technology goods. Some observers believe the country can keep up the pace for the next few years as the Commonwealth Games and other grand projects approach completion. But there is real uncertainty about what may follow. If foreign direct investment, which is still at over US$5 billion a year, starts to decline after 1998, there is concern that Malaysia will not have the capital base of its own to sustain the dream of full industrialization by 2020.

With its labour shortages and rising wage rates, Malaysia has no choice but to ascend the technology ladder. The central problem is that the Malaysian economy has relatively little depth. Manufacturing exports are still dominated by foreign multinationals, particularly in electronics. Although fears have been widely expressed that Malaysia's increasingly tight labour market and rising cost base might deter investment in the long run, interest in the country remains strong. For example, Taiwanese companies have expressed disappointment with the performance of some of their other Asian investments, including those in mainland China. In 1995, Taiwanese inward investment in Malaysia, however, tripled to over US$0.4 billion (Baker, 1995d).

The manufacturing industry will continue to lead the economic growth, but also along the way, enhance the country's export competitiveness in the international market. The competitiveness of the manufacturing industry does not depend simply on the competitive advantage derived from its natural endowment, but also on the deliberate and concerted efforts by both the public and private sectors to formulate strategies that will promote greater efficiency and productivity in the manufacturing industry to ensure its competitiveness.

References

Awang, S. (1994), 'Aiming For The Perfect Balance in Enrolment', *Sunday Star*, Kuala Lumpur, 31 July, pp. 25-6.

Baker, G. (1995a), 'Miracle Loses Lustre', *Financial Times*, 19 September, p. 3.

Baker, G. (1995b), 'The High-tech Trail Blazer', *Financial Times*, 19 September, p. 6.

Baker, G. (1995c), 'More Opening Up Needed', *Financial Times*, 19 September, p. 4.

Baker, G. (1995d), 'Japan and Taiwan — The Big Spenders', *Financial Times*, 19 September, p. 2.

Bank Negara Malaysia (1993), *Bank Negara Malaysia Annual Report 1992*, National Printing Press, Kuala Lumpur.

Bartlett, C. and Ghoshal, S. (1989), *Managing Across Borders: The Transnational Solution*, Harvard Business School Press, Boston, MA.

Cooke, K. (1995), 'Mahathir Takes the Economic High Road', *Financial Times*, 19 September, p. 1.

Clifford, M. (1996), 'Can Malaysia Take That Next Big Step?', *Business Week*, February, p. 106.

Elek, A. (1996), 'Pacific Economic Cooperation: Policy Choices For The 1990s', in Das, Dilip (ed.), *Emerging Growth Pole — The Asia-Pacific Economy*, Prentice Hall, Singapore.

Financial Times (1995), 'Survey of Malaysia: Key Facts', 19 September, p. 3.

Goodhart, D. (1994a), 'Where Chips Eclipse Smelters', *Financial Times*, 30 August, p. 2.

Goodhart, D. (1994b), 'Islam and Gigabytes', *Financial Times*, 30 August, p. 13.

Ho P. (1991), 'Managing Industrialization in Malaysia', in Institute of Strategic and International Studies, *World Bank Colloquium on Environmental Issues in the Region*, National Printing Press, Kuala Lumpur.

Joynt, P. (1991), 'International Dimensions of Managing Technology', *Journal of General Management*, 16(3), pp. 73-84.

Malaysia, (1991a), *The Second Outline Perspective Plan*, National Printing Press, Kuala Lumpur.

Malaysia, (1991b), *Sixth Malaysia Plan*, National Printing Press, Kuala Lumpur.

Malaysia, (1996), *Seventh Malaysia Plan*, National Printing Press, Kuala Lumpur.

Malaysia Industrial Development Authority (MIDA) (1995), *MIDA Annual Report 1994*, National Printing Press, Kuala Lumpur.

Malaysian Ministry of Science and Technology, (1992), *Action Plan For Industrial Technology Development,* National Printing Press, Kuala Lumpur.

McGrath, M. (1992), 'Manufacturing's New Economies of Scale', *Harvard Business Review,* May-June, pp. 94-102.

Middelmann, C. (1995a), 'Skilled Labour Runs Short', *Financial Times,* 19 September, p. 3.

Middelmann, C. (1995b), 'Luster Slips From Sell-offs', *Financial Times,* 19 September, p. 6.

Middelmann, C. (1995c), 'Survey of Malaysia: Shift to a higher gear', *Financial Times,* 19 September, p. 4.

Montagnon P. (1996), 'Tigers Pause for Breath', *Financial Times,* 12 August, p. 17.

Page, S. (1994), *How Developing Countries Trade - The Institutional Constraints,* Routledge, London.

Saiwa Bank (1995), 'Investment In Asia', in Saiwa Bank (1995), *Annual Investment Report,* Kuala Lumpur, pp. 6-13.

Seiji, N and Karen, E. (1996), 'The Characteristics of Asia-Pacific Growth Triangles', *Journal of the Asia Pacific Economy,* 1(1), pp. 123-134.

The Economist (1994a), 'Malaysia's problems with prosperity', 16 July, pp. 31-2.

The Economist (1994b), 'Who's Nicst (newly industrialized Asian countries)', 13 August, pp. 31-2.

The Economist (1994c), 'Private Money, Public Friends: Malaysian infrastructure', 22 October, pp. 81-2.

The Economist (1995), 'Asia's Competing Capitalisms', 24 June, pp. 16-7.

The Economist (1996), 'Keep an Eye on Current Affairs: South -East Asia', 9 March, p. 72.

World Bank (1991), '*Growth, Poverty, Alleviation and Improved Income Distribution in Malaysia: Changing Focus of Government Policy Intervention*', Report No. 8667-MA, Washington D.C., May.

World Bank (1995), *World Development Report 1995,* Oxford University Press, New York.

6 Foreign Direct Investment in China: Patterns, Processes, Prospects

IAN G. COOK and YONGJIANG WANG

Introduction

The changes in the Chinese economy in recent years have been both dramatic and far-reaching. A key element in these changes has been the influx of foreign direct investment (FDI), which has facilitated considerable restructuring, initially in the production, and subsequently the consumption, sectors of the economy. The objectives of this chapter are to summarize the changing pattern of FDI in the People's Republic of China since 1979, the year when the National People's Congress issued the country's first Law on Chinese-Foreign Joint Ventures; to explore the origins and nature of this investment and analyse the situation in the 1990s in which 'China Fever' hit the market and led to an unprecedented upsurge in FDI, notwithstanding the Tiananmen incident in 1989; and to assess some of the benefits and disbenefits of foreign direct investment to both foreigners and Chinese alike. Finally, we conclude by speculating about the prospects for FDI in the future.

Why foreign investment? The changing global situation

In explanation of the reason for high rates of FDI, it is pertinent, firstly, to consider the changing global context in which investment patterns operate. The second half of the 1980s, for example, witnessed a marked growth in FDI, from approximately $47 billion in 1985 to $132 billion in 1989 (All Figures $US unless specified). Flows to 'developing countries' (including China) increased at a faster rate than those to 'developed countries', with the main recipients being the countries of East Asia and Latin America. Within East Asia, Japan was the largest Organization for Economic Cooperation and Development (OECD) foreign direct investor, with 47.8 per cent of OECD FDI 1980-89. The United States came next with 31.3 per cent and then the United Kingdom with 7.6 per cent. China was by far the biggest recipient, with 37 per cent of FDI from OECD investors (the main source of FDI), compared to 24.6 per cent to Malaysia or 12.7 per cent to Thailand, next largest beneficiaries (*Finance and Development*, 1992). This huge rise in FDI came about, according to *Finance and Development* (published by the International Monetary Fund (IMF)/ World Bank), due to such factors as: increased integration of the global economy through finance and ownership, which enhanced opportunities for investment beyond and across national boundaries; changing structure of the world economy as many countries abandoned restrictive practices against FDI, just as they had done previously for foreign trade; and changing attitudes in developing countries, which began to actively seek private sources of capital by 'redefining their development strategies, liberalizing their economies, and implementing a range of new policies' (ibid, p. 50).

In other words, globalization trends (see Waters, 1995, for an introduction to key themes of globalization), allied to the growing acceptance (whether reluctant or otherwise) of the key role for the market (as opposed to state intervention) in economic development, coupled also with the decline of effective alternatives to market forces in East Europe and elsewhere, stimulated this massive outpouring of investment from the OECD in particular. In the 1990s, this outpouring of funds has reached even higher levels, and, arguably, 'FDI in the postwar world has been the late-twentieth-century equivalent of the Portuguese and Spanish explorers of the late fifteenth century. It is capital in search of new economic horizons to chart, conveyed by computer rather than by ship' (Simone and Feraru, 1995, p. 336). FDI, to these authors, is of 'extraordinary importance' because it is the means of 'technology transfer', central to human civilization at the current time (ibid, p.336). At the global level, 'China is now the largest recipient of FDI in the developing world' (Wooldridge, 1995). It is tempting to assume that this pattern of Chinese dominance will continue indefinitely, but it is nevertheless necessary to remind ourselves not only that China contributed markedly to such trends but also that it was affected by them. China, notwithstanding its continued position at the top of the FDI league table for developing countries, is, like any other nation, potentially vulnerable to any changes in the global scenario towards alternative patterns of investment, such as, for example, towards patterns of OECD investment at home rather than abroad, to investment in 'new' locations such as Vietnam or India, or to, say, investment on environmental rather than strictly economic criteria. It is always possible that a switch in global investment priorities could occur, to the possible detriment of foreign investment in the People's Republic of China (PRC), and, of course, such a switch could be prompted by internal changes in the PRC itself. Such a possibility will be discussed further below, at the conclusion to the chapter.

Why foreign investment in China?

Two decades ago it would have been almost impossible to predict that China would lead the league table of FDI, and, although the external factors noted above helped to set the preconditions for investment in China, internal factors have contributed strongly towards this outcome. In the modern era (see Wang for discussion of historical aspects, focusing on joint ventures (Wang, 1995)), foreign investment in China owes much to the resolution of the continuing debate within the Chinese Communist Party (CCP) as to the correct path to socialism. The main point of tension lay between those, like Mao Zedong, who preferred China to follow a model which stressed such values as self-help and self-reliance, with the minimum of interaction with the global capitalist economy, and those like Deng Xiaoping, who were more willing to open up China to market forces, albeit under the ultimate control of the CCP leadership. The 'Four Modernizations' — of Agriculture, Defence, Industry plus Science and Technology — were argued for by those who wished to open up the Chinese economy in the 1950s, again in the early 1960s and then conclusively since 1979 when the 'Dengist model' triumphed over alternatives. The 'Open Door' policy was a key element in this, as Zhao Ziyang noted in his Washington visit of 1984: 'China has opened its door and will never close it again...China always keeps its door open to friends' (Quoted, for example, in Chossudovsky, 1986, p. 138).

Not that the door had opened only in 1979 — the *rapprochement* with the United States and other Western countries began in the early 1970s and was mirrored in a marked expansion of foreign trade during that decade (Howe, 1978). The drive for foreign funds came as it was realized that the Four Modernizations could not be achieved without considerable foreign assistance, both financial and technological. As Xue Muqiao, one of the leading economists responsible for the new policies declared:

> To be able to repay our debts, we must work out an overall plan for the use of foreign investment...[initially] Priority should thus be given to the more profitable light industrial enterprises which need less investment and take a shorter time to build. Their products can soon be exported, enabling us to repay our debts. Big projects constructed with foreign investment, such as oil-mining and coal-mining, should be built on the basis of compensatory trade, that is, repayment for foreign investment in the form of exports. We may also build some badly needed projects, such as iron and steel plants, within the limitations of our resources. Even if they do not produce large quantities of exports, they will help us reduce imports and save foreign exchange. In short, we should balance our foreign exchange payments so as to minimize our foreign debts.
> (Xue Muqiao, 1981, p. 263)

Note that there was to be a sequence of preferred investment, and that foreign debts were to be minimized. Nor was self-reliance to be altogether forsaken:

> It is necessary to handle correctly the relationship between self-reliance and the adoption of advanced foreign technology. By bringing in advanced technology, we do not mean depending on foreign aid but improving our own scientific and technological level and our ability to build the country through self-reliance.
> (ibid, p. 263)

Several years later, other influential Chinese economists articulated the benefits of utilization of foreign capital as being:

1. To make up for the insufficiency of domestic funds and to help expand a country's economic construction;
2. To promote the setting up and development of new industrial sectors;
3. To strengthen the weak links in the national economy and to help develop backward economic sectors and regions;
4. To raise the technical and managerial level by importing advanced technology and equipment, production skills and management expertise;
5. To accelerate changes in the import and export structure, and to expand exports; and
6. To raise the employment rate.
(Liu Guoguang et.al., 1987, p. 503)

These postulated benefits illustrate the rationale for the encouragement of foreign investment and also act as a touchstone against which to evaluate the influx of foreign funds. The authors also noted that, during the Cultural Revolution, the use of foreign capital was labelled as 'worshipping things foreign and fawning on foreigners' (ibid, p. 504), an attitude which 'led to the practice of binding ourselves hand and foot against making use of foreign funds — a practice which could only produce adverse effects on the country's economic growth' (ibid, p. 504). By the late 1980s, two major factors restricting China's economic development were recognized as being 'insufficient funds' and 'backward technology', and 'That's why we regard attracting foreign funds and technology as an important aspect of our opening to the outside world' (Wang Huijiong and Li Boxi, 1989, p. 165).

It is now clear that China had been faced with a major choice after the Cultural Revolution: forward or backward. Forward? China could not stand alone (or with Albania) in its continuation of relative isolation from the rest of the world, but nobody in China knew what the foreigners would bring into China if China were to open up to the outside world. The Chinese folk-memory of the West was informed both by the suffering faced by generations of Chinese as a result of Western intrusion from the 19th Century on and also by the propaganda by the party and state against Western imperialism. Backward? Few, if any, believed that China would ever catch up with the West, despite this being a declared aim of the government and another part of the propaganda. People were tired of endless political struggle and disillusioned of any economic progress under the existing regime. *Qiong ze si bian*, an ancient Chinese proverb, means poverty makes people think about change. Ironically, after 30 years of revolution, China was in a situation in which the national economy was overreliant upon outmoded technology as well as being riddled with inefficiencies. Not only had China neither caught up with Britain nor overtaken the United States, but it had even been left behind by many nations or areas, such as the Four Little Dragons in Asia, which were originally similar to, or even poorer than, China. A crisis point had been reached and the era of reform was, after much debate and upheaval, ushered in.

As a result, in July 1979, the National People's Congress issued the country's first Law on Chinese-Foreign Joint Ventures. Thus, China officially announced its commitment to welcome foreign investment into the country and the wish to protect the legal interests of foreign investors. Since then, China began its new history of importing and utilizing FDI by setting up various businesses involving foreign capital. There were four main categories of such business: the Chinese-foreign equity joint venture (EJV); the contractual joint venture (CJV); the wholly foreign-owned enterprise (WFOE); and the cooperative business operation (CBO) (The latter is also called a 'Contractual Joint Undertaking' and differs from a joint venture in that the CBO does not have to be an economic entity set up inside China as a single legal entity, and the Chinese and foreign investors can cooperate with each other as separate legal entities. The forms and amounts of investment, the rights and obligations of the parties concerned are all specified in a contract. CBOs have remained unimportant within the broad pattern of FDI.). In a nutshell, an EJV is a limited liability company in which foreign investment is 25 per cent or more, contributed in cash, capital goods, industrial property rights or other means, and the EJV normally has a fixed lifespan which may be extended. The CJV is aimed more at capital or technological input from the foreign side, with the Chinese supplying land, labour or other resources, and distribution of profits (which may not be according to the initial proportion of investment from the partners) and other matters are spelt out in the initial contract. Finally, the WFOE:

> shall mean an enterprise established within the territory of China in accordance with the relevant Chinese Laws with its entire capital being invested by foreign investors and such terms shall not cover the branches of foreign enterprises and other economic organizations established within the territory of China.
> (Foreign Investment Administration and China Economic and Trade Consultants, Corp., 1993, p. 304).

The three waves of foreign investment

The previous two sections show, firstly, that not only were funds available within the global economy (due to structural change), but that, secondly, the Chinese government had moved to a strategy which recognized the need for FDI and would aim to develop the infrastructure to facilitate this. However, there were considerable obstacles to be overcome before the external and internal factors could be harmonized. FDI in China has not been a straightforward unilinear process since 1979, rather it has been a cyclic process of expansion with peaks and troughs. In our previous paper (Wang and Cook, 1993) we showed that following the promulgation of this Law on

Joint Ventures, by the end of 1988, foreign investment in China had experienced two waves of investment, and speculated that 1993 would be the end of the third wave of investment. In fact the latter did not end, in terms of utilized value, until 1994, which turned out in many ways to be even more of a boom year than the 'China Fever' year of 1992. This section summarizes the main features of each of these successively greater waves of FDI impacting upon China:

The first wave of foreign investment (1979-1985)

Before focusing on the detailed picture of foreign investment in China, several caveats must be presented. Firstly, it is extremely difficult to pinpoint the precise sources of investment . Most data sources list *countries* as the origins of investment flows, rather than institutions or individuals from which they originate. And so, although much is made of Hong Kong investment in China, for example, or more recently Taiwan and South Korea, such countries may be conduits for Japanese, US or European investments which are consequently much harder to trace. This situation is particularly problematic when investments originate from illegal activities and there has been some concern that 'hot money' from drug trafficking is being 'laundered' via property investments in South China. Further, 'A part (one-third, according to some estimates) of Hong Kong's investments in China are 'round trip' investments by mainland investors seeking the three-year tax holiday that was available to foreigners until 1994' (Petri, 1995, pp. 37-8). We feel that the 'one-third' estimate is probably exaggerated, but, although we focus here mainly on national patterns of investment, due to the restrictions on data availability, it must be remembered that capital *flows*, and in this case it is the sum total of contrasting flows which constitute the Figures quoted below. Also, as Murray points out, the Chinese government announces the highest possible figures for foreign investment 'in the hope this will encourage others to jump on the seemingly unstoppable investment bandwagon. Equity from the Chinese side is often included in the value of the project inflating the size of the apparent inflow' (Murray, 1994, p. 111). There is a significant difference between FDI which is seemingly *contracted* and that which is actually *utilized* (or *disbursed*), with the latter Figure being much smaller. We shall have recourse, therefore, to both sets of Figures where appropriate.

Foreign investment can be via loans, either as bilateral aid or multilaterally via the World Bank for example, or as Foreign Direct

Investment into the EJVs, CJVs, WFOEs and CBOs noted above. Recently, portfolio investment has also become possible into some Chinese limited companies. After 1979 it was not an easy task at first both for the Chinese government and ordinary people to think about using foreign capital within a socialist country, bearing historical and political reasons in mind. Consequently, at the very beginning of the reform, foreign investment was mainly limited into some special areas set up by the government such as Special Economic Zones (SEZs). As is now well known, in August 1980, a year after the promulgation of the first joint venture law, China established three SEZs in Guangdong Province — at Shenzhen, Zhuhai and Shantou — and a fourth one was set up in Xiamen, Fujian Province, in October of the same year.

At that time, just as the Chinese were uneasy, so too were foreign investors, who were still suspicious about investing in China, being wary of the stated aims of the PRC leadership, and of the many restrictions with which the joint ventures were faced. Also, of course, both sides in these developing partnerships were breaking new ground and there was doubt, mistrust, uncertainty, and a recipe for 'marital breakdown' in the contrasting cultures from which both sides came. Investors, for example, sought a free hand for hiring and firing of employees (possible in theory but difficult in practice — see Chossudovsky, p. 149), repatriation of profits, location of activity and other features of their usual business practice. In contrast, their opposite numbers sought to ensure that proper bureaucratic procedures were followed, that key decisions were given clearance from the local, provincial or national hierarchy, that maximum benefits would flow to the Chinese side and so on. Not surprisingly, therefore, most initial interest in investing in China came from (or via) Hong Kong or Macao, where potential investors were often 'Overseas Chinese' with ties of family, kinship and history, with South China especially. This cultural dimension was to become a key factor in the development of FDI.

Initially, however, the PRC was able to establish better links with foreign agencies rather than business lenders, and so, as Table 6.1 and Figure 6.1 illustrate, foreign loans grew more rapidly than FDI in the early 1980s, but even there progress was relatively slow. Such FDI as did occur was mainly involved with the processing and assemblage business. Between 1979 and 1982, according to official statistics, there were only 992 foreign investment projects set up in the whole of China. The actually utilized foreign capital in the three years 1979-82, therefore, was approximately $1.17 billion compared to $6 billion of contracted foreign investment.

Table 6.1 Foreign Capital Utilized in China Between 1979-1994 (US$ billion)

Year	FDI	Loans
1979-82	1.17	10.69
1983	0.64	1.07
1984	1.26	1.29
1985	1.66	2.69
1986	1.87	5.01
1987	2.31	5.81
1988	3.20	6.49
1989	3.39	6.29
1990	3.49	6.54
1991	4.37	6.89
1992	11.01	7.91
1993	27.52	11.19
1994	33.77	9.27

Sources: Data 1979-91, Huang, F., 'Foreign Direct Investment in China', *Jingji Kongzuozhe Xuexi Ziliao* (Study Material for Economic Workers), Beijing, No.72, 20 November 1992, pp. 5-15; Data 1992-4, State Statistical Bureau, *China Statistical Yearbook 1995*, China Statistical Publishing House, Beijing, p. 554.

Figure 6.1 Utilized FDI and Foreign Loans, 1983-1994 US$bn

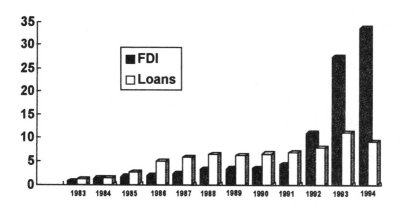

This relatively poor investment level was gradually improved during the following three year period, and foreign investment reached an initial peak, both in number and value, in 1985. This improved situation reflected growing confidence among potential investors, encouraged via the efforts made by the government of the PRC, including the introduction of tax relief, simplification of application procedures, and provision of other investment incentives. In 1983, foreign investment began to grow significantly. In that year 470 new projects were established with $1.73 billion of contracted FDI, and $0.64 billion of utilized foreign capital respectively. During 1984 and 1985, along with the deepening of economic reform and increasing confidence of the government both in dealing with and using foreign capital, China took further steps to attract such capital. After the decision to allow Hainan (then an administrative region of Guangdong) to apply some of the policies especially designed for SEZs in October 1983, China further opened 14 coastal cities for foreign investment in April 1984. This was followed, in February 1985, by the establishment of three coastal triangular economic zones. These were the Yangzi River delta, the Pearl River delta and a triangular area in southern Fujian. As a result of these initiatives, 1856 new projects were set up in 1984 and 3073 in 1985 respectively, about 4 times and 6.5 times of the number compared to 1983, with a sharp increase both in utilized and contractual values, as Table 6.2 illustrates. The spatial dimension to FDI is also of importance, therefore, in improving our understanding of the processes underpinning these growth patterns.

Phillips and Yeh provide a tabular summary of the pattern of foreign investment in China in 1985, prior to the real 'take-off' in the late 1980s. At this point Japan and the World Bank dominated the provision of foreign loans, with 50.9 per cent and 23.3 per cent of the loan total respectively, while Hong Kong and Macao (taken together) provide 48.9 per cent of direct foreign investment, followed by the United States with 18.3 per cent (Phillips and Yeh, 1990). Britain, incidentally, provided only 1.1 per cent of foreign loans but 3.6 per cent of FDI ($26.7 million and $71.4 million respectively). Foreign loans, according to their Figures, totalled $2.5 billion and FDI just under $2.0 billion, apparently a rough parity compared to a heavy preponderance of foreign loans over FDI in the period 1979-85 as a whole, $15.7 billion to $6.0 billion respectively (ibid, p. 234). However, Figure 6.1, taken from a Chinese source which employs utilized rather than contracted FDI shows that the disparity between loans and FDI continued at a roughly 2:1 ratio throughout the 1980s.

Table 6.2 Foreign Direct Investment in China, 1979-1994, by Number and Amount (US$ million)

Year	No.	Contracted Amount	Utilized Amount
1979-83	1,392	6,340	1,803
1984	1,856	2,650.5	1,258
1985	3,073	5,931	1,659
1986	1,498	2,834	1,875
1987	2,233	3,709	2,314
1988	5,945	5,297	3,194
1989	5,779	5,560	3,393
1990	7,276	6,567	3,487
1991	12,978	11,977	4,366
1992	48,764	58,124	11,007
1993	83,437	111,436	27,515
1994	47,549	82,680	33,767

Sources: Data 1979-1990, *Saishin Nitchuu Gooben Jigyoo* (Japanese-Chinese joint ventures), Commercial Law Centre, Inc., Tokyo, Japan, 1991, pp. 17-18; 1991 data, Huang, F., 'Foreign Direct Investment in China', *Jingji Kongzuozhe Xuexi Ziliao*, Beijing, No.72, 20 November 1992, p. 9; data 1992-4, State Statistical Bureau, *China Statistical Yearbook 1995*, China Statistical Publishing House, Beijing, p. 554.

Figure 6.2   Number of FDIs 1983-1994

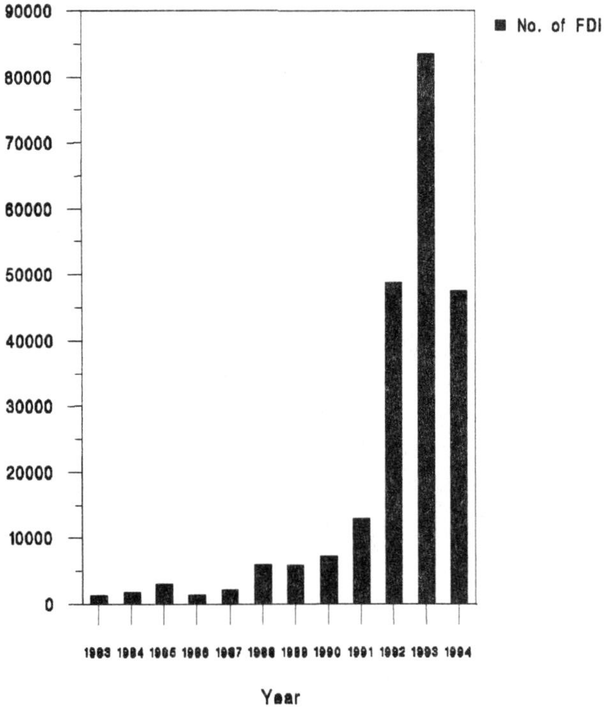

One of the characteristics of the form of foreign investment during this first investment wave was the domination of CJVs, which were led mainly by investments from Hong Kong and Macao. Out of 6321 foreign invested projects between 1979 and 1985, 3823 of them were CJVs, which represents more than three-fifths of the total number as Table 6.3 indicates. Note especially how few in number WFOEs and CBOs were during this wave, with the Chinese government refusing to encourage these forms of FDI due to the control which the foreign investor could exert over the enterprise. It was still, therefore, foreign investment with a considerable number of strings attached.

The second wave (1986-1988)

Foreign investment reached its peak both in number and value by 1985 in its first wave.   Problems involving the smooth operation of many foreign invested enterprises were mostly left unresolved, and often became vital for many newly established businesses. Such problems included poor infrastructure and legal environment for foreign investment, government bureaucracy, restrictions on domestic sale of joint venture products, lack of hard currency and constraints on management procedures. Many of these problems were directly or indirectly derived from the then extant political economy of China. The normal operation of many existing foreign invested enterprises was adversely affected, and frustrated many foreign investors and managers. Contrasting outlook and objectives of the Chinese compared to the foreign partner added to these problems, exemplified by the difficulties faced by the Chinese-American automobile joint venture, Beijing Jeep, which eventually had to be secretly bailed out of a cash flow crisis following high level negotiations with both the PRC and United States (US) governments (Mann, 1989; Murray, 1994). For such reasons, many potential foreign investors were understandably put off. Many Japanese companies, for example, hesitated to invest in China, notwithstanding that the pressure of the strong Yen for Japanese overseas investment was high, and many of them simply sought alternative destinations for their money within South East Asian countries. Consequently, the number of new foreign direct investments in China dropped dramatically in 1986 and 1987 (despite the total sum showing a small increase). In 1986, only 1498 new projects were registered, less than half that of the previous year. Note, however, as Figure 6.1 shows, that indirect foreign investment increased markedly, partly perhaps due to a time-lag within the institutional system of World Bank and other lending.

The Chinese government, partly under pressure from foreign investors, did not hesitate to respond to this decrease in FDI. In October 1986, the State Council issued the 'Provisions for the Encouragement of Foreign Investment' (the 22 articles), followed by a series of central regulations to implement them, and also by a flurry of municipal and provincial-level regulations. The Provisions clarified the legal environment for joint ventures. Investment in advanced technology and export-capable sectors was encouraged. Guarantees were given to secure autonomy of joint ventures from external bureaucratic interference and to eliminate many local costs about which foreign investors had complained loudly. At the same time, in order to attract more foreign investment, new investment incentives, such as favourable tax and customs treatment, were offered. These improvements in China's investment environment put China into a better position in the fierce competition with its Asian neighbours for investment

Table 6.3 Foreign Direct Investment in China 1979-1994, by Type (US$ million)

Year	EJV			CJV			WFOE			CBO		
	No.	Contract Amount	Utilized Amount	No.	Contract Amount	Utilized Amount	No.	Contract Amount	Utilized Amount	No.	Contract Amount	Utilized Amount
1979-83	190	315.4	173.2	1,123	3,229.9	758.5	48	371.4	83.1	31	2422.9	788.1
1984	741	1,066.6	254.7	1,089	1,484.0	465.0	26	99.9	14.9	n.a.	n.a.	522.9
1985	1,412	2,030.0	579.9	1,611	3,496.2	585.0	46	45.7	13.0	4	359.6	480.6
1986	892	1,375.2	804.5	582	1,358.1	793.8	18	20.3	16.3	6	80.8	260.3
1987	1,395	1,950.4	1,485.8	789	1,282.6	620.0	46	471.2	24.6	3	4.7	183.2
1988	3,909	3,133.9	1,975.4	1,621	1,624.0	780.0	410	480.6	226.2	5	58.6	212.2

Year	EJV			CJV			WFOE			CBO		
	No.	Contract Amount	Utilized Amount	No.	Contract Amount	Utilized Amount	No.	Contract Amount	Utilized Amount	No.	Contract Amount	Utilized Amount
1989	3,659	2,659.0	n.a.	1,179	1,083.2	n.a.	931	1,653.8	n.a.	10	203.7	n.a.
1990	4,093	2,680.0	n.a.	1,317	1,260.0	n.a.	1,861	2,440.0	n.a.	5	190.0	190.0
1991	8,395	6,080.0	2,299.0	1,778	2,138.0	764.0	2,795	3,667.0	1,135.0	10	92.0	160.0
1992	34,225	n.a.	n.a.	5,742	n.a.	n.a.	8,789	n.a.	n.a.	n.a.	n.a.	n.a.
1993	48,945	n.a.	n.a.	8,669	n.a.	n.a.	19,030	n.a.	n.a.	n.a.	n.a.	n.a.
1-6-1994	14,924	n.a.	n.a.	3,714	n.a.	n.a.	6,803	n.a.	n.a.	n.a.	n.a.	n.a.

Sources: Data 1979-1990, *Saishin Nitchuu Gooben Jigyoo* (Japanese-Chinese joint ventures),Commercial Law Centre,Inc., Tokyo, Japan, 1991, pp. 17-18; 1991 data, Huang, F., 'Foreign Direct Investment in China', *Jingji Kongzuozhe Xuexi Ziliao* (Study Material for Economic Workers), No.72, 20 November 1992, p. 9; data 1992-4, Toshiaki Sugida, 'Kaigai Chokusetsu Tooshi to Shoyuu Keitai no Sentei', JETRO *Chuugoku Keizai* (China Economy), No. 345, September 1994, p. 31.

(Pearson, 1991). Furthermore, in July 1988, in order to attract more investment from Taiwan, China formulated and promulgated the 'Provisions for the Encouragement of Investment by Taiwan Compatriots' As a result of the efforts noted above, the number of foreign investments increased steadily in 1987 compared to the previous year, and reached a peak by 1988. In 1988, 5945 new projects were set up, which was an increase of 166 per cent compared to the number of 2233 in 1987. In 1988 nearly $5.3 billion foreign investment was contracted, and $3.19 billion was in actual use, which were respectively an increase of 43 per cent and 38 per cent on those of the previous year. Also, during this second wave, the number of EJVs increased dramatically. In 1986, it first surpassed that of the CJVs in that year, and increased substantially throughout the period. By 1988, this number reached more than 2.4 times that of the contractual joint ventures. The reason for this increase seemed to be the improvement in the legal environment, and the preference of the Chinese government for EJVs. Perhaps it also reflected the recognition by some foreign investors of the special economic conditions in China, that the use of an EJV is more suitable for them in terms of securing vital scarce resources of raw materials and energy, in which they can more or less rely on their local Chinese partners (Commercial Law Centre Tokyo, 1991).

The third wave (1989-1994)

For many foreigners, China always seems to be a mystery or puzzle. The '4.6' incident (Tiananmen) which happened in 1989 in Beijing under the eyes of the world's media shocked most of the people both inside and outside of China. This was definitely a tragedy which should never have happened. Immediately afterwards, foreign businessmen were withdrawn from China and economic sanctions by major Western countries were applied to the PRC. 'In the wake of Tiananmen, the growth of foreign investment in China came to a halt' (Lardy, 1994, p. 64). For a period, the world seemed to be frozen as regards China, and China seemed to be forgotten, or perhaps forbidden, to foreign businesses. However, history sometimes fools people. As Lardy put it 'many observers were surprised when the actual inflows [of FDI] remained on a plateau of about $3.7 billion rather than falling precipitously' (ibid, p. 64) and such surprise turned to shock when the news of China's 12 per cent plus economic growth in 1992 reached the outside world. More surprise came with the news that 44,000 foreign invested ventures were registered within the first **six months** of 1993. This Figure was more than twice the total number registered between 1979 and the end of 1989. Clearly, China experienced another wave of foreign investment with new heights, which made China the main destination for new funds in the world's fastest growing region (*Financial Times*, 14-6-1993). This wave of investment continued, as far as utilized FDI was concerned, into 1994, coming to an end during that year.

After entering 1989, foreign investment continued to soar in the first half of the year, despite clear signs of overheating in the Chinese economy and government measurements to curtail overall economic growth. Between January and June of 1989, utilized FDI (all forms) rose 21.5 per cent over the same period in 1988. Contracted investment rose even more by 44.2 per cent. However, the '4.6' incident, as the Chinese refer to it, in 1989, became the immediate trigger of subsequent decline of foreign investment in the second half of the year. Although the average value of contracted and utilized investment for the whole year did not drop compared to 1988, the number of newly registered foreign investment projects did decrease by 2.8 percent to 5779 (Huang 1992). In particular, the decline in foreign investment after June appeared to be particularly dramatic for Western and Japanese investors (Pearson, 1991).

However, China's reform and open policy did not change after the incident as many Western businesses feared. On the contrary, at the Fifth Plenary Session of the Thirteenth Central Committee held in November 1989, although the decision was made by the new leadership to introduce tough retrenchment policies for the domestic economy, the Party restated its open door policy. It reassured the outside world that China would: a) continuously take active measures to encourage the use of foreign capital, import of advanced technology and exchanges in science and technology with foreign countries; b) while implementing laws and regulations concerning foreign investment, further improve the investment environment for FDI, and attract more foreign investment by making existing joint ventures a success and using them as models; c) continue to encourage the development of an export-oriented economy in the coastal areas and maintain the basic policies for SEZs and other coastal development areas.

Despite these measures, after Tiananmen China was faced with severe pressure from the outside world, especially from the Western industrialized countries via economic sanctions. There were numerous speculations about foreign investment and the fate of joint ventures in China. However, partly due to the government's recognition of the severity of foreign reaction to the investment environment in late 1988 and the political situation in 1989, particularly concerning Western and Japanese reactions, attempts were made to amend the 1979 Joint Venture Law. In April 1990, the National People's Congress passed several amendments to the existing Joint Venture Law which included the following three main areas: 1) to enable foreigners to act as joint venture board directors; 2) to eliminate time limits on joint ventures; and 3) not to apply nationalization on joint ventures, but if it is necessary to do so, appropriate compensation would be made (Imai, 1990). In addition, a series of relevant laws and regulations were promulgated in 1990, which include 'Provisions Concerning Encouragement of Investment from Overseas Chinese and Hong Kong and Macao Compatriots', 'Details for Implementing the Law on Foreing-Funded Enterprises' and the 'Provisional Administrative Measures for Land Developed and Managed by Overseas Investors'. In the same year, China also acceded to the 'Convention Concerning Settlement of Investment Dispute Between State and Citizens' (*Beijing Review*, 21/27-6-1993).

These new laws, regulations and measures indicated the determination of the Chinese government to adhere to its open door policy and its eagerness to attract more foreign investment. The improvements made to the investment environment helped counterbalance the negative impact of Tiananmen, and, by including those measures promulgated previously, China has successfully formed a reasonably sound legislation system for joint ventures and foreign-owned enterprises, providing effective legal protection for the legitimate rights and interests of foreign businesses. In particular, the two separate Provisions regarding investment from Honk Kong/Macao and Taiwan effectively promoted investment from Hong Kong, Macao, Taiwan and other overseas Chinese, post-Tiananmen. It was reported, for example, that Taiwanese business people were the first to return afterwards (Pearson, 1991).

Due to such efforts made by the Chinese government, despite the economic sanctions imposed by some Western countries, foreign investment, especially investment by overseas Chinese, did not drop. Asian nations often seemed to regard Tiananmen in a different light to the West, and, indeed, many Asian neighbouring countries, such as Malaysia, Singapore, Indonesia and South Korea were even rushing to improve their relationship with China in order to get a better chance to be involved with China's economic development. Between 1990 and 1992, China restored diplomatic relations with Indonesia and established diplomatic relations with Singapore, Brunei, Israel and South Korea (Wei Mu, 1992). At the same time, the relationship between Mainland China and Taiwan also improved dramatically. These new diplomatic and political developments have encouraged new investment from these countries, especially from South Korea, Taiwan and Singapore. In 1990, a total of 7276 new investment projects were approved which was 29% more than the previous year, with approximately $6.57 billion in contractual value and $3.4 billion in utilized value. Then in 1991 newly approved projects reached nearly 13,000 in total, a 65 per cent increase compared with 1991 (see Tables 6.1, 6.2 and 6.3 for details).

In 1992, after Deng Xiaoping's visit to the south urging the country to speed up its reform and economic development, a huge new wave of foreign investment swept across the country. Following Mr Deng's appeal, the government swiftly took a series of new strong measures to quicken its reform and opening up. During 1992, China opened more cities for foreign investment along the sea coast, border areas and rivers. In the meantime, China broadened its sectors for utilizing foreign capital, such as retailing, real estate, foreign trade, finance, insurance and transportation. Thus, in 1992 alone, nearly 49,000 joint ventures, cooperative enterprises, and wholly foreign-owned ventures were established, exceeding the total number of the previous 14 years. According to Chinese official statistics, these newly established projects involved $58 billion in contracted foreign capital, which is nearly five times the Figure for 1991. A total of $11 billion foreign funds was poured into the country, more than double the year before. This momentum was maintained and even surpassed in 1993, with more that 83,000 ventures and an amazing $111 billion of contracted investment, according to official sources. Such a momentum could not, however, be indefinitely maintained, and by 1994, although the amount of utilized FDI continued to climb, as Table 6.2 shows, the number of investments began to reduce, as did the total of contracted investment.

In addition, interestingly, as can be seen in Table 6.3, the number of WFOEs in 1990 exceeded that of the CJVs for the first time. There were 1861 wholly owned foreign enterprises recorded in 1990 with $2.44 billion contracted value, compared with 1778 and $1.26 billion respectively for contractual joint ventures. This trend was followed by a further increase in 1991, in which 2795 new projects were set up. These projects involved nearly $3.67 billion in contracted value and $1.14 billion in utilized value, compared with $2.14 billion and $764m respectively for 1778 new CJVs set up in 1991. This development seems to be an indication of the confidence gained by many foreign investors concerning their business operations in China, and a pointer to the improvement of the investment environment in China. Because of the sharp increase of wholly foreign-owned enterprises in the early 1990s, some even predicted that WFOEs will be dominant by the end of this century (Huang, 1992), but although the number increased again in 1993 to 19,030 the data suggests a dip by 1994, and in any cases EJVs remain popular.

The impact of foreign direct investment

In 1992, at the 14th Congress of the Communist Party, China officially announced the adoption of the market economy into its reform programme. This policy was confirmed at the 8th National People's Congress in spring 1993. Thus, China's 15 year old reform entered a new historic period. Of course, it would be wrong to think that a market economy has only recently begun in China. In fact, as many scholars have pointed out, the Chinese are among the most entrepreneurial people in the world. However, the market economy has only recently really taken off, and the authors are struck through their recent visits by people's changing perceptions, the change of attitude towards the market, and also by the explosion of entrepreneurial spirit among the Chinese people. Undoubtedly, these kinds of changes have significant implications for China's ongoing reform and economic development.

The dazzling China market

Probably as a reflection of such changes, a 'market fever' started to spread over the entire country, from the second half of 1992. This was followed by a tremendous inpouring of foreign investment. For example, Shanghai became a magnet for foreign investment, especially in the Pudong area (Cook, 1993, 1995; *Financial Times*, 2-6-93). In 1992, for example, 2012 projects were set up with $3,357m of contractual foreign investment, which exceeded the totals of the previous 12 years both in number and value. In the first 5 months of 1993 another 1559 such enterprises were set up to bring the grand total to 4848 in the city, involving some $10 billion of foreign capital. Utilized FDI in Shanghai was over $3 billion in 1993 and just under $2.5 billion in 1994 (State Statistical Bureau, 1995). Similarly, foreign investment in Beijing has also reached new heights. By mid-May 1993 the city had approved 1242 new projects which made the accumulated number of foreign invested enterprises a record high of 5011 involving $6.4 billion of FDI. The total contractual foreign investment was $12.2 billion by that time. Utilized FDI was $667 million in 1993 and, for the first time, over one billion dollars ($1.372 billion) in 1994. According to Beijing's overall development plan, in the near future Beijing's key sector for attracting foreign investment will be the tertiary sector. Foreign investors are encouraged to invest in projects such as public construction, transport, energy development, new construction materials, petrochemicals and the automobile industry.

Another major city, Tianjin, has also made tremendous strides in attracting foreign investment. According to municipal official Figures, by the end of July 1993, Tianjin had approved 2298 foreign funded enterprises involving $1.49 billion foreign capital, an increase of 2.8 times and 1.52 times on the Figures for the same period in 1992. To mid 1993, 4896 foreign funded enterprises were set up in Tianjin with contracts worth $5.78 billion in foreign capital, and, as with Beijing, utilized FDI was over one billion dollars for the first time in 1994 (State Statistical Bureau, 1995).

Since 1992, a significant change in the spatial pattern of foreign investment is the spread of investment activities, which used to be concentrated into certain areas such as the SEZs, Guangdong, Fujian and other coastal areas. For example, in early 1993, more than 3,000 new foreign invested ventures were established in the five provinces or regions in South-Western China (ie. Guangxi, Sichuan, Guizhou, Yunnan and Tibet). This was 2.5 times the total number (1200) of the previous years. These new ventures involved nearly $2 billion investment in total with $770m foreign direct investment. Despite this, however, investment in Guangdong and Fujian remain at a very high level, with utilized FDI in Guangdong in 1994, for example, reaching $9.46 billion (State Statistical Bureau, 1995).

Increasing competition

In general, until the early 1990s, the majority of the existing enterprises with foreign involvement were small businesses employing a handful of people in each. Hong Kong and Macao investors are behind the bulk of these smaller businesses. But, since 1992, this picture has been changing rapidly. Many world-famous multinationals, such as America's Motorola, Dupont, IBM; Japan's Mitsubishi or Matsushita; plus Philips etc, started to invest in China, especially in large-scale projects. Many of these involve the high technologies for which China has been longing.

Table 6.4 Foreign Direct Investment in China, 1988-1994, by Origin (Contract Basis) (US$ million)

		1988	1989	1990	1991	1992	1993	1994	1995
HK + Macao	No.	4,771	4,244	5,001	8,879	31,892	49,134	25,527	n.a.
	Value[a]	3,583	3,244	3,944	7,507	41,531	76,753	48,692	40,096
	Value[b]	2,095	2,078	1,913	2,487	7,709	17,861	20,174	20,060
Taiwan	No.	430	539	1,103	1,735	6,430	10,948	6,247	n.a.
	Value[a]	219	432	890	1,389	5,543	9,965	5,395	5,850
	Value[b]	22	155	222	466	1,051	3,139	3,391	3,162
US	No.	269	276	357	694	3,265	6,750	4,223	n.a.
	Value[a]	370	641	358	548	3,121	6,813	6,010	7,470
	Value[b]	236	284	456	323	511	2,063	2,490	3,083
Japan	No.	237	294	341	599	1,805	3,488	3,018	n.a.
	Value[a]	276	439	457	812	2,173	2,961	4,440	7,592
	Value[b]	515	356	503	533	710	1,324	2,075	3,108

		1988	1989	1990	1991	1992	1993	1994	1995
Singapore	No.	105	78	72	169	742	1,751	1,443	n.a.
	Value[a]	137	111	104	155	997	2,954	3,738	8,670
	Value[b]	28	84	50	58	122	490	1,180	1,851
South Korea	No.	2	9	47	230	650	1,748	1,849	n.a.
	Value[a]	0.4	15	46	137	417	1,557	1,806	
	Value[b]	n.a.	4	13	40	120	374	722	
UK	No.	21	19	23	36	126	348	390	n.a.
	Value[a]	42	32	119	132	287	1,988	2,748	
	Value[b]	34	29	13	354	38	221	689	
Germany	No.	22	19	13	24	130	320	314	n.a.
	Value[a]	47	149	46	558	130	249	1,233	
	Value[b]	15	81	64	161	89	56	259	

		1988	1989	1990	1991	1992	1993	1994	1995
Thailand	No.	29	30	28	52	407	809	424	n.a.
	Value[a]	38	57	42	108	723	1,074	781	
	Value[b]	6	13	7	20	83	233	235	
France	No.	12	11	16	24	140	305	226	n.a.
	Value[a]	23	10	12	10	289	236	248	
	Value[b]	23	5	21	10	45	141	192	

Note: 1) [a] Contract value; [b] Implementation value. 2) Figures for South Korea for 1988 and 1989 are based on Korean sources which include only cases approved by the South Korean Government; quoted in JETRO *China Newsletter*, No. 97, Mar.-Apr. 1992, p. 15.

Sources: Edited based on Figures from the Ministry of Foreign Trade and Economic Cooperation, China; China Statistics Yearbook, quoted in *Saishin Nitchuu Gooben Jigyoo*, p. 59, JETRO *China Newsletter*, No. 96, Jan.-Feb. 1992, pp. 11-12; No. 109, Mar.-Apr. 1994, p. 16; Figures for 1994, *People's Daily* (Overseas Edition), 7.4.1995; Figures for 1995, *Nihon Keizai Shinbun* (Japan Economic News), 6-5-1996.

Competition among foreign companies is intensifying. Japanese companies, which had been reluctant in responding to China's call for more investment and technology transfer in the 1980s, began to make substantial investments, as Table 6.4 shows. As can be seen, Japanese investment in China, slow to take off in the 1980s, rose markedly from 1991 to 1992, and once more from 1992 to 1993 and 1994. Although, as Wang notes (Wang, 1995), there are differing estimates from Chinese and Japanese sources, the story is broadly the same, that while Japan's foreign investment was declining elsewhere, investment in China showed exceptional growth. By 1994, it was reported in Japan that successive groups of Japanese businessmen were flocking to China in order to do business there (JETRO *China Newsletter*, July-August 1994). In April 1993, for example, Japanese carmaker Suzuki unveiled its project to become the first Japanese firm to make automobiles in China (*The Economist*, 24-4-1993). In Dalian, a 50 year project — the 2.2 square kilometres Dalian Industrial Park — involving more than 20 Japanese companies, began with government assistance from both countries (*News Bulletin*, Japan-China Investment Promotion Organization, 18-3-1993). The project itself is to provide industrial sites mainly for Japanese companies and to offer a model for Japanese investment in China. In 1995, Japanese investment increased dramatically, and Japan became the third largest source of foreign investment after Hong Kong and Taiwan (*Nihon Keizai Shinbun* (Japan Economic News), 6-5-1996).

Despite the increased importance of Japanese investment, however, the most fierce driving forces behind the 1990s investment boom in China were Taiwanese and South Korean companies. Both of these are late starters, as Table 6.4 indicates, but their speed of business expansion in China is remarkable. According to official Chinese estimates, the stock of Taiwanese investment in mainland China jumped from $3.4 billion at the end of 1991 to $9 billion at the end of 1992. Unofficial guesses in Taiwan put the amount of cash even higher, at between $15 billion to $25 billion (*The Economist*, 22-5-1993), and official data suggests that investment in 1993 and 1994 was even greater, rising to nearly $10 billion of contract value in 1993 alone, for example, as Table 6.4 shows.

In the 1980s and into the 1990s Hong Kong has been the biggest investor in China, and some $21 billion of direct investment was pumped into the mainland, at least twice as much as Taiwan, by the early 1990s (*The Economist*, 24-7-1993). In the past, however, because of political reasons and Taiwan's ban on direct trading and other economic links with the mainland, many businesses from Taiwan were required to go through

Hong Kong. This, therefore, reduced the ostensible Figure for Taiwanese investment in China. By 1993 the Taiwanese situation had changed dramatically. In April 1993, for example, representatives from the two sides of the Taiwan Strait held their first quasi-official talks in Singapore. For several years after that, relationships between the two sides improved rapidly, fuelling the boom of Taiwanese investment in the mainland, until the controversy over PRC missile-testing and war games in the pre-election period in Taiwan, February-March 1996, called a, probably temporary, halt to business expansion between the two. In theory at least, Taiwan enjoys more advantages over Hong Kong in terms of language, culture and industrial bases. For example, Taiwanese businessmen speak *putonghua* ('common speech', or Mandarin), which is China's official language. But most Hong Kong businessmen only speak Cantonese, which, although of undoubted importance, is only one of dozens of local dialects in China. China's economic boom is gradually spreading further to the north and other inland areas from the Cantonese-speaking Guangdong province, where Hong Kong businesses have been predominant. This gave Taiwanese businesses an advantage in their involvement with China's further economic development, as it spread further afield. The Taiwanese investment boom in the Yangtze Delta area is one indication of this. There were, by 1993, nearly 4,000 Taiwanese-funded enterprises in this area, which accounted for one fourth of the Taiwanese total in mainland China by the end of March (*People's Daily*, 25-8-1993). In the first six months of 1993, Taiwanese investment in the mainland increased 5.7 times compared with the same period in 1992, well above the average rate of 1.8 times for foreign investment and became China's second largest source of foreign investment after Hong Kong.

The (South) Koreans are also among the new forces of foreign investment upsurge in China. The Koreans are known to be willing to invest in any industry which the Japanese do not favour; and to transfer technology into China where the Japanese may be reluctant to do so. The formation of formal diplomatic relations between China and South Korea in August 1992 helped South Korean companies in China to develop their new business. By the end of 1992, companies from South Korea had initialled agreements worth $616m in China with much more in the pipeline (*Financial Times*, 14-6-1993), as Table 6.4 indicates for 1993 and 1994. As Fu-Kuo Liu notes, China became, by late 1994 'the most preferred country and has been the number one for investment by South Korean enterprises' (Liu, 1996, p. 159), with the political desire for stability in the Korean peninsula further enhancing the economic imperative for closer ties between South Korea and China.

Evaluating foreign investment in China

Beginning in 1992 'China Fever' hit the market. We have seen, above, the impact of this on FDI, and on the tremendous increase in investment from Japan, Taiwan and South Korea in particular. How to evaluate this is difficult. For example, as noted above, how certain can we be of the *origin* of investment when it is given statistically at a national level only? We know that much Hong Kong investment actually originated from Taiwan, but we do not know whether that holds true equally for, e.g. UK investment as well, and there are some worries about the precise origins and nature of 'foreign' investment (Perry, 1993). More research is required, therefore, at the micro-level of the firm, on the investments themselves, and the precise source of funding for these.

Then there is the impact of foreign investment on China itself. The authors are in agreement on the need for the PRC to integrate more fully into the global economy, and FDI is an important element in promoting integration. Foreign investment, nonetheless, is a mixed blessing, and the authors are less in agreement on the relative benefits and disbenefits of FDI. Firstly, on the positive side, foreign investment can lead to many of the benefits noted above by Liu Guoguang and his colleagues. Thus, for example, investments have expanded China's economic construction, aided the development of new industrial sectors and strengthened many of the weak links in the national economy. Management skills have been generally enhanced and new technologies introduced, while exports have shot up, in large part due to this extra investment, and foreign-invested firms now have a key role in export growth (Lardy, 1994). Despite such undoubted successes, however, it is doubtful, whether investments have as yet helped significantly to 'develop backward economic sectors and regions' nor has the employment rate been sufficiently raised. For example, Itoh and Shibata quote Japanese sources to show that the significant Japanese electrical machinery industry employed nearly 43,000 workers in China by end 1993 (Itoh and Shibata, 1995). Although this is a fair number, it was still less than those employed by those companies in Taiwan and Thailand, for example, and much less than those employed in Malaysia, where the total was just over 118,000. Given the scale of China's labour surplus, which some estimates suggest could reach 200 million, the size of the employment problem in China is readily apparent. Moreover, FDI is, notwithstanding its greater spatial extension than in the 1980s, still heavily concentrated into the coastal provinces in general and into urban centres in particular (Cook, 1998). The huge surplus of employment in China's rural areas has continued to increase, despite investment in Township and Village Enterprises (TVEs), and many people still remain cut off from the gains which FDI can bring.

In addition, FDI can heighten inflation as too many funds are attracted too quickly into the economy, which can then overheat. It can warp the structure of the economy as foreign investors have priorities which differ from those of the State, perhaps especially for investment in property rather than industrial development (For example, by far the two largest categories for investment by Hong Kong listed companies in the early 1990s were 'Infrastructure' and 'Property', with each being 10 times or more the value of the next category, 'Industrial Manufacturing' (*Financial Times*, 2-9-93)). The 'get rich quick' mentality which underlies 'China Fever' can have a knock-on effect on indigenous entrepreneurs, who seek fast returns rather than long term investments, perhaps thereby increasing corruption and 'spiritual' or 'cultural pollution'.'. FDI can also increase foreign debt because foreign loans, eventually, need to be repaid, while repatriation of profits can adversely affect the balance of payments (although China's foreign exchange restrictions attempt to limit this).

There are serious issues with FDI, but perhaps the most fundamental one for the future of the PRC is that foreign investment may pose, via the forces unleashed, a fundamental challenge to the bureaucratic-authoritarian system itself, a challenge which does not seek to *confront* state power, instead it increasingly bypasses and thus *subverts* it. New economic, communication and cultural linkages are being created via this investment; linkages which cross provincial and international boundaries and transform 'vertical' relations (within the internal hierarchy of the state) into 'horizontal' ones across space and across borders. The 'new regionalism' in which new spatial allegiances develop is one aspect of this, as the contributors to our previous volume illustrate, and 'The new situation can result in regional concepts and regional identities supplanting national concepts and national identities, and regionalism may supplant nationalism for the people in the areas most affected by these changes' (Cook, Doel and Li, 1996, p. 2). Thus, as regards China, the changes in the South, centred on Guangdong-Hong Kong and Fujian-Taiwan for example, may pose challenges to

Beijing's authority, an authority which, historically, has often been marginal in these distant provinces.

Cook and Li have explored this issue further, presenting three alternative scenarios for the future of China, summarized as 'no substantial change', 'China shrinks' and 'China expands', respectively (Cook and Li, 1996). Each of these has contrasting possibilities for the future of FDI in China. In the first, the PRC continues much as at present, and despite internal tensions dissent would be muted via continued economic growth and consumerism. The possibilities for FDI, if not necessarily for democracy and human rights, would continue to be good in such a scenario. In the second, China would 'deconstruct' (Goodman and Segal, 1994) into smaller parts, and although prospects for FDI would be good in certain areas (such as South China) in the short term, Cook and Li regard this as a 'nightmare scenario' due to the potential bloodshed and upheaval which such an outcome would engender; prospects for FDI, therefore, would seriously diminish over time, as economic opportunities were reduced. Their final scenario, of an expanded China, is more unpredictable in its impact, and could lead either to enhanced opportunities for FDI in a larger and more prosperous China, or to diminished opportunities as China became an aggressive state more concerned with military expansion rather than economic growth.

The Chinese authorities seek to control and limit such potential dangers of FDI, acting periodically to modify legislation on development zones, for example, or to restrict credit and ensure that resources are directed towards such priority areas as spending on infrastructure (Walker, 1995). The positive benefits of FDI are emphasized by the Chinese government, but, as Smith notes in a critical review (Smith, 1993), the authorities may be riding the proverbial tiger, a tiger which has become immensely more strong in the 1990s. More research is required to evaluate the pluses and minuses of this great wave of investment, but it is clearly not an unmitigated 'good'. To sum up, therefore, and despite the question mark over some of the official data, the scale and pace of foreign investment in China is exciting and dramatic. Whether the positive changes that such investment has unleashed outweigh the potential negatives is still rather early to judge. What *is* fairly certain is that these changes seem to be irreversible, even after the era of Deng Xiaoping, and even though the 'brakes' were put on by the PRC in 1994, China's latest 15 year development plan envisages a continuing important role for FDI. Notwithstanding the problems, and the negative features of foreign investment, what is clear is that the pattern and process of direct foreign investment will continue to have a considerable impact on the future shape and nature of China's economy and society.

References

Beijing Review (1993), 'Legislation for Foreign-Funded Firms', 21-27 June, p. 23.

Chossudovsky, M. (1986), *Towards Capitalist Restoration? Chinese Socialism After Mao*, Macmillan, London.

Commercial Law Centre Tokyo (1991), *Saishin Nitchuu Gooben Jigyoo* (Japanese-Chinese Joint Ventures), Commercial Law Centre Inc., Tokyo.

Cook, I.G. (1993), *Urban Issues in the West Pacific Rim*, paper presented to the British Pacific Rim Research Group, Liverpool John Moores University, May.

Cook, I.G. (1995), *Pressures of Development in China's Large Cities*, paper presented to the Symposium on International Urbanization in China, Shunde City, Guangdong, September.

Cook, I.G. (1998), 'Urban and Regional Pressures of Development', in Cannon, T. (ed.) *China: Economic Growth, Population and the Environment*, Macmillan, London (in press).

Cook, I.G., Doel, M.A. and Li, R. (1996), 'Introduction', in Cook, I.G., Doel, M.A. and Li, R. (eds), *Fragmented Asia: Regional Integration and National Disintegration in Pacific Asia*, Avebury, Aldershot, pp. 1-11.

Cook, I.G. and Li, R. (1996), 'The Rise of Regionalism and the Future of China', in Cook, I.G., Doel, M.A. and Li, R. (eds), *Fragmented Asia: Regional Integration and National Disintegration in Pacific Asia*, Avebury, Aldershot, pp. 200-219.

The Economist (1993a), 'Japan Ties Up the Asian Market', 24 April, p. 79.

The Economist (1993b), 'Taiwan: Twixt Handshake and Armlock', 22 May, p. 73.

The Economist (1993c), 'Japanese Manufacturing: Asian Promise', 12 June, p. 98.

The Economist (1993d), 'Taiwan and China: Feeding Mother', 24 July, pp. 71-2.

Finance and Development (1992), 'Recent Trends in FDI for the Developing World', Vol. 29, No.1, March, pp. 50-1.

Financial Times (1993a), 'Shanghai', 2 June.

Financial Times (1993b), 'China's Investment Revolution', 14 June, p. 21.

Financial Times (1993c), 'Long Slog to a Smooth Landing', 5 August, p. 15.

Financial Times (1993d), 'HK Investors Warm to Mainland Cooling', 2 September.

Foreign Investment Administration and China Economic and Trade Consultants Corp. (1993), *Investment in China*, Ministry of Foreign Trade and Economic Cooperation, Beijing.

Goodman, D.S.G. and Segal, G. (eds) (1994), *China Deconstructs: Politics, Trade and Regionalism*, Routledge, London.

Howe, C. (1978), *China's Economy: A Basic Guide*, Paul Elek, London.

Huang, F. (1992), 'Foreign Direct Investment in China', *Jingji Kongzuozhe Xuexi Ziliao* (Study Material for Economic Workers), No. 72, 20 November, pp. 5-15.

Imai, S. (1990), *Investment into China: Investment Environment and Joint Venture Case Study*, JETRO, Tokyo.

Itoh, Motoshige and Shibata, Jun (1995), 'A Study of the Operations of Japanese Firms in Asia: the Electrical Machinery Industry', in Chen, E.K.Y. and Drysdale, P. (eds), *Corporate Links and Foreign Direct Investment in Asia and the Pacific*, Harper Educational, Pymble, New South Wales, Australia, pp. 187-202.

Japan-China Investment Promotion Organization (1993), *News Bulletin*, No. 15, 18 March, pp. 54-5.

Lardy, N. R. (1994), *China in the World Economy*, Instititute for International Economics, Washington, DC.

Liu Guoguang et. al. (1987), *China's Economy in 2000*, New World Press, Beijing.

Liu, Fu-Kuo (1996), 'Industrial Development and the Impetus to Regional Economic Integration in Pacific Asia', in Cook, I.G., Doel, M.A. and Li, R. (eds) (1996), *Fragmented Asia: Regional Integration and National Disintegration in Pacific Asia*, Avebury, Aldershot, pp. 137-166.

Mann, J. (1989), *Beijing Jeep: The Short Unhappy Romance of American Business in China*, Simon Schuster, New York.

Murray, G. (1994), *Doing Business in China: The Last Great Market*, China Library, London.

Nihon Keizai Shinbun (Japan Economic News)(1996), 6 May, p. 8.

Pearson, M.M. (1991), *Joint Ventures in the People's Republic of China*, Princeton University Press, Princeton.

People's Daily (Overseas Edition) (1993a), 'Increasing Taiwanese Investment in the Mainland', 13 August, p. 5.

People's Daily (Overseas Edition) (1993b), 25 August, p. 5.

Perry, E. (1993), 'China in 1992: An Experiment in Neo-Authoritarianism', *Asian Survey*, Vol. XXXIII, No. 1, January, pp. 12-21.

Petri, P.A. (1995), 'The Interdependence of Trade and Investment in the Pacific', in Chen, E.K.Y. and Drysdale, P. (eds), *Corporate Links and Foreign Direct Investment in Asia and the Pacific*, Harper Educational, Pymble, New South Wales, Australia, pp. 29-55.

Phillips, D. and Yeh, A. (1990), 'Foreign Investment and Trade: Impact on Spatial Structure of the Economy', in Cannon, T. and Jenkins, A. (eds), *The Geography of Contemporary China: The Impact of Deng Xiaoping's Decade*, Routledge, London, pp. 224-248.

Simone, V. and Feraru, A.T. (1995), *The Asian Pacific: Political and Economic Development in a Global Context*, Longman USA, White Plains, New York.

Smith, R. (1993), 'The Chinese Road to Capitalism', New Left Review, No. 199, May-June, pp. 55-99.

Walker, T. (1995), 'China, Reason for Satisfaction', *Financial Times*, 6 October.

Wang, Huijiong and Li, Boxi (1989), *China Towards the Year 2000*, New World Press, Beijing.

Wang, Yongjiang (1995), *Japanese Joint Ventures in China: A Study in Sino-Japanese Business Relations*, PhD Thesis, University of Sheffield, Sheffield.

Wang, Yongjiang and Cook, I.G. (1993), *Foreign Investment in China and the Current Situation*, paper presented to the British Pacific Rim Research Group, Liverpool John Moores University, September, and, updated, to the Anglo-French Workshop on East Asia, School of Oriental and African Studies, November.

Waters, M. (1995), *Globalization*, Routledge, London.

Wei Mu (1992), 'Zhongguo Waijiao de Zuixing Xingshi' (the latest situation of China's diplomacy), *Wide Angle*, Hong Kong, No. 241, 16 October.

Wooldridge, A. (1995), 'Survey of Multinationals: Managing on the Frontier', *The Economist*, 24 June.

Xue Muqiao (1981), *China's Socialist Economy*, Foreign Languages Press, Beijing.

7 Managed or Mismanaged Trade? US-Japan Trade Relations During the Clinton Presidency

SIMON LEE

Introduction

Trade between the United States (US) and Japan provides the world economy with its most important bilateral trade relationship. In 1996, 27.2 per cent of Japan's exports and 22.7 per cent of its imports were accounted for by trade with the US, its most important trading partner. The bilateral trade relationship has also been the most politically sensitive, not least since the US recorded a $10 billion trade deficit with Japan in 1978. Between 1974 and 1989 no fewer than 24 of the 40 trade disputes in the Pacific addressed by US 301 trade measures involved action against Japan (Ryan, 1995, p. 342). In 1996, the US recorded deficits in both its trade balance ($83.6 billion) and its current account ($65.8 billion) with Japan. An earlier influential US commentator responded to this imbalance by suggesting that the US trade negotiating strategy had amounted to nothing less than the surrender by the US of its future prosperity (Prestowitz, 1988). In the face of US demands for corrective action, at least one Japanese politician (Ishihara, 1991) advocated a more assertive negotiating stance, whilst another (Ozawa, 1994) later suggested that nothing short of a Japanese political revolution would be sufficient to ensure a harmonious bilateral relationship in future. This chapter seeks to analyse the conduct of this vital and politically sensitive bilateral trade relationship during the Presidency of Bill Clinton. The chapter begins by analysing the broader global, regional and domestic context for trade relations during the 1990s. It then focuses upon the Clinton administration's trade policy inheritance before suggesting that the July 1993 United States-Japan Framework for a New Economic Partnership and the June 1995 US-Japan automobile dispute constituted the two most important landmarks during Clinton's first term of office. The chapter concludes by analysing the prospects for trade relations with Japan during Clinton's second term.

President Clinton's first term of office coincided with some major developments in the governance of world trade.[1] In institutional terms, at the global level the completion of the Uruguay Round of the General Agreement on Tariffs and Trade (GATT) has culminated in the establishment of the World Trade Organization (WTO) (Hoekman & Kostecki, 1995). At the regional level, the increasingly integrated European Union, the newly established North American Free Trade Agreement (NAFTA) and the more slowly evolving Asia Pacific Economic Cooperation (APEC) have provided important new arena for the expression of trade policy issues. In terms of ideas and debate, the discipline of international political economy has been much exercized by the extent and implications of globalization and regionalization (Gamble & Payne, 1996), the relationship between them (Geiger & Kennedy, 1996), and their impact upon important bilateral trade relationships-most notably between the US and Japan.[2]

Some (e.g. Ohmae, 1996) have suggested that globalization of trade and markets has become so far advanced as to render national economies increasingly redundant. Others (e.g. Hirst and Thompson, 1996) have remained sceptical about the extent of globalizations, and its impact upon the governance of world trade. The globalization of the international economy is neither a recent nor a universal phenomenon. Indeed, genuinely transnational corporations remain relatively rare and, in any case, Europe, Japan and North America possess the capacity, especially if policy is properly coordinated, to exert powerful influence over international flows of trade and investment (Hirst & Thompson, 1996, pp. 2-3). For some, globalization has represented a trap and a major threat to the prosperity of the developed world from which salvation can only be found in a rejection of GATT and its replacement by regionalized free trade (Goldsmith, 1993). For others, restriction or elimination of international trade is an erroneous fallacy (Hindley, 1994). Fortunately, for those fearing a zero-sum conflict between regional blocs characterized by exclusivity and protectionism, the evidence thus far is that the rationale of regionalism has been the removal rather than the erection of trade barriers (Gamble & Payne, 1996, p. 251).

In addition to the impact of developments at the global and regional levels, the trajectory of US-Japan trade relations during the 1990s has been heavily influenced by the performance of the respective domestic economies. There has been a prominent role reversal from the pattern of earlier postwar decades largely characterized by more rapid Japanese economic growth. For the US, the 1990s has been marked by a period of sustained growth both in its domestic economy and its total trade, the latter expanding by no less than 44 per cent between 1992 and 1996 (USTR, 1997). This buoyant performance has had a major beneficial impact upon the size of the US budget deficit, the principal legacy of the profligate years of Reaganomics. During fiscal year 1996, the budget deficit declined to $107 billion and for 1997, President Clinton has announced a revized forecast for the deficit of only $37 billion owing to higher than expected tax revenues. Indeed, his forecast is that the budget will be restored to a $20 billion surplus by 2002 after being deficit since 1969. This healthy performance has not improved the US current account. Indeed, during 1996, the US current account deficit increased to $165.1 billion, the worst trade performance since 1987 and the second worst in history. Despite improving for the second successive year, the US merchandise trade deficit with Japan stood at $47.7 billion — a fall of 19 per cent.

Part of the explanation for the continuing US trade deficit lies in the continuing weakness of demand in the domestic Japanese economy which has struggled throughout the 1990s to recover from the financial trauma induced by the collapse of the 'bubble economy'. This was the name given by the Japanese to the economic boom, fuelled by very low interest rates, which developed in Japan following the September 1985 Plaza Accord that led to a rapid appreciation in the value of the yen against the dollar. In an attempt to surmount their rising costs, Japanese companies embarked upon an unprecedented investment boom, raising Y85 trillion ($638 billion) between 1985 and 1990. This explosion in investment in the real economy was accompanied by a colossal expansion in lending to the consumer and property market, to the extent that by the end of 1989, Japan's property market was estimated to be worth over Y2000 trillion-or four times the value of US property. These speculative trends in turn helped to fuel a staggering rise in the Tokyo Stock Exchange which was worth 151 per cent of Japanese GDP on the 31 December 1989, the date of its all-time peak (compared with just 29 per cent of GDP in 1980) (Wood, 1992, pp. 6-8, 50). When the bubble economy burst, and share prices lost 48 per cent of their value by 1 October 1990, the loss in paper wealth was Y300 trillion ($2.25 trillion) or three times the then size of Third World debt.

Despite low real interest rates and the introduction of no fewer than six recovery packages by successive Japanese governments between August 1992 and September 1995, which together injected more than Y65 trillion yen into the domestic economy, the Japanese economy has rarely managed to grow at an annual rate less than half that achieved on average during the 1980s. The highest growth rate for 23 years, 12.7 per cent during the first three months of 1996, has proven unsustainable. At a time when the Japanese economy has been in more urgent need of decisive action than at any time since 1945, prospects for economic recovery during the 1990s have not been assisted by the onset of political instability and uncertainty, induced by successive high profile corruption scandals since the late 1980s and culminating in the end of nearly four decades of Liberal Democratic Party (LDP) hegemony in July 1993.

The subsequent period has been characterized by party fragmentation and realignment on both the Left and the Right of Japanese politics. Beginning with the eight-party coalition government led by the Japan New Party's Morihiro Hosakawa, Japan has been led by no fewer than four different Prime Ministers, each at the head of insipid, often minority and multi-party coalition governments. These administrations have included the shortest-lived premiership of Tsutomu Hata (only 59 days during 1994) and the first socialist Prime Minister for 47 years, the Social Democratic Party's Tomiichi Murayama. Although the LDP emerged from the October 1996 General Election as the largest single party, the current Prime Minister, Ryutaro Hashimoto has once again had to govern Japan as the head of a coalition government. The inability of Japan's political system to deliver an authoritative, single party and majority government, capable of decisive action independent of party factional bosses, continues to act as an important constraint upon the capacity of Japanese governments to play an assertive international political role commensurate with the economic power deriving from the world market share of Japanese multinationals.

From managed trade to aggressive unilateralism

Trade policy in the US has been characterized by an occasionally abrasive relationship between the Presidential and Congressional branches of government over who should take the leading role in defining and protecting US interests. Article 1, Section 8 of the US Constitution has granted control of the regulation of international commerce to Congress. However, this historical tradition of Congressional domination of US trade policy began to be challenged following the passage of the 1934 Reciprocal Trade Agreement Act which delegated trade strategy to the President and State Department. During the postwar Bretton Woods era, Congress was content to continue to delegate authority. For example, the 1962 Trade Expansion Act passed by Congress created the Special Representative for Trade Negotiations, which was renamed the office of the United States Trade Representative (USTR) in 1980. Once the US trade balance with the rest of the world began to move towards a deficit in the 1970s Congress became increasingly reluctant to delegate. Fast-track procedures for trade policy were introduced, giving Congress ninety days to respond to the President's trade strategy. Shortly before the election of Ronald Reagan, in 1979, Congress forced the President to reorganize the Executive branch. President Jimmy Carter's 1980 executive order raised the status in trade policy of the USTR by authorising it to make and administer US trade policy, lead all trade negotiations, and represent the US government in all major international trade organs (Ryan, 1995, p. 336; Grant, 1993, pp. 275-276).

A key trade policy objective of both the Reagan and Bush administrations was the reduction of the US trade deficit with Japan. Their triple failure to cut the deficit, restrain protectionist sentiment at home, and maintain good relations with the Japanese has been seen as 'one of policy as well as ideas' (Williams, 1994, p. 52). Williams has explained these shortcomings in terms of a failure of understanding, on the part of the Bush and Reagan administrations and their key policy advisors, that the trade friction with Japan reflected a transfer of power from Washington to Tokyo. This was illustrated above all by the ineffectiveness of Bush's 1989 Structural Impediments Initiative which sought no fewer than 240 politically expensive changes in Japanese business practices. Any pretence to free trade had long since been abandoned by the earlier Reagan administration in its early months of office when it forced the Japanese government to introduce voluntary export restraints (VERs) on Japanese automobile manufacturers. Further VERs were subsequently imposed on Japanese trade in steel (1984), machine tools (1986), and semi-conductors (1986). The management of trade was carried a further step forward in 1984 when four industries where the US was highly competitive — forest products, medical equipment and pharmaceuticals, electronic products (largely excluding semiconductors), and telecommunications — were singled out for some intensive bilateral negotiation with Japan.

Japanese compliance with this Market-Oriented Sector Selective (MOSS) trade initiative was agreed in January 1985 at a US-Japan summit. As a consequence of the initiative's introduction, from 1985 to 1987 US exports to Japan in the MOSS industries grew from average annual rates of -0.3 per cent to 25 per cent, equivalent to an average annual growth rate of 14 per cent — which itself exceeded the 6 per cent annual increase in total US exports to Japan during the same period (Lincoln, 1990, p. 151). To complement the MOSS initiative, during 1985 the Reagan administration also announced the establishment of a trade 'strike force' to address trade issues and initiate trade cases. Despite the fact that it was already operating a large number of discriminatory tariffs on imported manufactures, e.g. ball bearings (12 per cent tariff), motorcycles (30 per cent), and non-rubber footwear (18.5 per cent) (Grant, 1993, p. 276), in the autumn of 1986 the Reagan administration began to press Japan for further concessions, in the particular form of the liberalization of its domestic construction market to foreign contractors. When the resulting negotiations were stalled by the Nakasone government, the Trade Policy Review Group, including officials representing the Department of Commerce and USTR, threatened to invoke trade sanctions against Japan. This practice of threatening and indeed imposing punitive trade sanctions was maintained during the Bush presidency. For example, in 1990, the US imposed tariffs on Japanese milling machines even though the customer, Ford Motor Company, pointed out that the machines were three times faster than American machines. The following year saw the imposition of 63 per cent tariffs on Japanese flat screen displays for computers even though the customers, IBM and Apple, pointed to the absence of US suppliers.

These examples demonstrate how, although rhetorically committed to free trade, neither the Reagan nor the Bush Presidencies were characterized by the consistent exercise of free trade principles in the conduct of trade policy. This ambivalence toward the potential benefits and costs of liberalized markets was exemplified in US government policy toward inward foreign direct investment (IFDI). Kang has shown how during the 1980s US IFDI policy changed from one of benign neglect to one of cautious activism largely as a consequence of the domestic political reaction to increasing Japanese IFDI (Kang, 1997, p. 329). Whereas Japanese IFDI in the US stood at $4.7 billion or 6.2 per cent of the total stock in 1980, by 1990 it had multiplied to $83.5 billion or 20.7 per cent (second only to the UK's $108.1 billion) (Kang, 1997, pp. 318-19). The principal cause of tension was the October 1986 announcement by the US semiconductor manufacturer

Fairchild (ironically then a wholly owned subsidiary of the French company Schlumberger) that it was being sold to the Japanese manufacturer Fujitsu. The hostile domestic political reaction to the sale of Fairchild reawakened demands for tighter regulation of IFDI, culminating in the May 1986 Democrat-sponsored Foreign Investment Disclosure and Reciprocity Act which sought to restrict future IFDI in the US unless US companies and individuals could invest in the foreign investor's domestic economy on a reciprocal basis. Although a modified version of this Bill was voted down by the Senate, a subsequent Democrat-sponsored amendment to the 1988 Omnibus Trade Bill sought to give the President discretionary power to scrutinize and reject undesirable investment affecting 'products or key technologies essential to the US defence industrial base' (Congressional Record, House, 20 April 1988, H2118 cited in Kang, 1997, p. 325). The passage of this Exon-Florio amendment gave the Committee on Foreign Investment in the United States (CFIUS) the power to monitor and enforce performance requirements on IFDI. However, this extension of cautious activism did not act as a constraint on Japanese investment in the US. Between October 1988 and April 1992, the Japanese acquired no fewer than 399 high-technology businesses in the US (with the UK a distant second with only 65 acquisitions), equivalent to 66 per cent of total foreign acquisitions (Kang, 1997, pp. 320-321). Rather than being seen as a threat to US competitiveness, Japanese IFDI came increasingly to be seen as a vital external stimulus to the competitiveness of US companies.

During the 1980s, the US was increasingly willing and able to use its leverage over Japan in bilateral trade negotiations not merely to protect uncompetitive and declining industries but to reinforce and institutionalize its competitive advantage in the advanced technologies of the sunrise industries. The poor trade relations which the Clinton administration was eventually to inherit emanated from the decision taken by the Bush administration in May 1989 to use Section 301 of the 1988 Omnibus Trade and Competitiveness Act to name Japan (together with India and Brazil) as 'priority' trading partners which should be subjected to pressure to force them to remove trading practices deemed by the US to be unacceptable. For Bhagwati, this action indicated to its trading partners that the US was now prepared to embrace 'aggressive unilateralism' in its trade policy (Bhagwati, 1991, p. 1). The genesis of and potential for this 'aggressive unilateralism' in US trade policy toward Japan could be traced back to Section 301 of the 1974 Trade and Tariff Act which focused on 'unreasonable' trade practices that lay beyond the remit of GATT rights and obligations. Under Section

301, 'if the USTR determines that a foreign act, policy, or practice violates or is inconsistent with a trade agreement or is unjustifiable and burdens or restricts US commerce, then action by the USTR to enforce the trade agreement rights or to obtain the elimination of the act, policy, or practice is mandatory, subject to the specific direction, if any, of the President' (US Congress, 1989). Section 301 was consistently amended during the late 1970s and early 1980s, but it was not until September 1985 that Ronald Reagan declared that his administration's 'New Trade Policy' would make active use of the Section's provisions (Kuroda, 1991, p. 220). However, it was actually the Super 301 and Special 301 provisions of the 1988 Omnibus Trade and Competitiveness Act which threatened to conflict with the multilateral provisions of the GATT. Super 301 required the USTR to compile a list of countries with 'unreasonable' practices, and then lay down deadlines for the removal of these practices by the offending parties. Failure to comply by the set deadline would invoke retaliatory measures from the US (Bhagwati, 1991, p. 3). It was this measure which was deployed by the Bush administration against Japan in May 1989.

As with Super 301, Special 301 had been drawn up to deal with the increasingly sensitive issue of trade abuses of intellectual property rights (Blakeney, 1997, pp. 4-6). It was intended to eliminate 'unfair' practices and open up foreign markets to US manufacturers. Congress regarded Special 301 as a means to gain one-way concessions from trading partners but as Bhagwati has shown, from the very outset both Super 301 and Special 301 were operated under the mistaken assumption that they were legal under the GATT (Bhagwati, 1991, p. 33). This assumption was based on the fact that Congress has not formally ratified the GATT Treaty. The expectation among its trading partners, including Japan, was that the US would honour the multilateral framework provided by the GATT. If the US did not honour its multilateral obligations, what was to prevent other GATT signatories from following the US example by imposing their own measures against what they regarded as trading practices 'unfair' to their interests? Bhagwati concluded that the world trading system should not be predicated on the assumption that any single player, however, powerful, should be able to impose its own rules, and unilaterally profess their own legitimacy (Bhagwati, 1991, p. 36). The resort to such action by the Bush administration seemed to reflect a malady in US trade strategy toward Japan which was symbolized by Bush's own illness when visiting Japan prior to his unsuccessful 1992 Presidential election campaign.

Trade Policy at a Kantor

The first Clinton administration was somewhat unusual in that three of its key positions were to be occupied by several of the most influential academic commentators on the governance of world trade, each with their own distinctive perspective on the future conduct of US foreign economic policy. Robert Reich, who was to serve as Labor Secretary, contended in The Work of Nations that the US should prepare for the twenty-first century by recognising that in future there would no longer be national products, technologies, corporations, industries or economies. With geographical boundaries becoming increasingly meaningless, Reich contended that each nation's primary assets would be its citizens' skills and that therefore the primary political task would be to reward those possessing the skills and insight to contribute to the global economy (Reich, 1991, p. 3). In sharp contrast, in her analysis of trade conflict in high-technology industries, *Who's Bashing Whom?*, the future Chairperson of the Council of Economic Advisers, Laura D'Andrea Tyson advocated managed trade, i.e. trade controlled, directed or administered by government policies, as a means of promoting competitiveness. Free trade was no longer 'necessarily and automatically the best policy' because trade in high-technology industries was characterized by imperfect competition and had become a 'fertile breeding ground for interventionist policies' (Tyson, 1992, pp. 3-4). The correct US trade policy reponse would be a defensive strategy of 'cautious activism' for which manipulated rather than free trade would be the appropriate benchmark and aggressive unilateralism 'defensible as an interim response to foreign trading practices and structural barriers' (Tyson, 1992, p. 258). Jeffrey Garten, who was subsequently to serve Clinton between 1993 and 1995 as Under Secretary of Commerce for International Trade, joined other influential commentators (Thurow, 1992) in seeing the post-communist era as a struggle between the US, Japan and Germany (Thurow saw the European player in the 'Head to Head' global contest as the European Community rather than Germany alone). Garten argued that a 'cold peace' could yet be avoided by the Big Three if they remembered the damaging consequences for international trade of a leadership vacuum during the interwar years (Garten, 1992, p. 190).

The prospects for harmonious trade relations with Japan during the early months of the Clinton Presidency did not appear particularly auspicious. During the 1992 election campaign, Clinton indicated that he was in favour of free trade, but an advocate of fair trade. George Bush's formative years had been during the era of unrivalled US hegemony in the late 1940s and throughout the 1950s. His instinct for open markets was sustained to the final day of his presidency when he sanctioned the sale to a Japanese company of the sole US supplier of a new generation of laser disc drives used to improve the performance of the Patriot missile. In sharp contrast, Clinton's formative years politically had been during the troubled 1970s and 1980s-a period of declining US competitiveness in important world markets, such as consumer electronics and motor vehicles. He was expected to pursue a more mercantilist trade policy in accordance with Tyson's 'cautious activism'. This was more than borne out by his administration's first announcement on trade policy when the new Commerce Secretary, Ron Brown, imposed dumping duties on already declining Japanese steel exports to the US (together with steel exports from 18 other countries). The Japanese Foreign Ministry immediately urged the Clinton administration to make only 'truly impartial judgement' in its trade policy (*Financial Times*, 29 January 1993). Having seen the 1984 voluntary export restraint on Japan's steel exports to the US removed by the Bush administration as recently as March 1992, Brown's precipitative action prompted fears in Tokyo that there might be a revival of Super 301 actions. The Director General of the powerful and prestigious Ministry of International Trade and Industry (MITI) warned that Japan would contemplate retaliatory action in this eventuality.

Jagdish Bhagwati has contended that the Clinton administration wished to implement a shift in US trade policy towards Japan based on four principles each of which was based upon faulty economic analysis or politically unrealistic. First, that while the US market was open Japan's market was unfairly closed thereby giving the Japanese a considerable advantage over their US competitors. However, commentators were far from unanimous about the extent of closure of the Japanese market, the degree to which this could be measured by the share of imports in Japan's GNP, and the competitive advantage to be derived from closure. Second, Clinton's trade policy assumed that the US could make a unilateral assessment of Japan without recourse to validation by more impartial multilateral procedures. Bhagwati has contended that this policy could degenerate into a counterproductive rule by the law of the jungle (in which the US would inevitably be king!). Third, the Clinton administration assumed that a results-oriented approach to trade policy was justified by the 'informal' nature of Japanese market closure. Bhagwati has suggested that this was to overlook the fact that only markets and not governments could determine the appropriate levels of market share and imports. Fourth, the Clinton administration appeared to assume that Japan would only comply with US demands if it was threatened with the sanction of 301 tariff retaliation, illegal under the GATT's Articles. Bhagwati has contended that the notion that the Japanese could continue to be bullied into making one-way trade concessions was to fly in the face of the wider and changing realities of the US-Japan relationship (Bhagwati, 1996, pp. 265-266).

The prospects for avoiding a damaging trade war were not initially helped by the fact that the Big Three US automobile manufacturers had been the only industrial companies to be received by Clinton at Little Rock during his transition to office. As soon as Clinton was sworn in, the Big Three indicated that they were contemplating a \$45 billion law suit because they believed that Japanese and European automobiles were being sold more cheaply in the US market, thereby contravening US commercial law. During his conformation hearings, Ron Brown stated that he would not rule out the possibility of special protection for US industries. Fears of protectionism were also fuelled by Clinton's choice for the post of USTR. Mickey Kantor, a millionaire lawyer and Democratic Party insider, like his predecessor Carla Hills, had no prior experience of trade policy. He soon made it known that he would not be adopting a dogmatic approach to trade negotiations, declaring that he was not going to be caught in a theological debate about trade which did not lead to practical and pragmatic results. The one principle which Kantor would defend was the status of the US economy as the largest open market in the world. At the same time, Kantor announced that he would support Congressional opposition to proposals in the Uruguay Round of the GATT negotiations which proposed that US trade laws be subject to challenge by the GATT. In terms of his attitude toward the Japanese, Kantor indicated that he did not intend to adopt the approach to opening markets implict in the Bush Administration's Structural Impediments Initiative, by stating 'It is not my business to tell them how to organize society...It is my business to ensure that markets become more effective' (*Financial Times*, 29 March 1993). At the same time, Kantor did not envisage the US bearing sole responsibility for prosecuting trade negotiations because he believed that the Japanese no longer either stand aside or seek protection.

The 1993 Framework Agreement

Clinton informed the Japanese Prime Minister, Kiichi Miyazawa, at their April 1993 summit in Washington that his administration would be seeking specific targets for US exports in particular markets in Japan. The two premiers agreed to establish a joint panel to create a forum for discussing how to cut the Japanese trade surplus. However, Clinton's most instructive action had been to announce that his number one target for cutting the surplus was an appreciation in the value of the yen. The Japanese Foreign Minister was later to respond that it was 'extremely unusual for a head of state to refer to currency exchange rates and a departure from the norm for someone with top authority to say something like that' (*Financial Times*, 22 April 1993). Not to be deterred from the objective of a quantifiable approach to US-Japan trade, on a visit to Tokyo at the end of April, Ron Brown informed his Japanese audience that 'We are very serious about a results-oriented approach and measurable results and monitoring those results' (*Financial Times*, 23 April 1993). Despite the vigorous opposition of MITI officials to this suggestion, Brown announced that the US would be seeking to draw up two new bilateral agreements with Japan in order to address both structural and sectoral issues. Subsequently, Mickey Kantor chose to reveal at OECD ministerial discussions in May that the US would be presenting within a week fresh proposals for a policy framework to open up certain sectors of the Japanese economy. This framework was intended as a successor to the Bush administration's 1989 Structural Impediments Initiative.

At the outset of trade negotiations in Washington with Japanese trade representatives, it emerged that the US had targeted six sectors-automobiles, automobile parts, computers, supercomputers, electronics and semiconductors-regarded as particularly difficult for US suppliers to export to Japan. To help surmount Japanese resistance to his results-oriented trade strategy, Kantor urged Congress to revive the fast-track trade negotiating authority, albeit without the renewal of Super 301, because it was thought this might jeopardize GATT negotiations now at an advanced and critical juncture. For its part, the Japanese government responded to the threat of an extension of managed trade by publishing a report from an advisory committee to MITI which accused Japan's top 10 trading partners of unfair trading practices (*Financial Times*, 11 May 1993). The report claimed that a results-oriented approach to trade policy would lack objectivity and mistakenly associate trade imbalances with inadequate market access. It also drew a clear distinction between the unilateral approach to trade which the report claimed the US was without parallel in pursuing, and the multilateral approach which it argued was the best means to resolve trade issues, using the GATT dispute settlement mechanism 'whenever necessary and feasible' (*Financial Times*, 12 May 1993). However, Japan's negotiating position was somewhat undermined when a report from the Japan Fair Trade Commission found that the keiretsu sometimes obstructed their competitors, including foreign companies, from entering Japanese markets for glass, motor vehicles and paper products (*Financial Times*, 30 June 1993). However, the Commission had no plans to act against the companies concerned.

In the event, within its first seven months of office, the Clinton administration had negotiated the United States-Japan Framework for a New Economic Partnership (hereafter referred to as the Framework Agreement), the most important bilateral trade negotiation of Clinton's first term. The Framework Agreement, which was signed on the 10 July 1993, possessed two key objectives for US-Japan trade relations, namely a reduction in the Japanese trade surplus and increased foreign access to Japanese markets. These objectives were to be addressed by five main criteria. First, Japan undertook to signficantly increase its government's procurement of competitive foreign good and services and second, to reduce the regulation governing foreign firms operating in the domestic Japanese market. Third, bilateral negotiations would be undertaken to open up 'other major sectors' of the Japanese economy. Fourth, negotiations would improve 'economic harmony' by correcting longstanding macroeconomic imbalances in Japan's markets. Fifth, implementation of existing bilateral trade agreements would be monitored and/or renegotiated to improve market access. The Japanese Government had wanted a commitment from the US that these five criteria should not be interpreted as results-oriented targets but the Clinton administration resisted any such pledge. From the US perspective, the Framework provided an unprecedented package of objective quantitative and qualitative measures for evaluating the progress in opening up the Japanese market.

Although Japanese resistance to managed trade steadily increased in the wake of the Framework Agreement, not least at the February 1994 Washington Summit between Clinton and Prime Minister Morihiro Hosokawa, it was unable to prevent the Framework from having a major impact on the pattern of US-Japan trade in the sectors covered by the Agreement's rubric. For example, by November 1995, Mickey Kantor was able to proclaim that in the Clinton administration's first 33 months of government, the Framework Agreement had embraced no fewer than 12 of the 20 trade agreements reached with Japan. In those sectors covered by the Framework, US exports had expanded by more than 50 per cent - a growth rate more than 2.5 times greater than growth in other US exports to Japan. Moreover, by the end of February 1997, the USTR Designate, Charlene Barshefsky, was able to point to no fewer than 24 trade agreements with Japan, a dividend of 800000 jobs from US exports to Japan, and a growth rate in US exports to Japan during the previous three years no less than six times faster than the growth of Japanese exports to the US. Managed trade under the Framework Agreement appeared to have paid a handsome economic dividend.

It's the Auto Sector, Stupid!

Apart from the Framework Agreement, the other most important development in US-Japan trade relations during Clinton's first term came on the 27 June 1995 when the two nations found themselves on the brink of an unprecedented trade war. It is not surprising that it should be trade in automobiles and automobile parts which risked a meltdown in trade relations given that in 1994 no less than 58 per cent (or $38.3 billion) of the US $66 billion trade deficit with Japan had been accounted for by trade in this sector. This in turn constituted 23 per cent of the total US trade deficit with the rest of the world in 1994. Furthermore, foreign automobile manufacturers had won only 4.4 per cent of the Japanese market during 1994, compared with a 37 per cent foreign manufacturers' share of the US market (Stokes, 1996, p. 283). Mickey Kantor defended the US action, claiming that US manufacturers had exported only 400000 vehicles to Japan in the previous 25 years compared with the 40 million vehicles which Japan had shipped to the US.[3] Furthermore, eighteen months of bilateral negotiation under the Framework Agreement had failed to yield progress in the automotive sector. Frustrated by this lack of progress, the Clinton administration had initiated a Section 301 investigation of the Japanese market for automobile parts on the 1 October 1994. Nevertheless, the unilateral threat to impose 100 per cent tariffs (equivalent to almost $6 billion of duties) on Japanese luxury automobiles unless the Japanese agreed to voluntary import expansion (VIE) targets represented a very major escalation. The Clinton administration's triple demand was that Japan should reform its automobile inspection system, Japanese automobile dealerships should also sell US vehicles, and Japanese manufacturers should establish voluntary purchase plans for US-manufactured vehicle parts.

To outside observers, nothing, apart from a reluctance to make the necessary investment, was stopping the Big Three US manufacturers from either establishing their own dealerships networks for automobiles and automobile parts in Japan or indeed complying with vehicle inspection systems as they had done for decades in other major export markets. Indeed, Bhagwati has correctly portrayed the whole US-Japan automobile dispute as 'a monumental mistake' motivated by a combination of political, bureaucratic and industrial factors. Given the overriding contribution of trade in automobiles and automobile parts to the US trade deficit with Japan, the political dividend to be derived from a frontal assault on the Japanese automobile industry was apparent, not least because for any of Clinton's opponents to question his strategy would have been tantamount to condoning Japan's 'closed' markets. A major confrontation with Japan also offered Ron Brown the chance to demonstrate that the Commerce Department had an important role to play in opening markets, and should not be culled by a Republican Congress. From an industrial perspective, the high yen had long since encouraged Japanese manufacturers to move production of automobiles and automobile parts overseas. Therefore, the cost of compliance with the USTR's demands for more open markets was not likely to be high for Japanese manufacturers whereas the costs of non-compliance would be extremely high if punitive sanctions were imposed. What the dispute did signify was an important tactical shift in US trade policy with Japan because the Clinton administration was now targeting Japanese companies rather than the Japanese government itself. The US could have avoided resort to aggressive unilateralism by pursuing its grievances through the nascent WTO procedures. However, this would have risked the embarassing possibility either of losing its case, or of winning the case but finding that the principle of challenging domestic barriers to imports would then be used as a legal precedent against its own regulation of US markets (Bhagwati, 1996, pp. 270-275).

The US threat of unilateral imposition of punitive tariffs was eventually withdrawn on the 28 June when negotiations on the automotive sector were completed, eventually leading to agreement on the 23 August. The resulting Framework Agreement for US-Japan automotive trade contained no fewer than seventeen objective criteria in pursuit of the objective of significantly expanding the opportunities for sales of US automobiles and automobile parts in the Japanese market. The Agreement was supplemented by a plethora of 'voluntary' statements from Japanese manufacturers and dealerships indicating their intention to improve market access. However, the sum total of the Agreement was something less than a guarantee that the US trade deficit in automobiles and automobile parts would dramatically diminish. The chief Japanese negotiator was Ryutaro Hashimoto, the Minister of International Trade and Industry. With the backing of Japanese public opinion, Hashimoto steadfastly refused to accede to Kantor's demands for market-share targets for US exports to Japan. Kantor eventually retreated, claiming that Hashimoto had agreed to increase US market share by a specified amount when in reality all that Japan had agreed was to change its rules for vehicle inspections (Levinson, 1996, p. 6). The effect of the negotiation was to demonstrate that saying 'no' to the US might be an effective tactic in trade negotiations. For Hashimoto, the political dividend from his successful negotiation was accelerated promotion to the Japanese premiership the following January.

Bhagwati has concluded that the US-Japan automobile dispute has inflicted damage on the world trading system in a number of ways. First, aggressive unilateralism has damaged the cause of multilateralism because the threat of punitive tariffs violated the spirit if not the actual letter of the law at the WTO, which had taken seven long years of negotiation to establish. Second, the Clinton administration's actions undermined the credibility of the nascent WTO. Third, the dispute introduced a further source of instability and unpredictability into the world trading system by risking a titanic confrontation between a government with huge economic and political resources capable of blackmailing even powerful multinationals. Fourth, the demand for voluntary import expansion risked market distortion and trade diversion of contracts from competitive to uncompetitive firms. Fifth, however vehement its denials, the Clinton administration's recourse to VIEs constituted managed trade and nothing less than 'export protectionism'. Sixth, the dispute undermined the credibility of the Clinton administration's commitment to multilateralism and its moral right to leadership in world trade negotiations when it was transparently unprepared to abide by the rule of multilateral law. Finally, when they refused to capitulate to demands for a formal commitment to VIEs on automobiles and automobile parts, the dispute merely presented the Japanese with a fresh opportunity to outmanoeuvre the US in trade negotiations. It also gave the Japanese government renewed confidence to be more assertive in defence of its own interests and agenda, as demonstrated barely a few months later when the Japanese used their chairmanship of the 1995 Osaka APEC Summit to stall American attempts to set a formal timetable for the liberalization of trade and investment within the region. Therefore, the politically futile resort to aggressive unilateralism should be abandoned in future in favour of bilateral or impartial multilateral resolution of trade disputes through the WTO, thereby normalising trade relations between the US and Japan (Bhagwati, 1996, pp. 277-279).

Prospects for Trade Policy during Clinton's Second Term

US trade policy under the first Clinton administration has been roundly criticized for its use of aggressive unilateralism in the form of the threat of tariff retaliation (illegal under GATT), its willingness to demand managed trade through the imposition of voluntary import expansions, and its preoccupation with preferential trade arrangements under Article 24 of the GATT (Bhagwati, 1996, p. 262). To escape this scenario, one diplomatic source has recommended the creation by the year 2000 of a Japan-America Free Economic Area (Tong, 1996, p. 118). Drawing upon his own experience as Under Secretary of Commerce for International Trade during the first Clinton administration, and free from the bounds of office, Jeffrey Garten has warned the second Clinton administration that, since the key issue of trade liberalization was marginalized from the political agenda during the 1996 election campaign, it must now act with business leaders to create a new partnership. This partnership should be founded upon the recognition that Washington's influence over global markets has greatly diminished but that it nevertheless retains a critical role in assisting business to surmount regulatory, environmental and other obstacles to export markets (Garten, 1997, p. 68). Indeed, in recognition of the increasing dependence of the US economy upon export-generated growth, Garten has identified a framework of eight principles to create a successful partnership between Washington and business.

First, Garten has identified the need to reach a renewed consensus about the centrality of commercial interests in foreign policy in order to 'reignite the fervour for trade liberalization' which had inspired negotiations concerning the GATT, NAFTA and APEC during Clinton's first term. Second, the need for Washington and business leaders to construct a stronger constituency for open global markets among the business community and in Congress-not least because of the risk that globalization has weakened the political consensus for free trade. Third, the need for the administration and business to develop a better understanding of the interaction between business interests and human rights. Fourth, the need for the administration and business to make peace over the use of unilateral export controls for foreign policy purposes-so as to the use of multilateral rather than unilateral sanctions unless national security is threatened. Fifth, the need for Washington and business to cooperate to address congressional and public concerns about commercial diplomacy, not least charges of undue foreign influence. Garten advocated an increase in the federal budget for export promotion which had declined from $4.5 billion in 1994 to a planned $2.8 billion in 1997. Sixth, the need to reorganize the relationship between business and diplomacy, by consolidating trade financing agencies into one streamlined but powerful government-supported trade and investment bank. Seventh, the administration and business should assist the process of formulating and implementing political and economic reform in major emerging markets. Finally, Washington should clarify where the national interest may depart from that of the business community-not least in relation to states such as Libya, Iran and Iraq (Garten, 1997, pp. 72-79).

The broader economic context in 1996 has provided some grounds for optimism about the prospects for creating a Gartenesque partnership to deliver a less fraught trade relationship between the US and Japan during Clinton's second term of office. During 1996, the Japanese economy showed faltering signs of finally escaping from its longest postwar recession. In 1996, growth in industrial production of 2.6 per cent contributed to a real terms 3.6 per cent increase in Japan's GDP grew to $4564 billion (or $36263 per capita), the best performance among the Group of Seven (G7) economies. Inflation was negligible, recording a mere 0.1 per cent increase in the consumer prices' index while long-term interest rates stood at a paltry 3.1 per cent. The prospects of economic recovery were further sustained in the first quarter of 1997 by growth of 2.5 per cent, compared to the same period a year earlier (*Financial Times*, 15 July 1997). For his part, Bill Clinton was able to paint a very bullish picture of the US trade performance during his first term as President in his 1996 Annual Report on the Trade Agreements Program (USTR, 1997). Here the President reported that US sales to Japan during 1996 had increased by more than 6.3 per cent to $68.4 billion (accounting for 11 per cent of US goods' exports) despite the context of an appreciation in the value of the dollar from Y84 in April 1995 to Y114 in December 1996. Indeed, despite the sluggish performance of the domestic Japanese economy during Clinton's first term, US exports to Japan had risen by 43 per cent between 1992 and 1996, with exports to Japan oustripping Japanese imports to the US in 1996, which had fallen by more than $9 billion or 7.5 per cent. In fact, Japanese goods represented less than 14.5 per cent of total US imports in 1996, compared to almost 18.1 per cent in 1992. As a consequence, the US had managed to reduce its bilateral trade deficit with Japan by 22 per cent during 1996.

These macroeconomic grounds for optimism have to be set against less encouraging trends. The early months of Clinton's second term of office have been marked by a bilateral trade performance rather less favourable to the US. Although January 1997 was marked by Japan's lowest trade surplus with the rest of the world for 13 years, its surplus with the US rose sharply (by 81.6 per cent to Y298.34 billion, compared with the previous month) following a significant weakening of the yen against the dollar. From its record high of Y79.75 against the dollar in April 1995, the yen had depreciated by around 50 per cent to reach Y127 in trading on the 10th April, its lowest level against the dollar for five years (*Financial Times*, 11 April 1997). US trade performance has markedly deteriorated as a consequence. During April, for example, the US recorded a $4.8 billion trade deficit with Japan (following a $4.6 billion deficit in March), its worst performance since the previous October. Reflecting this overall trend, the pattern of trade in the politically sensitive and strategically important automobiles and automobile parts sector witnessed a 25.6 per cent decline in July 1997 in sales of imported automobiles in Japan-the fourth consecutive month in which overseas sales had fallen dramatically when compared to a year earlier. Most importantly, sales of US-made automobiles had declined by an average of 34.3 per cent compared to a year earlier. The impact had been heaviest on Japanese automobiles manufactured overseas (including those produced at US plants) which had declined by 55.6 per cent (*Financial Times*, 7 August 1997).

These Figures suggest that the August 1995 Framework Agreement on automobiles and automobile parts has been less effective in improving the US trade performance in this sector than was suggested by upbeat assessments emanating from the Clinton administration during the 1996 election campaign. The suspicion of the current USTR, Charlene Barshefsky, is that recent market trends in favour of Japanese companies reflect Japanese attempts to slow down the pace at which both new dealerships to sell US automobiles are being opened and the Japanese market for automobile parts is deregulated. The Japan Automobile Manufacturers' Association was able to report a 22.3 per cent rise in

Japanese automobile exports to the US during the first six months of 1997, the strongest growth since 1980 and the first year-on-year increase for more than a decade (*Financial Times*, 29 July 1997). Future prospects of avoiding the rekindling of protectionist sentiment in the US will not have been helped by a report from the Economist Intelligence Unit (EIU, 1997) suggesting that the Japanese automobile industry is on course for a longer term assault on world markets, not least the US market, because of the weakening yen and Japanese manufacturers' success in cutting costs. Indeed, the report has forecast that Japan's share of new automobile sales in the US will increase from the current 30 per cent to 35 per cent by 2005 (*Financial Times*, 6 May 1997).

Salvation through Japanese Deregulation?

At the June 1997 G7 Denver Summit, attempts were made in negotiations between key members of the Clinton and Hashimoto administrations to ease tension over Japan's growing current account surplus. To counter Clinton's concerns over the Japanese trade surplus, Hashimoto affirmed his government's commitment to deregulation of Japan's domestic markets. Indeed, the two leaders launched a new framework initiative through which Japan will consult the US on how best to deregulate some of its most important markets, namely financial services, telecommunications, medical equipment and housing. At the same time, in a further attempt to defuse fears of renewed confrontation over trade, Japan's finance minister, Hiroshi Mitsuzaka informed the US Treasury secretary, Robert Rubin, that Japan remained committed to stimulating its economic performance and avoiding a further rise in its current account surplus. For his part, Rubin agreed to cooperate in attempts to avoid excess volatility in currency markets (*Financial Times*, 21 June 1997). The fundamental problem confronting the Hashimoto Government is that it has little scope for changes in its economic policy which would stimulate the domestic economy, potentially increase demand for U.S. imports and thereby satisfy Washington's concerns. In terms of fiscal policy, in April 1997, the Japanese government introduced a potentially deflationary package of tax increases, including a rise from 3 per cent to 5 per cent in sales tax, in an attempt to address Japan's budget deficit. Spending cuts announced in June planned to cut general government expenditure by 0.5 per cent or Y200 billion. Japan cannot reverse these tax increases or increase public expenditure merely to satisfy US opinion. At the same time, monetary policy offers no immediate solution because interest rates have been at a record low since September 1995. This means that deregulation is the principal policy instrument remaining to the Hashimoto Government to stimulate the Japanese economy.

History suggests that there is nothing straightforward about the process of deregulating a major economy. For example, Bailey et al. have shown how trade liberalization in the US during the middle decades of the twentieth century was neither inevitable nor irrevocable: US domestic politics, institutional choice, and the international economy interacted to promote trade liberalization (Bailey, Goldstein & Weingast, 1997, pp. 309, 337). Domestic political institutional innovation, in the form of the 1934 Reciprocal Trade Agreements Act which delegated responsibility for trade strategy to the President and State Department, led both directly and indirectly to increased world trade, and this increase in trade in turn encouraged members of Congress and foreign actors to give greater importance to the liberalization of international markets. By comparison, there has been a lesser degree of inevitability about the liberalization of Japanese trade in the 1990s. Here too domestic politics, institutional choice, and the international economy have interacted to promote trade liberalization but it has been external political and market factors and their impact on domestic institutions have played a far more salient role than was the case in the US half a century ago. Previous Japanese deregulation initiatives during the early 1990s foundered on the entrenched opposition of powerful domestic interests. What may have transformed the immediate and future prospects for deregulation is the perception by certain previously sceptical domestic interests, not least those in the debt-ridden, beleaguered financial sector, that deregulation could be a vital spur to renewed international competitiveness and market share.

Although the absence of numerical targets for managing trade may primarily account for the Hashimoto Government's willingness to sign up to the new bilateral trade agreement at the 1997 Denver G7 Summit, Michio Nakamoto has argued that there are several other reasons why Japan should so placidly embrace regular consultations with the US over further deregulation of its domestic economy. First, the length and difficulty of escaping from the post-bubble economy recession of the early and mid-1990s has convinced many previously sceptical politicians and bureaucrats that restructuring and deregulation of the domestic economy is a priority that should be undertaken and at an unprecedented pace. Second, Japanese companies have generally been much slower than their competitors in exploiting the competitive advantage to be gained from locating overseas. Although, the ratio of overseas to domestic Japanese manufacturers tripled from 3 per cent in 1985 to 9.1 per cent in 1995, this is still a much lower ratio than the 26 per cent Figure for US manufacturers in 1995. Deregulated domestic markets will afford the opportunity for Japan to increase its attractiveness to the foreign direct investment (FDI) which has provided a major stimulus to the economic performance of other leading industrialized economies. Japan's ratio of inward to outward FDI of 13.6 per cent in 1994 is indicative of the previously hostile domestic climate for foreign investors, especially when compared to the 1.2 per cent FDI ratio for the US in 1994 (Nakamoto, 1997, p. 3).

If deregulation is to spur Japanese competitiveness, it will need to avoid the sources of tension in trade negotiation which have characterized recent bilateral negotiations on market liberalization. For example, in the telecommunications sector, despite the progress on liberalization made in WTO negotiations, the US has continued to press for greater liberalization of the domestic Japanese market in the belief that Nippon Telegraph and Telephone (NTT) has continued to discriminate against foreign suppliers in its procurement of equipment. In the aviation sector, US demands for an 'Open Skies' policy have been confronted by Japan's preference for more limited liberalization because of its fears of US domination of the lucrative trans-Pacific market. Given these problems, perhaps the greatest hope for reducing tension in the US-Japan bilateral relationship may be the rising political salience of the US-China trade relationship. In June 1997, for example, the US trade deficit with China rose 9.1 per cent to $3.8 billion whereas the deficit with Japan fell 25 per cent to $3.63 billion. It seems inevitable that the US-China trade relationship will become the most important bilateral relationship in the world economy. Indeed, the degree to which China will displace Japan as the US's most important trading partner in the first half of the next century has been illustrated by the first official Chinese acknowledgement that China's economy will become the biggest in the world by 2030. A study produced by the Chinese Academy of Social Sciences (CASS), has forecast that China's economy will be larger than Japan's by 2010 and will overtake the US by 2030 when its GDP of $155000 billion will be greater than the US's $131110 billion. Indeed, CASS is confidently forecasting that by 2050, China's GDP of $383000 billion will be double that of the US (*Financial Times*, 7 August 1997). In this future market scenario, it may be the US which finds itself the object of Chinese aggressive unilateralism.

Notes

1. Governance is the term which has been coined to reflect the fact that economic management is no longer the sole province of the state but is now 'a function that can be performed by a wide variety of public and private, state and non-state, national and international institutions and practices' (Hirst & Thompson, 1996, p. 184).

2. Regionalization has been defined as 'those processes which deepen the integration of particular regional economic spaces' (Payne & Gamble, 1996, p. 258).

3. It is ironic that after 13 years of being ranked in second place behind Japan, in 1994 the US overtook Japan to once again become the world's largest automobile producer (12.3 million vehicles compared to Japan's 10.6 million).

References

Bailey, M., Goldstein, J. & Weingast, R. (1997), 'The Institutional Roots of American Trade Policy: Politics, Coalitions, and International Trade', *World Politics*, 40, April, pp. 309-338.

Bhagwati, J. (1991), 'Aggressive Unilateralism: An Overview', in Bhagwati, J. & Patrick, H. (eds), *Aggressive Unilateralism: America's 301 Trade Policy and the World Trading System*, Harvester, London.

Bhagwati, J. (1996), 'The US-Japan Automobile Dispute: a Monumental Mistake', *International Affairs*, Vol. 72, No. 2, April, pp. 261-279.

Blakeney, M. (1997), Trade *Related Aspects of Intellectual Property Rights: A Concise Guide to the TRIPS Agreement*, Sweet & Maxwell, London.

EIU (1997), *World Automobile Forecasts 1997*, London.

Gamble, A. & Payne, A. (eds) (1996), *Regionalism and World Order*, Macmillan, London.

Garten, J. (1992), *A Cold Peace: America, Japan, Germany, and the Struggle for Supremacy*, Times Books, New York.

Garten, J. (1997), 'Business and Foreign Policy', *Foreign Affairs*, Vol. 76, No. 3, pp. 67-79.

Geiger, T. & Kennedy, D. (1996), *Regional Trade Blocs, Multilateralism and the GATT*, Pinter, London.

Goldsmith, J. (1993), *The Trap*, Macmillan, London.

Grant, R. (1993), 'Trading Blocs or Trading Blows: the Macroeconomic geography of US and Japanese Trade Policies', *Environment and Planning A*, Vol. 25, pp. 273-291.

Hindley, B. (1994), *The Goldsmith Fallacy:Why Open Trade and the GATT are Best*, Centre for Policy Studies, London.

Hirst, P. & Thompson, G. (1996), *Globalization in Question: The International Economy and the Possibilities of Governance*, Polity Press, Cambridge.

Hoekman, B. & Kostecki, M. (1995), *The Political Economy of the World Trading System: From GATT to WTO* , Oxford University Press, Oxford.

Ishihara, S. (1991), *The Japan That Can Say No: Why Japan will be First among Equals*, Simon & Schuster, London.

Kang, C.E. (1997), 'US Politics and the Greater Regulation of Inward Foreign Direct Investment', *International Organization*, Vol. 51, No. 2, pp. 301-33.

Kuroda, M. (1991), 'Super 301 and Japan', in Bhagwati, J. & Patrick, H. (eds), *Aggressive Unilateralism: America's 301 Trade Policy and the World Trading System*, Harvester, London.

Levinson, M. (1996), 'Kantor's Cant: the Hole in Our Trade Policy', *Foreign Affairs*, Vol. 75, No. 2, pp. 2-7.

Lincoln, E. (1990), *Japan's Unequal Trade* , The Brookings Institution, Washington.

Nakamoto, M. (1997), 'Common Goal with US', *Financial Times Survey: Japan*, 15 July, p. 3.

Ohmae, K. (1996), *The End of the Nation State: The Rise of Regional Economies*, Harper Collins, London.

Ozawa, I. (1994), *Blueprint for A New Japan: The Rethinking of a Nation*, Kodansha, London.

Prestowitz, C. (1988), *Trading Places How we are Giving Our Future to Japan and How to Reclaim It*, Basic Books, New York.

Reich, R. (1991), *The Work of Nations: Preparing Ourselves for the 21st-Century Capitalism*, Simon & Schuster, London.

Ryan, M. (1995), 'USTR's Implementation of 301 policy in the Pacific', *International Studies Quarterly*, Vol. 39, pp. 333-350.

Stokes, B. (1996), 'Divergent Paths: US-Japan Relations Towards the Twenty-first Century', *International Affairs*, Vol. 72, No. 2, April, pp. 281-291.

Thurow, L. (1992), *Head to Head: The Coming Economic Battle among Japan, Europe and America*, Nicholas Bradley, London.

Tong, K. (1996), 'Revolutionising America's Japan Policy', *Foreign Policy*, Vol. 105, Winter, pp. 107-124.

Tyson, L. (1992), *Who's Bashing Whom? Trade Conflict in High-Technology*, Institute for International Economics, Washington.

US Congress (1989), *Overview and Compilation of US Trade Statutes*, US Congress, Committee on Ways and Means, Washington.

USTR (1997), *1996 Annual Report of the President of the United States on the Trade Agreements Program* United States Trade Representative, Washington, Homepage: http://www.ustr gov/reports/tpa/1997/part3.html.

Williams, D. (1994), *Japan: Beyond the End of History*, Routledge, London.

Wood, C. (1992), *The Bubble Economy: The Japanese Economic Collapse*, Sidgwick & Jackson, London.

Index